S0-ABC-172

DESTINATION NORMANDY

0 11557 03535 3

The Stackpole Military History Series

THE AMERICAN CIVIL WAR

Cavalry Raids of the Civil War
Ghost, Thunderbolt, and Wizard
Pickett's Charge
Witness to Gettysburg

WORLD WAR I

Doughboy War

WORLD WAR II

After D-Day
Armor Battles of the Waffen-SS, 1943–45
Armoured Guardsmen
Army of the West
Australian Commandos
The B-24 in China
Backwater War
The Battle of Sicily
Beyond the Beachhead
The Brandenburger Commandos
The Brigade
Bringing the Thunder
Coast Watching in World War II
Colossal Cracks
A Dangerous Assignment
D-Day Deception
D-Day to Berlin
Destination Normandy
Dive Bomber!
A Drop Too Many
Eagles of the Third Reich
Eastern Front Combat
Exit Rommel
Fist from the Sky
Flying American Combat Aircraft of World War II
Forging the Thunderbolt
Fortress France
The German Defeat in the East, 1944–45
German Order of Battle, Vol. 1
German Order of Battle, Vol. 2
German Order of Battle, Vol. 3

The Germans in Normandy
Germany's Panzer Arm in World War II
GI Ingenuity
Goodwood
The Great Ships
Grenadiers
Hitler's Nemesis
Infantry Aces
Iron Arm
Iron Knights
Kampfgruppe Peiper at the Battle of the Bulge
Kursk
Luftwaffe Aces
Massacre at Tobruk
Mechanized Juggernaut or Military Anachronism?
Messerschmitts over Sicily
Michael Wittmann, Vol. 1
Michael Wittmann, Vol. 2
Mountain Warriors
The Nazi Rocketeers
On the Canal
Operation Mercury
Packs On!
Panzer Aces
Panzer Aces II
Panzer Commanders of the Western Front
The Panzer Legions
Panzers in Normandy
Panzers in Winter
The Path to Blitzkrieg
Penalty Strike
Red Star under the Baltic
Retreat to the Reich
Rommel's Desert Commanders
Rommel's Desert War
Rommel's Lieutenants
The Savage Sky
A Soldier in the Cockpit
Soviet Blitzkrieg
Stalin's Keys to Victory
Surviving Bataan and Beyond

T-34 in Action
Tank Tactics
Tigers in the Mud
Triumphant Fox
The 12th SS, Vol. 1
The 12th SS, Vol. 2
The War against Rommel's Supply Lines
War in the Aegean
Wolfpack Warriors

THE COLD WAR / VIETNAM

Cyclops in the Jungle
Expendable Warriors
Flying American Combat Aircraft: The Cold War
Here There Are Tigers
Land with No Sun
Phantom Reflections
Street without Joy
Through the Valley

WARS OF THE MIDDLE EAST

Never-Ending Conflict

GENERAL MILITARY HISTORY

Carriers in Combat
Desert Battles
Guerrilla Warfare

DESTINATION NORMANDY

Three American Regiments on D-Day

G. H. Bennett

STACKPOLE
BOOKS

Copyright © 2007 by G. H. Bennett

Published in paperback in 2009 by
STACKPOLE BOOKS
5067 Ritter Road
Mechanicsburg, PA 17055
www.stackpolebooks.com

DESTINATION NORMANDY: THREE AMERICAN REGIMENTS ON D-DAY, by G.
H. Bennett, was originally published in hard cover by Praeger Security International,
an imprint of Greenwood Publishing Group, Inc., Westport, CT. Copyright © 2007
by G. H. Bennett. Paperback edition by arrangement with Greenwood Publishing
Group, Inc. All rights reserved.

No part of this book may be reproduced or transmitted in any form or by any means
electronic or mechanical including photocopying, reprinting, or on any information storage or retrieval system, without permission in writing from Greenwood Publishing Group.

Cover design by Tracy Patterson

Printed in the United States of America

10 9 8 7 6 5 4 3 2 1

ISBN 978-0-8117-3535-3 (Stackpole paperback)

The Library of Congress has cataloged the hardcover edition as follows:

Bennett, G. H. (George Henry), 1967–
    Destination Normandy : three American regiments on D-Day / G. H. Bennett.
p.cm. — (Studies in military history and international affairs, ISSN 1537-4432)
    Includes bibliographical references and index.
    ISBN 0-275-99094-X (alk. paper)
1. World War, 1939–1945—Campaigns—France—Normandy. 2. United States.
Army. Infantry Regiment, 116th. 3. United States. Army. Parachute Infantry Regiment, 507th. 4. United States. Army. Infantry Regiment, 22nd. I. Title.
D756.5.N6B43 2007
940.54'21421092273—dc22   2006025916

Dedicated to:
The fallen

And to:
Those men and women on both sides of the Atlantic who continue
to remember them

Contents

List of Illustrations

Acknowledgments

With thanks to:

In Britain: Professor Jeremy Black of Exeter University; my colleagues at the University of Plymouth, Jill Keenan, Clare Hamling, Nikki Girvin, and Sandra MacDonald; the Cultural Office, U.S. Embassy, London; National Archives UK; Plymouth City Library; Nottinghamshire Record Office; West Country Studies Library; Ian Rayment and the staff at the University of Plymouth Library; Sidmouth Town Library; Exmouth Town Library; the BBC People's War Web site teams in Devon and Cornwall; the Devon Record Office; the Leicestershire Record Office; Jim and Margot Stanger of the 29th Infantry Division Association; and Steve Mutton.

In the United States: The National Archives; the staff at the Franklin D. Roosevelt Library; Stanley Kowalski; the Virginia, Maryland, Fairfield, and Stamford historical societies — in particular Dennis Barrow, Librarian, Fairfield Historical Society; Renee Kilsh (Army Art Curator) and the staff of the U.S. Army Center of Military History, Carlisle, Pennsylvania; and Dick Brodeur.

In France: The staff at the diocesan archives at Coutances; the staff at the departmental archives at St. Lo; the mayor of Graignes, Monsieur D. Small; and Sebastian of Hotel 6 Juin.

Introduction

We are at the crisis of the war. We must open our second front on the continent of Europe this month, & my feeling is that we shall do it within the next few days. There is a general feeling of uneasiness & an intense longing for the end of the war—though no one wishes to throw up the sponge & make a patched up peace with Hitler. Most people think that owing to dilatoryness [*sic*] or disclination [*sic*] to make the plunge, we missed our chances last year. The campaign in Italy has been a bitter disappointment. . . . The Anzio business seems to have been grossly mismanaged. . . Little is said openly about the prospects of our invasion attempt—but I think that most people have their fears. We have not been lucky in our landings hitherto—& these will be the biggest of all. Unless we have found some new leaders. . .we shall not make a success of our landings—& so far after 5 years of war we have found very few geniuses among our generals. Most of the men who will take part in the fighting will be new to battle—& despite rigorous training, men may fail in the real thing. The only preparation for war—is war—& our men for the greater part have not had the preparation the Germans have. I forsee a lot of fighting close to the places of landing with our men—difficult to re-inforce— hemmed in by superior numbers—unable to move forward. The likelihood of our being able to push the Germans out of occupied Europe is a very remote one—the possibility of our fighting our way through Germany to Berlin—well beyond the realms of possibility.[1]

These dark diary thoughts voiced on the eve of the invasion of Europe belonged not to a soldier or politician but to Sydney Race, an inspector of schools in Nottingham, England. In 1944 it was apparent to the generals, the politicians, and the ordinary people in Britain, the United States, and Europe that Allied progress in the war had been painfully slow. Germany still controlled the continent, even though the

Russians were making steady progress in the East. Preparations for a second front in Western Europe had been underway since 1942, but by mid-1944 many civilians wondered, despite the preparations, whether the invasion would ever be launched. The extent to which the generals, and the large numbers of untried British, Canadian, and American troops, relished the prospect of storming the beaches of occupied Europe was open to question in the minds of Sydney Race and other observers. Many wondered at the outcome of the invasion, which seemed to offer a myriad of possibilities, from disaster possibly leading to a negotiated peace, to partial success leading to attritional fighting inland from the invasion beaches. Few would have predicted that the greatest gamble of the war would result in the defeat of the enemy in a little under a year.

This final climactic campaign in Europe would involve thousands of American soldiers, a significant proportion of whom would be killed or wounded in action. From different states, enlisting in different cities, training at camps spread across the United States, they would have nothing in common other than death in the same battle and burial alongside one another. For many Americans involved in the opening phases of the final campaign in Europe, their first and final battle would be in Normandy, and their burial place would be above Omaha Beach in the American Cemetery at Colleville-sur-mer. Each year thousands of people visit the cemetery to view the white tombstones, which hold only the briefest of information: name, rank, regiment or unit, home state, and date of death. It is a place of reflection and stillness disturbed only by the quiet continuing rumble of the waves on the beach below. What strikes the visitor is that while every state in the Union is represented on the headstones, the casualties come from a comparatively small number of units. In particular the bulk of the casualties in Normandy were sustained by a handful of infantry regiments.

The 1940s and 1950s saw the publication of a plethora of regimental histories. Usually based on an inadequate range of sources, many were labors of love for a former officer of the regiment. They provided rather limited insights into the world of the American infantryman, his regiment, and the war in Europe. Later historians preferred to write from the perspective of the divisional level, which made for simplicity of narrative. With the rise of oral history in the 1970s, historians attempted to combine a foxhole eye view of combat together with a wider tactical and strategic appreciation. Using oral history, new light could be cast on those things for which documents either did not exist or were insufficiently detailed.[2] Despite this, the middle ground of military history, the regimental level, has steadily receded from view since 1945. It offers neither the functional ease of writing about divisions and the "big picture," nor the emotional engagement of the oral history view from the foxhole. And yet, with the wide variety of sources (both oral and documentary) now available, it can offer a valuable way to understand the levels above and below it, from the level of division to the level of the individual soldier. Examining D-Day, the lead up to it, and the aftermath, from the perspective of the regiment can offer new insights into the final campaign in Europe, the history of the American army and the experiences of the American infantryman.

This book will explore this level and D-Day through the lives of three particular units. The 22nd Infantry Regiment, part of the 4th Infantry Division, would land on Utah Beach on June 6. Part of the regular army, it could trace its lineage back to the War of 1812. Its experiences on D-Day and immediately thereafter involved waging a war of siege against German strongpoints across a flooded hinterland behind the beaches, rather than a modern war of fire and maneuver. Elsewhere, the 116th Infantry Regiment would be cut down on Omaha Beach. This National Guard unit from Virginia, landing as part of the 29th Infantry Division, would live up to its proud history that stretched back to the Civil War. Despite taking heavy casualties, it would force its way off Omaha Beach and achieve the near impossible task of breaking through Hitler's Atlantic Wall at one of its most formidable points. Further inland, the 507th Parachute Infantry Regiment, part of the 82nd Airborne Division that had already distinguished itself in the Mediterranean Theater, would suffer the worst misdrop of any American parachute unit on D-Day. With the job of protecting the flank of the American landings on the Normandy beaches, it would fight not as a unit but as a number of groups isolated from each other and often without any other support. Measuring its heritage in months rather than years, the 507th would write the first pages of its own history. Instead of fighting around two rivers as they had expected, their battlefield would be a vast swampland where control of bridges, roads, and dry land were the principal military objectives. The commanding officers of our three regiments would experience fates as different as their regiments. One would win a Silver Star for gallantry. Another would spend the remainder of the war in a German prisoner of war camp, and another would be relieved of his command for the performance of his regiment judged insufficiently successful by the generals above him. Fate could be very unkind to regiments and their commanding officers.

For the men of the 116th, 22nd, and 507th (Parachute) infantry regiments, D-Day was both a date and a symbolic moment of destiny for individuals and nations. D-Day was effectively an elastic moment in time in June 1944. To the men of the 116th, the morning of June 6 was indeed their greatest challenge. For the 22nd, their moment of decision would come almost a week later as they finally broke through key German strongpoints that had delayed the advance from Utah Beach. For the 507th, D-Day was an unending desperate fight to survive until they could link up with forces from the beaches. For some D-Day would last for 24 hours: for others it would last 10 days or more.

For the soldier, the regiment provided his neighborhood, the battalion his home, and his company a surrogate military family. The regiment provided a soldier's identity, and regiments varied greatly in their character. Some, particularly National Guard units, reflected a locality; some a particular function (such as the Parachute Infantry Units); some a proud lineage; and others the personality of a dominant commanding officer. Most reflected a combination of these attributes. There were good units and bad, hard-luck outfits that sustained heavy casualties and could not be completely relied upon. The best units could identify themselves by the number of tricky operations which they were called on to undertake.

The American infantry regiments that fought in Normandy were divided into three battalions. Three regiments (nine battalions) formed a division. Divisions were clustered into corps and corps into armies. Soldiers had limited identification with the division whose insignia they sported on their shoulder. Corps and army level were too remote for most soldiers to really identify with or understand unless they were led by a particularly strong personality. A regiment might provide a soldier with his neighborhood and the regiment his home, but a George S. Patton could provide an omnipotent god-like figure—remote, mythic, all-seeing, and all powerful.

Regiments varied greatly and mere statistics and unit numbers could not obscure the fact that they amounted to separate communities with vastly differing identities. Such differences between units were perhaps a reflection of the rapid growth of the American military in the 1940s. The U.S. Army at the outbreak of World War II was in a parlous state. In 1939 there were only five regular army divisions. With a growing sense of emergency, especially after the fall of France in June 1940, a Selective Service Act was brought in requiring the registration of men aged 21–35. Over 900,000 men were drafted for one year. In August 1941 this was lengthened to eighteen months. At the same time, between 1940 and 1941, the National Guard was federalized. This involved thirteen weeks of mobilization training. Nevertheless, with just 11 regular army divisions in 1941, the U.S. Army remained seriously understrength as it prepared to go to war.

A typical infantry regiment in 1943 numbered 3,118 men. Approximately 871 men could be found in each of its three battalions with medical detachment, service company, headquarters company, and other detachments accounting for the remaining men. Each battalion would have four 193-man rifle companies (1st Battalion—A, B, C, D; 2nd Battalion—E, F, G, H; 3rd Battalion—I, K, L, M). The rifle companies were the primary combat unit of the American infantry. Below company level were 41-men platoons composed of three twelve-men squads plus the platoon leader and his team. The offensive power of each regiment began with the squad, led by a sergeant with a corporal as second in command. The M1 Garand rifle, firing an eight-round clip at distances of up to 600 yards, was the basic infantryman's weapon, equipping seven of the 10-men fire team of each squad. A Browning Automatic Rifle (BAR) team would make up the rest of the fire team. With a 20-round box magazine, the BAR gunner was supported by two assistants to lay down heavy supporting fire at the rate of 60 rounds per minute. Comparatively slow by contemporary standards, the BAR carried great stopping power and the speed at which the M1 Garand could lay down fire meant that the U.S. Army squad could produce an enviable volume of fire on any target.[3] Comparatively few men carried that icon of American warfare and gangsterdom: the Thompson submachine gun. They were, however, along with carbine versions of the M1 Garand, in greater use with American airborne regiments. The regiment and its subunits represented a deadly brotherhood in which men were joined in the profession of arms. The regiment was not only a home, it was a house of education. Paul Fussell, a lieutenant in the 103rd Infantry Division, later commented: "Melville's Ishmael says that a whale-ship was his Yale College and his Harvard. An Infantry Division was mine, the 103rd, whose dispirited personnel wore a colorful green and yellow cactus on their left shoulders. These hillbillies and Okies, drop-outs and petty criminals were my teachers and friends."[4]

In addition to covering the combat performance of our three regiments, this book will also provide background insights into the experience of the American solider in Britain before D-Day. The regiments that would be tested on D-Day took time to form and develop. June 6 was the end of a very long road for most of the men who went through it. The men of the 116th Infantry Regiment had been in Britain preparing for D-Day since 1942. The men of the 22nd and 507th were in Britain for only a few months before embarking on General Dwight D. Eisenhower's "Great Crusade" to liberate Europe. All of them had to get used to living and training on a small cramped island off the coast of occupied Europe. Beset by shortages and bombed cities, the American soldier had to get used to a different culture and landscape in which he would train for the promised invasion. That process of training was lengthy and difficult, and the U.S. Army would sustain heavy casualties as part of it. Just how many casualties is even today not completely clear. What is clear is that some of the things that went wrong on D-Day became apparent in the training program, and yet nothing was done, or could be done, to offset the dangers that would later cost lives.

Trying to understand the American experience on D-Day is a difficult process. The documentary record in the National Archives in Washington is in places very fragmentary. The U.S. Army's Center for Military History at Carlisle in Pennsylvania has done a magnificent job of working with veterans, recording their experiences and serving as a place to which they can donate letters, diaries, and memories. Excellent work has been done by the D-Day museum in New Orleans and the National D-Day Memorial in Virginia. The documentary record is not really the problem for the historian. What matters more is the lack of visual sources for D-Day and the cultural baggage that goes with our picture of the past. In the American mind, D-Day has become an episode of mythic proportions—a national Calvary where the blood of one generation was spilled for the sake of the next and the liberty of all mankind. Few of those landing on the beaches in 1944 would have wanted to see it that way on June 6. In addition, our picture of the landings has become skewed in the public consciousness.

While working on another book I stumbled across a collection of photographs in the Franklin D. Roosevelt Presidential Library at Hyde Park in upstate New York. The archive in the Roosevelt Library is as remarkable as the man it honors. Roosevelt was interested in everything and a collector of many things. His archive contains letters written by Oliver Cromwell, the logs of eighteenth-century British warships, and accounts in Dutch of the settlement of New York State. This is not to mention the small matter of the 40 tons of private papers that he accrued during a busy life, and a remarkable presidency, from 1933 to 1945. Roosevelt realized the value and importance of history and was magpie like in his devotion to saving every scrap of paper for the future. Nevertheless, it was still somewhat of a surprise to come across a collection of nearly 2,000 photographs from the Second World War, which the library was finishing cataloguing. Those photographs had been given to the library by Olin Dows, a photographer working for the army historical section, and by his stepson Luis Browne. Dows had followed the troops training in England. In the aftermath of D-Day, he had followed them to France and had documented some of the fiercest fighting in Normandy, the Ardennes, and beyond. A quick glance at the photographs revealed that Dows had real talent as a photographer and that most of his photos had never been published. Even more remarkably some 250 images depicted US troops training in North Devon at the American Army's Assault Training Center, centred on Woolacombe on the coast. Significantly and poignantly the troops that Dows had photographed belonged to the Regimental Combat Team of the 116th Infantry Regiment, 29th Infantry. These were the men who had been part of the spearhead for the landings on Omaha Beach. Many of the men Dows pictured training for D-Day had not lived to see June 7. The multitude of photographs were a reminder of how few visual resources the historian has for the actual D-Day landings.

Some 3,000 men died on Omaha Beach as the price of breaking through the German Atlantic Wall. By First World War standards—British Prime Minister Winston Churchill, for one, envisaged a level of slaughter on D-Day equivalent to a day's offensive during that war—3,000 dead was mercifully small. However, to 3,000 families and to the American nation, the price was traumatically high. While the Allied political and military leadership were relieved at the scale of the losses, some wondered whether something had gone wrong on Omaha Beach. Understanding what took place on that beach was, however, a very difficult undertaking. This was partly due to the confusion on the battlefield, wartime secrecy, and a reluctance to relive their experience on the part of survivors and veterans. It was also due to a lack of visual sources on the battle. Robert Capa of *Life Magazine* waded ashore on Omaha Beach on June 6 and quickly began to snap the carnage around him. He shot off 106 photographs before boarding a landing craft. Arriving in Portsmouth, Capa had his photos rushed to London for developing. The rush continued at the developing studio in London with the result that a dark room assistant destroyed all but eight of Capa's images, and even they were blurred.[5] In addition to Capa's photography, color movie footage of the landings was shot by a Coast Guard camera crew under the direction of Hollywood director John Ford. Like Capa's photographs, Ford's film was also rushed to London. There it was viewed by Eisenhower, heavily edited, and transferred to black and white for newsreel release.[6] Unsurprisingly, the edited film did not show the full horror of Omaha Beach. It had been sanitized for public consumption. Images of American dead on Omaha Beach were not released until after the war. By the 1990s, when the Eisenhower Center began to search for Ford's original color film, all traces of it had disappeared.[7] Interestingly, the opening images of *Saving Private Ryan*, with its jerky camera movements, narrow angle, and bleached colour, simulated how Ford's beach scenes might have looked. The overall effect was to confront the viewer with what appeared like newly discovered archive footage. As one reviewer commented: "it's almost impossible to believe that this could be staged—this must be some long-lost footage from the invasion that we've never seen before."[8] With the visual reality of Omaha Beach being formed in the public mind by just a handful of Capa's photographs, and Ford's sanitized film, most people could not envisage what took place on Omaha Beach.

What also of other episodes in the invasion of Europe? While Omaha Beach had received the attention of Steven Spielberg, other episodes have been completely over-shadowed by the carnage of the one near disaster which the Allies faced on June 6. In cinematic and cultural terms, the American airborne landings which preceded the fight for the beaches revolves around Private John Steele of the 82nd Airborne. His stick of paratroops came down directly on top of the small French town of St. Mere Eglise. Most of them were mowed down by the German troops already in the town square overseeing the efforts of local French people to put out a fire resulting from Allied bombing. Steele's parachute caught on the steeple of the local church and he was trapped there as his comrades were shot down around him. Wounded, he played dead until he was eventually brought in and captured by the German troops using the steeple as an observation point. In the 1960s, Cornelius Ryan's book *The Longest Day* and the resulting film told Steele's story, making him an iconic figure for the parachute landings.

Similarly, Ryan's book and film made the story of Utah Beach that of Brigadier General Teddy Roosevelt. Landing in the first wave several hundred yards from the correct position, Roosevelt is claimed to have said "We'll start the war from right here," and in so doing made the decision to bring the subsequent waves ashore at a spot which proved far more advantageous than that which had been intended. Working tirelessly in the hours and days following the initial landing, Roosevelt demonstrated outstanding personal courage and leadership of the highest order. The award of the Congressional Medal of Honor served as recognition of his work. Unfortunately the order was made posthumously, as Roosevelt died from a heart attack less than a week after D-Day. For a generation, Henry Fonda as Roosevelt and Red Buttons as Steele in the film version of *The Longest Day* summed up the stories of Utah Beach and the American paratroop landings.

The American landings on D-Day have passed into legend in a process in which Hollywood rather than historians have played the leading role. This is not to say that the two have not on occasion worked hand in hand. Spielberg's approach towards the opening stages of *Saving Private Ryan*, backed by the authority of Steven Ambrose, is meticulous in its approach, but the problem is that the images are so powerful as to sum up D-Day for the postwar generation. By examining the landings from the perspective of our three regiments, we have three cross-sections—cutaways if you will—through D-Day. The reader will hopefully appreciate the wider view this offers.

Just as D-Day is the stuff of legend for an American audience, so it is for a European audience. For many in Normandy, the celluloid pictures of heroism and liberation cover darker memories of the Gestapo and SS and of heavy bombing of population centers. Cities like St. Lo and Caen were destroyed by American bombs in an attempt to save American lives. Liberation came at a high price for many in Normandy. The civilian dead are not grouped neatly into one beautiful cemetery like that at Colleville-sur-mer.

The legacies of D-Day remain very much alive in Britain. Across the southwest of Britain, reminders of the American presence in the lead up to D-Day litter the landscape, from the sites of former American hospitals to storage depots, parade grounds, and training facilities. Almost every little community across the southwest which hosted American troops during the war has its story to tell. The American army has passed into local folklore. "They were so rich that at the end of the war they dug big pits and pushed all their surplus equipment into it, even motorbikes" is a story repeated regularly across the southwest. In addition to such tales, a lot of reliable and detailed information on the American presence during the war has been unearthed in particular communities. In particular, Mr. Ken Small of Slapton in Devon fought a lone crusade in the 1980s to establish the facts of Operation Tiger, a D-Day exercise off the coast of South Devon that had ended in the deaths of over 700 American soldiers and sailors. His successful efforts to memorialize the disaster, revolving around the recovery of an M4 Sherman medium tank from the seafloor off South Devon, acted as a spur to others in Devon, Cornwall, and Dorset. They began to research and to try to memorialize the history of American units stationed in their communities during the war. Organizations such as the 351st Tribute Fund, which sought to memorialize the 351st Shore Engineer Regiment and other American forces stationed in Exmouth in Devon during the war, showed other communities what they might achieve.

The memorial stone to the 351st Shore Engineer Regiment in Phear Park in Exmouth has now been joined by a further memorial to the dead of the September 11, 2001, attacks on the United States. On that day, the actions of one man saved many lives. Rick Rescorla, the security chief for Morgan Stanley Bank, ensured that casualties among the staff of the bank were minimal. As a young man in the Cornish town of Hayle in Britain, Rescorla had been in awe of the Americans stationed in the town in preparation for D-Day. He wanted to be like them. Thus he was set on a course which would lead to a distinguished career in the Seventh Cavalry, life in America, and a hero's death on September 11. D-Day continues to echo through to today and beyond, even as the men who spearheaded it pass away.

CHAPTER 1

Operation Bolero and the Clash of Cultures

In April 1942, four months after the Japanese attack on Pearl Harbor had brought the United States into the war, American and British planners met to discuss the invasion of Europe. Only by a direct assault on Hitler's European empire, and a drive on Berlin, could the end of the war be guaranteed. This was despite the champions of heavy bombing, who argued that Hitler could be defeated through airpower and a costly land campaign avoided. The talks were long and arduous, the Americans preferring a direct strategy of a seaborne assault across the narrowest section of the English Channel followed by a drive through France to Germany. While the Americans preferred an attack on the Pas de Calais, the most obvious place for a cross-channel landing and hence the most heavily defended, the British preferred an attack on the coast of Normandy. An assault there had a number of advantages, not the least of which were that it was a less obvious point of attack and that the ports of Plymouth, Portsmouth, and Southampton were handily placed for such an assault. The British view eventually prevailed.

Further compromises also had to be reached on a range of subsidiary issues: Should the landing take place at night or at dawn? To what extent should any landing be preceded by a period of bombardment of enemy defenses from the air and from the sea? Should smoke be used? How quickly and how far should initial advances be made beyond the beachhead? How many troops would be needed for the initial and follow-up operations? What use should be made of airborne troops? How many landing craft and other resources would Allied planners need to devote to the operation? These were all critical questions, and on the outcome of the invasion perhaps hung the outcome of the war. If the invasion failed with heavy loss of life, might public opinion in the United States and Britain prefer a negotiated peace to further years of struggle? A defeat on the coast of Normandy might have the most profound repercussions militarily and politically. Every aspect and every potentiality resulting from a landing on the coast of northern France had to be worked out. For example, by

1943 the British and Americans were comparing their estimates on the number and nature of the casualties that they would face in the opening phases of the campaign.[1] American planners envisaged that on D-Day, 13.33 percent of troops would be drowned. Breaking through the German defenses would cost 25 percent of all the troops involved and a further 3 percent per day as the bridgehead was enlarged. Of the 25 percent initial casualties, 25 percent would be fatalities, 55 percent wounded, and a further 20 percent gassed. The threat of gas remained a constant worry for those planning for D-Day. Given that casualties would need evacuation and treatment, Allied planners were forced to come up with an assessment of the range of casualties that would need treatment. They determined that 43 percent would be stretcher cases and 57 percent would be classed as walking wounded. This would allow other planners to calculate the sea- and airlift capacities necessary to deal with the problem of wounded. An evacuation plan involving aircraft, ships, mobile field hospitals, hospital trains, and hospitals in the United Kingdom could then be worked out. This was one of many problems that the planners needed to address.

Once plans had been established, dress rehearsals were conducted to test their effectiveness. The first of these, Exercise Jantzen, took place in August 1943 with a follow-up, Exercise Harlequin, held the following month. Incorporating experience derived in the Mediterranean and Pacific, the planners tested, refined, and retested the plans that had been drawn up so meticulously. Considerable care was taken to define areas of responsibility and control and areas of overlap or common interest. The difficulties were not always reconciled. For example, in forecasting the number and nature of casualties on D-Day, American planners ignored the Evett's Rates used by British and Canadian forces in forecasting likely numbers of casualties. A post–D-Day administrative assessment of planning for the operation noted: "there was some difficulty in reconciling the respective estimates although a considerable measure of agreement was finally achieved."[2]

To prepare for the invasion, the U.S. Army, Navy, and Army Air Force commenced a steady buildup starting in 1942, codenamed operation Bolero, which would see the 29th Infantry Division brought to Britain. Other divisions would join them as the buildup continued in 1943. By July 1943 it was estimated that some 1,345,000 Americans would be stationed in England by April of the following year.[3] A timetable for their arrival was carefully prepared which saw the number of Americans stationed in Britain rising from 181,000 in mid-1943 to the final total in April 1944. Housing, provisioning, and training such a large army away from home called for a massive effort ranging from building hospitals to barracks, storage facilities, and supply depots. In all, some £50 million would be spent on providing the infrastructure to support the American occupation of Britain.[4] The administrative effort to locate and secure the services of such things as commercial laundries to support the American presence demanded considerable time and attention on the part of the British army's southern command. Land had to be found for the purposes of creating vast vehicle parks. On Merseyside, served by the ports of Wallasey and Liverpool, Aintree, Haydock, and Arrowe Park had capacity for over 7,500 vehicles. At the vehicle parks some assembly and cleaning after storage and transport across the

Atlantic would be carried out. Gasoline and oil storage facilities also had to be established at places such as Bovey Tracey (Devon), Malmesbury (Wiltshire), and Dorchester and Wimborne (Dorset). Suitable sites for ammunition depots had to be identified and developed at Launceston and Fowey in Cornwall.

The provision of sufficient hospital beds to support the American presence and to cater for the eventual flow of casualties resulting from the invasion was an even greater headache. The provision of base facilities placed heavy demands on the supply of British labor, already in short supply as a result of the war. In the county of Devon alone, hospitals had to be established at places such as Stover, Plasterdown, and Axminster with additional room made available for American troops in existing hospitals at Exeter and Tiverton. Many of the new hospitals were constructed to an identical 834-bed specification. Materials were in short supply, and inevitably the building program for D-Day threatened to fall behind schedule. In total, 34 of the 834-bed hospitals were planned. A further 16 hospitals (1,086 bed-type), and one hospital of 750 beds, were also built. Over 16,500 beds in existing hospitals were also made available to incoming American forces and plans were to convert several barracks in southern England to hospital use. In total 90,864 beds, at a cost of over 15 million pounds, were to be provided to support the American army in England and in the opening phases of the invasion of Europe.[5] In addition, 60 landing ships would be converted to carry casualties back from France to hospitals in England, and eight specialized hospital carriers would be available to deal with the more seriously wounded casualties.[6] An evacuation plan was worked out whereby casualties requiring more than 180 days' treatment would be taken back to the United States.

Workshop and storage facilities close to suitable road and rail links had to be identified or constructed at places such as Plymouth, Exeter, Launceston, Cullompton, and Ottery St Mary. The vast G50 depot at Taunton in Somerset had over a million feet of covered storage and over 600,000 feet of open storage. It would hold everything from medical supplies to ration packs in preparation for the invasion.

American dead posed their own set of problems. In July 1942, under the Key Plan for the Reception, Accommodation and Maintenance of the U.S. Forces, first edition, it was agreed that Brookwood Cemetery in London would be the principal burial ground for American forces in England and Wales.[7] Receiving cemeteries in Northern Ireland and Scotland were also identified. To ease the process of burial, and in recognition that accidents in training would inevitably occur, the American military sought and obtained an exemption from British law, which required that inquests had to be held into accidental or suspicious deaths.

In the seven months before May 1944, the anticipated date of the invasion, the southwest of England resembled a vast armored camp, with GIs sleeping in tents or quonset huts, or boarding with local families. Officers, generally speaking, had the pick of the accommodations, often taking over large country houses, such as Parnham House in Dorset, for elements of the 1st Infantry Division. Ports like Brixham, Dartmouth, and Plymouth were full of an assortment of landing craft and supply ships which would carry the troops across the channel. Everywhere across the land, vast dumps of material could be found camouflaged along key routes which would carry the assault troops to ports of embarkation. The roads rumbled with convoys of American military vehicles, and on the trains heavy equipment and troops were moved from disembarkation ports in the north to holding areas in the south.

The American soldiers stationed in the southwest of England, where the majority of U.S. troops were based, found themselves in a strange situation. Thousands of miles from home in a foreign country, they trained for an invasion that never seemed to come. To the east, British and Canadian forces similarly trained for the invasion that they would spearhead, with the British landing on two beaches in Normandy, the Americans two, and the Canadians one.

In the meantime American troops spent their time training and doing their best to relax in a Britain hit by wartime shortages. To try to avoid friction between the troops and their hosts, on their way over on the *Queen Mary* in 1942, the men of the 29th Division, like the divisions that would follow them, were given talks about life in Britain. They were also issued with *A Short Guide to Life in Great Britain.* The guide advised that contrary to American folklore, the British were reserved but not unfriendly, and that all troops had to behave in a diplomatic manner. Boastful and loud behavior were to be avoided, and on no account were the British to be underestimated or ridiculed for the performance of their forces earlier in the war. Considerable efforts were made in the guide to emphasize that in spite of their differences, the British and Americans had a great deal in common: "There are also important similarities – our common speech, our common law, and our ideals of religious freedom were all brought from Britain when the Pilgrims landed at Plymouth Rock. Our ideas about political liberties are also British and parts of our own Bill of Rights were borrowed from the great charters of British liberty."[8] Together with a handy guide to the incomprehensible British currency of pounds, shillings (bobs), florins, thruppences, and farthings, the guide offered handy insights into British life, from weights and measures to the nature of football in Britain. The tone was calculated to appeal to the common soldier:

> Britain may look a little shop-worn and grimy to you. The British people are anxious to have you know that you are not seeing their country at its best. There's been a war on since 1939. The houses haven't been painted because factories are not making paint— they're making planes. The famous English gardens and parks are unkempt because there are no men to take care of them, or they are being used to grow needed vegetables. British taxicabs look antique because Britain makes tanks for herself and Russia and hasn't time to make new cars. British trains are cold because power is needed for industry, not for heating. . . . The trains are unwashed and grimy because men and women are needed for more important work than car-washing. The British people are anxious for you to know that in normal times Britain looks much prettier, cleaner neater.[9]

The main points of the guide would subsequently be reiterated in soldier's publications such as *Yank* under headings such as: "For Yanks not at Oxford: Or How a fighter with the A[merican] E[xpeditionary] F[orce] can keep Himself and his British Hosts Happy while visiting the Tight Little Isle."[10] Information films entitled

Welcome to Britain and *Know your Ally* provided further means to get the message across.

In recognition of the significant regional differences that GIs would encounter, the U.S. Army also prepared a *Guide to Northern Ireland* for the large number of GIs who would find themselves stationed there. Production of the guide was particularly urgent. Under Operation Magnet, the 34th Infantry Division and 1st Armored Division were to arrive in Northern Ireland between January and June 1942. By the end of that month the American presence in Northern Ireland had grown to over 41,000 men. The guide would be an invaluable means for these men to navigate the social and religious problems of Northern Ireland. American troops were counseled to live up to the high image held by the Irish people of the United States and its people. Religion was identified as a particularly thorny issue: "In America we ask, 'Where do you come from?' In Ulster they ask, 'What church do you belong to?' If the question is put to you, tell the truth and then change the subject."[11] Irish girls were identified as a particular cultural problem: "Irish girls are friendly. They will stop on the country road and pass the time of day. Don't think on that account that they are falling for you in a big way. Quite probably the young lady you're interested in must ask her family's permission before she can go out with you." The guide was not distributed to all the American units that passed through Northern Ireland during the course of the war. Remarkably, it does not appear to have been distributed to the men of the 82nd Airborne Division who were based there in 1943–44.[12]

Despite the preparation and warnings, on arriving in Britain most Americans were shocked at the cultural differences. Writer and historian Paul Fussell, who served as a second lieutenant in the 103rd Infantry Division, captured the shock particularly well:

> Britain was a world away from the environment the boy Yanks knew and loved. For one thing cars were tiny and drove on the wrong side of the road. Victuals were vastly different: the food was cottony and bland, the beer soft and lukewarm. When after a lot of disgusting beer a boy sought a place to urinate, he found the fixtures laughably archaic. Bathtubs were not overly common, showers virtually non-existent. It seemed to rain all the time, and there was little central heating only tiny gas stoves that hardly worked. Everything seemed called by a different name: a drugstore (which sold only drugs) was called a chemist's, and condoms tended to be sold by hairdressers, ie barbers. The coinage was irrational and required constant study if one were to avoid being cheated.[13]

Most GIs, however, quickly accepted the hospitality of British people, who went out of their way to make them feel welcome. The British populace was remarkably accommodating towards their American guests. As one reviewer put it on the BBC:

> It is impossible to be reserved with a fellow who smiles, goes on chewing, and at the same time shows a perfect set of teeth. Their elasticity is infectious, and we for the most part have thawed quickly. One fellow said, "I have been in this country a few months, nearly all the time in towns, or as you like to call them Cities. But this village life is different. In

the village your people do speak to each other, you call your shopman by his Christian name, and well—even the dogs seem to belong to everyone, not the owner."[14]

Just as the U.S. Army had prepared its soldiers for life in Britain, the British government had tried to prepare its citizens for the arrival of American troops. As early as mid-1941 the British Foreign Office began to recognize how little British people knew about the United States. A report by the Foreign Office's Research and Press Service called attention to the "deplorable" state of American studies in Britain: 'The serious study both of American history and institutions and of contemporary America is notable in Britain by its absence'.[15] The most practical outcome of these concerns was the British equivalent of *A Short Guide to Great Britain*. A short pamphlet entitled *Meet the US Army* was prepared for the Board of Education by the Ministry of Information. Available at just four pence, it was written by British writer Louis MacNeice. It contained a guide to the American regions and explanations of the American currency system, the nature of American sports, and American life. What was particularly striking about *Meet the US Army* was its central rationale, which was to acknowledge differences to prevent misunderstandings on which German propaganda might seek to capitalize:

> You defeat enemy propaganda not by denying that these differences exist, but by admitting them openly and then trying to understand them. The truth here expressed applies equally to us in Britain. We must avoid all easy or romantic or prejudiced generalisations. We must neither think of Americans as a entirely different species from ourselves nor expect them to act in all things exactly as we do. A comprehensive comparative analysis of the U.S.A. and Britain is beyond the scope of this pamphlet; its purpose is to instance a few facts which will remove the A.E.F from a show-case labelled merely 'Allies' or 'Soldiers'—or, for that matter, merely 'Americans'—and set them in a perspective where they will appear as human beings—like us and unlike us, but more the former than the latter.[16]

In addition to *Meet the US Army,* the British Board of Education set up short courses in several cities, including Exeter and London, to educate teachers about America, and the BBC devoted some of its programming to informing its listenership about North America.

Accommodations had to be made all around. Stanley Kowalski, a GI from New Haven, Connecticut, reached Britain in 1944, as a replacement for an infantry division. One of his officers warned him and the other new arrivals to use their canteens in local pubs short of glasses. Like so many other Americans brought up on lager-style beer, his first sip of English bitter disgusted him, "but after the seventh canteen I didn't care any more." Relationships inevitably flowered between English girls and American men. Not all of these were harmonious and occasionally commanding officers would have to explain "their responsibilities" to some of their troops. Sex would not be the only area of contention between troops and their hosts.

CHAPTER 2

Three Regiments and the Mind of the GI

THE 116TH INFANTRY REGIMENT—29TH INFANTRY DIVISION

The U.S. Army's 29th Infantry Division had a long and distinguished record before the Second World War when it was among the earliest American units sent to Great Britain. The constituent elements of the division could trace their histories back to the Civil War, during which they had fought on opposite sides. A National Guard division, in 1917 it had been activated for service overseas, arriving on the Western Front in July 1918. It had suffered 787 men killed in action, and 4,783 wounded in action before the armistice on November 11, 1918. It had remained on active service until May 1919 when the division returned to the United States and was stood down. During the twenties and thirties the component elements of the 29th Division were kept busy with training for war. Routine training was punctuated by regular activations to deal with natural disasters and to ensure order during individual disputes. As a result of a strike by mill workers in Danville, Virginia, in November 1930, the 116th Infantry Regiment was called in by John Pollard, governor of Virginia, to restore order. In January 1931 another element of the division, the 246th Field Artillery Regiment, was called in to relieve the 116th. It was not until February 10, 1931, after the end of the strike, that the foot patrols were called off and the checkpoints closed.

Even before America entered into the war, the 116th Regiment had begun to undergo a process of rapid change. In the spring of 1941 the first draftees from Virginia, Kentucky, and Tennessee were posted to the unit. Other men left the regiment as they retired or went onto officer training to staff a rapidly expanding army. In the late spring of 1941 a further batch of draftees reached the regiment. This time they were from the north, from Maryland, and many were Catholics of Italian and Polish extraction. This made for a strange clash of cultures within a regiment whose members were largely drawn from Virginia and whose families originally came from the

British Isles. However, accommodations were quickly made as Marylanders learned to speak hillbilly and Southerners picked up some of the sharper sounds of the suburbs of Philadelphia.

The men of the 29th, and the 116th in particular, had a keen sense of who they were, representing their communities in rural Virginia and a past that connected them to Stonewall Jackson and the critical battles of the Confederacy.

> Its gray, Thank God, we fought and bled
> For a great cause now left unsaid
> Our pride is our Confederate dead
> For we are the sons of Lee
>
> Next to the gray are bars of blue
> For men whose strife with us is through,
> Who are now our comrades strong and true,
> Invincible in unity.
>
> Now see the lines of snowy white.
> It means we're pure in God's own sight;
> Its God's will, and by God we'll fight,
> For Freedom and liberty.
>
> Now for the background red as gore;
> It stands for days of long before,
> When we mastered the cannon's roar.
> We were then artillery.
>
> In the cross at the top behold,
> Our sacrifice in France is told.
> Valhalla claims our flower of gold,
> For it is the Fleur de Lis.
>
> "Ever Forward" to the Hall of Fame,
> We march again to honour the name,
> Of our regiment we proudly claim,
> The 116th Infantry.[1]

After the Japanese attack on Pearl Harbor had brought the United States into the war, in February 1942 the division was reorganized at Fort Meade near Washington, DC, leaving it with three infantry regiments, including the 116th. The reorganization also had the effect of making the 29th Division an almost solely Virginia-Maryland affair. The division received new equipment, such as 105-mm guns for the artillery.

The regiment's stay at Fort Meade saw other transformations. Life at the base brought home to many the seriousness of the months that lay ahead. The regiment's officers pushed the men hard to transform occasional soldiers, who had perhaps joined the National Guard as a means to supplement family incomes hit hard by the depression, into a unit that would be a match for any regular regiment, American or otherwise. New uniforms and weapons were issued and discipline was strict. The men had to get used to living in barrack blocks, 40 men to a dormitory with a foot locker at the aisle end of the two rows of 20 cots. Olive drab blankets and white sheets (three of each were issued with one at the laundry at any one time) were laid out on each bed with military precision. In each dormitory, two small private rooms accommodated two sergeants who would see to it that military discipline was enforced at all times.

At the farewell dinner at Fort Meade on March 14, 1942, Miss Madeliene Carroll, an English film actress, was made the daughter of the regiment. It was a symbolic appointment. Born in West Bromwich in England in 1906, she had appeared in 21 films before starring in *Virginia* in 1941. This film led to the invitation for her to become the daughter of the regiment. At the dinner she remarked: "I am half British and half French so I have already seen a lot of war... [She received the invitation to become daughter of the regiment in 1941] at a time when America thought they could stay out of the war, and I don't blame them for feeling that way."[2] The link between Virginia, England, and France would later be emphasized in more costly ways.

From April to September 1942, the reorganized division carried out extensive training in the South of the United States before going to Fort Blanding, Florida, to prepare for overseas deployment. Most enjoyed their time at Fort Blanding, in a beautiful setting with a white sandy beach. In September 1942 the division moved to Camp Kilmer, New Jersey. Kilmer would serve as the principal holding camp for GIs about to ship to Europe. Barbed wire and the military police ensured that there would be no second thoughts about going overseas. Most of the division embarked on the British passenger liner *Queen Mary* on September 26. The voyage was notable for several reasons.

The first was that many men received their first taste of life on the ocean wave. Seasickness, combined with cramped accommodations and inadequate food, created an experience that most preferred to forget. The second major feature was that during the voyage, the *Queen Mary* collided with the HMS *Curacao,* a British light cruiser. *Curacao* was cut in two and sank, quickly taking 332 members of her crew to their deaths. It was yet another reminder to the men of the regiment that in war there will inevitably be casualties. Collision damage to the bow of the *Queen Mary* was such that she was forced to drop her speed dramatically. This made her vulnerable to enemy attack. To augment the ship's defenses, Browning automatic rifle teams were stationed along the decks of the *Queen Mary.* Fortunately their marksmanship was not tested, although as the *Queen Mary* docked and the disembarking GIs could see the damage to the ship's bow, some wondered how they had avoided joining the crew of the *Curacao* in their watery grave.

The rest of the division followed the *Queen Mary* across the Channel to the United Kingdom on October 5. Although destined for the British Army Barracks at

Tidworth in the south of England, the division landed in Scotland in order to minimize the risk of attack from enemy aircraft and submarines. Once at Tidworth, the troops began to train for the projected Allied invasion of Europe. By comparison with the delights of Fort Meade or Fort Blanding, their new British accommodations left a lot to be desired. Twin bunks, straw mattresses, no pillows, and unheated barracks were features of Tidworth that the men of the 116th Infantry Regiment would long remember.

In 1943 the 29th Infantry Division arrived in Devon, spreading itself across the border between Devon and Cornwall with its headquarters at Tavistock to the north of Plymouth. The 116th Infantry Regiment was quartered across West Devon. The First Battalion was based on the outskirts of the small Devon town of Ivybridge, on the very edge of Dartmoor. The main base was Uphill camp on the Exeter road, which could house up to 1,500 men in huts, while officers were based at Stowford House. A fuel depot was based at Wrangaton and, as D-Day approached, some 2,500 additional troops were housed in tents in and around Ivybridge. Ivybridge was ideally placed for the military training grounds on Dartmoor, and a grass airstrip was built near Ivybridge at David's Cross to allow Piper Cub aircraft to bring in VIPs to watch the exercises.

Commanded by Lieutenant Colonel John Metcalfe, the First Battalion, 116th Infantry Regiment, consisted of companies A (Captain Taylor Fellers), B (Captain Ettore Zappacosta), C (Captain Bertier Hawks), and D (Captain Walter Schilling). To the north of the First Battalion, on the edge of the village of Bridestowe, were the Second Battalion under Major Sidney Bingham. It comprised companies E (Captain Lawrence Madill), F (Captain William Callahan), G (Captain Eccles Scott), and H (Captain George Boyd). The Third Battalion, under the command of Lieutenant Colonel Lawrence Meeks, included companies I (Captain Jack Flora), K (Captain William Pingley Jr.), L (Captain Charles East), and M (Captain Charles Kidd). This battalion, together with the Headquarters, Anti-Tank, Cannon, and Service companies, were based north and east of the city of Plymouth, which had been heavily bombed earlier in the war.

At the same time, some men from the division volunteered to form the 29th Ranger Battalion. It was envisaged that the elite Rangers would spearhead the division's assault on the coast, and in 1943 there were no ranger units in the United Kingdom. Three officers and 15 men from the 1st Ranger Battalion formed the nucleus of the new unit. The selection process was rigorous, and all men were volunteers. The 29th Rangers trained separately from the rest of the division, starting with the five-week course run by British Commando instructors at Spean Bridge in Scotland. Members of the 29th Rangers took part in a number of commando raids against the coast of enemy-occupied Europe. For example, in September 1943 they were involved in a raid against an enemy radar station on the Ile d'Ouessans. This small island off the coast of Brittany had a radar station and a small garrison. Operating from Falmouth in Cornwall, the raiding party attacked the radar station in the early hours of September 3, destroying the station and eliminating the garrison. Slowly but surely, the 29th Rangers gained valuable combat experience. However, in 1944 with other Ranger battalions stationed in the south of England, it was decided to disband the 29th Rangers and return the men to their original units.

22ND INFANTRY REGIMENT—4TH INFANTRY DIVISION

In time the 29th Infantry Division would be joined by the other units as part of the Bolero plan. The buildup would take time, and most American units would spend only a few months in England before embarking for France. Like the 116th Infantry Regiment, the 22nd had a proud history, and it too was to play a leading role in the plans for an Allied invasion of Europe. However, unlike in the 116th, it took some time for the men of the 22nd to understand what fate had in store for them. From its inception in 1812, the 22nd Infantry Regiment had become one of the core units of the regular U.S. Army. Its work was often dull and mundane. During the First World War the men of the 22nd had the ignominious task of guarding the docks at Hoboken. It was unglamorous and unrewarding work for one of the U.S. Army's oldest infantry regiments. The 1920s and 1930s saw the regiment continuing to play a worthy, if unspectacular, military role, working alongside the American Red Cross and the Civilian Conservation Corps as part of President Franklin Roosevelt's New Deal for the American public. As the pace of army reform

Men of 29th Rangers washing on Dartmoor (Olin Dows collection, Franklin D. Roosevelt Presidential Library)

29th Rangers making coffee on Dartmoor, July 1943 (Olin Dows collection, Franklin D. Roosevelt Presidential Library)

gathered pace in the late 1930s, the regiment began to see changes as horse transport was replaced by more modern means. By 1940, with Europe in the midst of war, the regiment was brought up to a higher state of efficiency. Maneuvers in Louisiana and South Carolina were conducted with a sense of expectation of what might be around the corner for the regiment. With the attack on Pearl Harbor, the regiment was dispersed throughout Georgia to guard vital installations. Increasingly intense combat training was conducted in 1942 and 1943, and in February 1943 the regiment received a new commanding officer in the form of Colonel Hervey A. Tribolet. Amphibious training in Florida followed. In the warm waters off Florida, the regiment learned the basics, rehearsing boat loading, unloading, and logistical planning time and time again. Many men within the regiment suspected that the training would all be in vain and that, as in the First World War, they would provide the last line of defense if the enemy got as far as Hoboken or Trenton.

507TH PARACHUTE INFANTRY REGIMENT—82ND AIRBORNE DIVISION

While the 22nd Infantry Regiment was one of the oldest units in the American army, the 507th Parachute Infantry Regiment was one of the newest. In late June

1940 the U.S. Army recognized the potential of paratroop infantry by forming a Parachute Test Platoon at Fort Benning, Georgia. In May 1940 German parachute forces had played a key role in the opening phases of the German attack in the West. Paratroops seemed to be a key part of the war of mobility, which the Germans had shown could be waged to swift and devastating conclusion. Paratroops could be used to seize key objectives many miles ahead of any advance and could tie down disproportionately large numbers of enemy forces. Airborne forces could dislocate the enemy front line by constituting a threat from the rear. The U.S. Army was not about to be left behind in the new warfare. After several weeks of training and initial evaluation drops, the 501st Parachute Infantry Battalion was formed in October 1940. From the outset the paratroops were encouraged to see themselves as an elite outfit—tougher, more highly trained, and more disciplined than regular units. The parachute regiments were further distinguished by the fact that they were all volunteers. Their distinctive uniforms, with high brown jump boots, helped the process by which the parachute infantry regiments became elite units. The new arm attracted mavericks such as Colonel Howard Johnson, who had qualified as an officer in the U.S. Navy before transferring to the army. He volunteered to train as a parachutist and went on to handpick many of the officers who later formed the 501st Parachute Infantry Regiment.

Other regiments formed in the wake of the 501st. The 507th Parachute Infantry Regiment was activated at Fort Benning on July 20, 1942, Colonel George Millet Jr. commanding. The process of forming a new parachute infantry regiment involved building up a cadre of qualified officers and noncommissioned officers (NCOs). It was somewhat disrupted by the attack on Pearl Harbor, the emergency delaying the normal flow of men through training. Pearl Harbor affected the formation of the regiment in other ways. The influx of volunteers following the Japanese attack ensured that the 507th would be led predominantly by citizen soldiers. The paratroops were glamorized in army recruitment posters. The fact that paratroops received extra "jump" pay was another incentive. Jump pay increased the pay of a private by $50 a month. Basic pay for a private in the army was a mere $21. Officers received an extra $100 a month in jump pay.

After selection and basic training, airborne candidates would attend jump school. To complete jump school they would have to complete five descents by parachute. This was coupled with heavy doses of physical training to ensure that the American paratrooper was among the most fit of the combatants of the Second World War. By July 1942 the 507th had received enough men from jump school that its training exercises were becoming ever more complex. In September the regiment as a whole went to training areas in Alabama to commence large-scale training. During this phase of training, many members of the regiment received experience landing in trees and in marshland. For example, on October 30 a small group of officers made a deliberate landing into a lake in Georgia to test the difficulties of a descent into water. The test was not wholly reassuring, although the presence of a safety boat prevented any serious injury. Training was punctuated by athletics, sport, and weekend passes. Boxing, wrestling, and swimming, along with other competitions, kept the men busy outside of training. In March 1943 the regiment arrived in Louisiana to take part in large-scale maneuvers, during which the three battalions would practice landing and assembly.

Following the end of the Louisiana maneuvers, the regiment left for a new home in Alliance, Nebraska. There they continued to train and to undertake public duties to maintain public morale and encourage support for the war effort. In November 1943 the 507th received its orders for overseas deployment.

To some in the new regiment, the commanding officer, Lieutenant Colonel Millet, cut rather a strange figure. A "somewhat overweight oldster" was how one second lieutenant remembered him. He excited the wonder, the loyalties, and the hatred of those around him. On one occasion he made a parachute jump wearing tennis shoes instead of jump boots. While he built up a regimental basketball team to almost professional standards, winning in 24 of their 26 games (outscoring their opponents by a total of 1,160–540), he otherwise showed little interest in the kind of team sports that other commanding officers would embrace as a vital part of physical training for their regiments.[3] However, the team of officers that Millet built up around himself had great loyalty towards their commanding officer. Whatever his personal quirks, training and maneuvers in Nebraska and Louisiana showed that the regiment was quickly coming together as a battle-ready formation. That made the interminable wait for an overseas deployment and action all the harder.

THE GI MIND-SET

As disparate as our three regiments may seem, they did have much in common. Most significantly, the men who made up the American spearhead for the invasion of Europe shared a common mind-set. They believed in their country and wished to restore their American values to the European continent. The intricacies of Nazism and Italian fascism were lost on most of them, although the American press had done its best to explain and educate and, from 1939, had given full coverage to the Battle for France, the Battle of Britain, and the ongoing Battle of the Atlantic. The American boys trusted their government, and if President Roosevelt said that they had to fight overseas for American values, then resignedly they would go. Most knew little of Europe, but they associated it with many of the political and religious problems that had led their ancestors to emigrate to the United States. That being said, most recognized cultural and familial ties with Europe. Stories, tradition, family connections, accent, and even culinary practice meant that Americans were steeped in aspects of European culture, even if they professed general ignorance about the continent. For most, the war would mark their first visit overseas to a mythic land of their ancestors.

In any case they knew that America represented the most modern, most dynamic, most perfect and progressive society on earth. American industry was the most productive and advanced. While they might fear for their individual futures, few doubted the outcome of the war. America simply could not lose. American weapons, particularly aircraft, were the best. The first powered flight of Wilbur and Orville

Wright had taken place in North Carolina, not Northern Europe. America was the land of modernity, backed by the unlimited resources of North and South America. Hollywood was the capital of the cinema industry, and Detroit the capital of the automotive trade. Army recruits from Manhattan to rural Tennessee knew the rhetoric of American modernity.

Many of the assumptions of the green troops of the 101st Airborne and the 4th and 29th infantry divisions were shared by the men of the 1st Infantry Division and 82nd Airborne. Together they would spearhead the attack on the French coast on D-Day. The 1st Infantry Division, which would land alongside the 29th on Omaha Beach, rated as veterans of a crack outfit. They had landed in North Africa in Operation Torch in November 1942, losing 167 killed and missing in the process. At the Kasserine Pass in February 1943, the division was on the receiving end of a mauling from the German Afrika Korps. In July 1943 the division spearheaded the Allied landings on Sicily along with the 82nd Airborne.

The men of the Big Red One exemplified some of the psychological traits of a veteran infantry unit. To a certain extent they were shared by the dogfaces of the 4th and 29th divisions, but by 1944 the 1st Infantry Division had seen so much action that within its ranks perceptions and prejudices were especially marked. To the men of the Big Red One, all other units were inferior, and soldiers in noncombat units barely deserved the name. Faded fatigues and worn equipment were a badge of honor, and efficiency in drill was a sure sign of absence from the battlefront. All officers serving behind the front were especially detested. Perceptions about their high pay and the privileges they enjoyed behind the front did not endear them to line infantrymen.

Special opprobrium was reserved for the high command. The decision, after the landings in Sicily, to remove the 1st Division's popular commander, Major General Terry Allen, was regarded as a public rebuke by the men who saw him as a soldier's soldier. That his similarly well respected deputy, Brigadier General "Teddy" Roosevelt Jr., was also moved to the 4th Infantry Division was a further blow to the men of a veteran unit who wondered why the high command always seemed to call their number when there was work to be done. Allen's replacement, Major General Clarence Huebner, had his work cut out in reigning back a division which felt that it had done its share of fighting and dying while the 4th and 29th infantry regiments had enjoyed an easier life in the United States and England.

The GI also enjoyed an interesting relationship with God. One 82nd trooper recounted in his memoirs:

> It has been said that there are no atheists in foxholes. In fact, many men did turn to God in those extreme circumstances. Some also felt that a loving God would not place them in these circumstances where random death was everywhere, and the good had as great a chance of dying or being horribly maimed as the bad. Fatalism was a middle ground. Stated simply, fatalism can be defined as accepting whatever happens after taking all the possible positive actions for the benefit of oneself and one's unit. Generally speaking, a soldier in the proximity of extreme danger for the first time relied on religion for support, but after repeatedly seeing the randomness and unfairness of how death and

wounding happened around him, this sole dependence on religion ended for most. Religious explanations for what was happening seemed inadequate. Fatalism became a more acceptable psychological function. This is not to say that men completely abandoned religion, most simply adapted to a new psychological defense against their terrible circumstances.[4]

The thing that most GIs hated above all else was training, which was unrelenting both stateside and in England. In England, Dartmoor—a vast, wet expanse of moorland in the southwest—held a special attraction for the American army. The 116th was one of the first units to come to loathe the landscape of steep heather-covered hills, fast-flowing streams, and peat bogs. It was the same landscape of misery in which Sir Arthur Conan Doyle had set his Sherlock Holmes mystery *The Hound of the Baskervilles*. Above the 116th, in base camps in Devon, Dartmoor would loom dark and forbidding on the horizon.

CHAPTER 3

Early Training and the Buildup to June 6, 1944

The training of the 116th Infantry Regiment was relentless, but not entirely rigorous. Exercises on Dartmoor were particularly detested as two 25-mile, and one 40-mile, hikes per week became routine. The barren and bleak heartland of the moor on which the troops would march and conduct live firing exercises was generally loathed. So familiar did Dartmoor become to the men of the 29th Infantry Division that General Gerhardt, the division commander, named his jeep "Vixen Tor" after one of the Dartmoor Tors (peaks). The jeep survived the war and currently resides in the museum of the 5th Infantry Regiment in Baltimore, Maryland. That a myth about a witch revolved around Vixen Tor probably seemed appropriate to the long lines of troops forced to trudge the moor as part of their training. What seemed particularly ridiculous to the troops came about when they were taken to Dartmoor to start training for the amphibious assault to liberate France. Captain Charles Cawthon, who was in command of Headquarters Company, 2nd Battalion, later wrote:

> GI's training had started off in a fumbling way, for there was only a vague idea of what we had to do. At first, it was all conducted on land, using homemade mock-ups of landing craft. Dartmoor was probably as good a land area for this as any, for it seemed afloat in rain. Its vast, rolling pitching stretches of spongy turf were usually clouded in mist—a desolate eerie, sometimes bleakly beautiful place. We came to know, but never to love, Dartmoor as we tramped across it, shivered in its cold winds and slept on its liquid surface.[1]

When not sleeping out on the moor, accommodations for the troops in Devon were mostly in quonset (nissen) huts hastily erected by the British to receive incoming American troops. Food was generous by the standards of wartime Britain, but not generous by the standards of the wartime United States. PFC Felix Branham, age 22, of T Company, 116th Infantry Regiment, later remembered:

116th Infantry Regiment Assault Training, Dartmoor, 1943 (Olin Dows collection, Franklin D. Roosevelt Presidential Library)

We were in a British barracks at Crown Hill outside of Plymouth. It was some six or eight miles from the edge of the moors, which is a miserable, horrible place to be at any time, much less training. We were hungry all the time, on half rations. We would go to the mess hall, and you could smell the food, and you would wind up getting half of what you expected. You'd get half an orange, half a slice of bread. You would get maybe a small ladle of powdered eggs—horrible. If someone has never tasted powdered eggs, you can't imagine how they tasted or what they looked like.[2]

Across the southwest of England, thousands of troops awaited the invasion growing increasingly restive in an alien environment. They griped about their day-to-day life to each other, in letters home, and occasionally in poetry:

A Yank in the ETO [European Theater of Operations]

Where the heavy dew whips through the breeze,
And you wade in mud up to your knees.
Where the sun don't shine and the rain blows free,
And the fog's so thick you can hardly see.

Where we live on Brussels sprouts and spam
(And those powdered eggs aren't worth a damn)
In town you eat their fish and spuds,
And wash them down with a mug of suds.

Open-air haircut for soldier of the 116th Infantry Regiment (Olin Dows collection, Franklin D. Roosevelt Presidential Library)

You hold your nose while you gulp it down
It bites your stomach, then you frown
For it burns your tongue, makes your throat feel queer,
It's rightly called bitter, it sure ain't beer.

Where prices are high and queues are long
And those GI yanks are always wrong,
Where you get Scotch for four bits a snort,
And those limey cabbies never stand short.

And the pitch black nights when you stay out late
Its so bloody dark you can't navigate
There's no transportation, so you have to hike,
And you get knocked on your can by a goddam bike.

Where most of the girls are blonde and bold
And think a Yank's pockets are lined with gold.
And there's Piccadilly Commandos with painted allure
Steer clear of them or you are burned for sure.

This isle's not worth saving, I don't think
Cut those ballons loose—let the damn thing sink.

I'm not complaining but I'll bet you know
Life's rougher than hell in the E.T.O.[3]

PFC John Barnes joined A Company of the First Battalion, 116th Infantry Regiment, based at Ivybridge in February 1944. With most of the unit made up of men from Virginia, Barnes, a New Yorker, found himself a little out of place. He found the men eager for action. They had trained and trained for months and wanted to get on with the job that they had been preparing for. Barnes felt that he was far from ready but soon found himself caught up in the routine of training:

> Within a few weeks the four platoons of A Company were reorganized into six boat teams. I felt gloomier than ever, but the boys were right. We were going to be the assault force as combat opened on the northern shores of France. Our training became very serious. We learned to attack pillboxes as a team. I was in Boat Team Number Two under Lieutenant John Clements. Out on the moors we would practice landings from an imaginary boat. Men would line up in three columns.... The first three out of the boat were riflemen. They would fan out when the ramp came down and take-up protective-fire positions. Next came two men who carried bangalore torpedoes, long lengths of pipe containing dynamite. These were shoved under barbed wire to blow a pathway. The next men were designated as wire cutters to help clear the gap. Then came machine gunners to cover us, next ... mortar gunners and ammo carriers. Lastly, a flamethrower team and a dynamite team to get close to the pillbox and blow it up.[4]

THE 22ND INFANTRY REGIMENT ARRIVES IN ENGLAND

While PFC Barnes felt himself unready for the task clearly confronting the 116th Infantry Regiment, the men of the 22nd Infantry Regiment, 4th Infantry Division, had no idea what their task might be. January 1944 found the regiment at Fort Jackson in South Carolina. For several months it had been practicing amphibious landings in Florida and Georgia. Although it was one of only three regular army regiments that had not seen action, most considered it unlikely that the regiment would be committed to action imminently. Many of the men had gone home on furlough over Christmas, and on their return to Fort Jackson they tended to dismiss the rumors of imminent action. However, Colonel Hervey Tribolet, commanding officer of the 22nd Infantry Regiment, held a closed meeting with the officers of the three battalions to confirm that the rumors were true. Hurried preparations were made for overseas deployment. New equipment and clothing were issued, and soldiers prepared to leave their families. Decisions had to be made about a range of domestic issues, including whether to sell cars that might otherwise stand idle for months. On January 7 the regiment went to the railhead at Fort Jackson to begin the journey north. Their destination was Camp Kilmer, New Jersey. At the camp telephone calls in and out were forbidden, the mail was censored, and visitors forbidden. The men did at least receive 12-hour passes to New York City while being sworn to the strictest secrecy.

Assault Training at Ivybridge (Olin Dows collection, Franklin D. Roosevelt Presidential Library)

At Camp Kilmer further training took place in the use of scramble nets and in combating enemy gas attack. The men were issued new gas masks and sent into gas chambers to test their effectiveness. It underlined the fact that Allied planners expected the Germans to bombard the invasion beaches with gas shells. Each man was given a detailed physical examination and inoculations against various diseases. Chaplains did good business holding services and talking to the men who were preparing themselves for overseas departure and probable combat.

On January 14 the regiment was placed on six-hour alert to be ready to move. Two days later the regiment loaded onto trains destined for the port of New York. A little after midnight, the men detrained and loaded onto ferries which would take them across the Hudson to a waiting transport. There was a sense of excitement and apprehension:

> The ferries pulled into the pier and personnel quickly unloaded and moved into a spacious inclosed loading platform. Once inside, companies were formed and moved to designated ramps awaiting roll call and boarding orders. While the troops were lined up, Red Cross workers distributed cakes, candy doughnuts, and coffee to each individual. About 0300 hours ... the men boarded the transport. It was not quite what they expected to find. They had visions of a tremendous vessel with luxurious rooms and facilities; instead it was an ocean-grey coloured transport converted to carry troops in large numbers. There were no luxuries, no large scale beds or chairs, only iron beds hung from the walls and bracings throughout the ship. Before daylight approximately five thousand men had boarded the *Capetown Castle*, at the time the eighth largest transport

in the British fleet. In addition to the 22nd Infantry, there were personnel from headquarters units of the 4th Division.[5]

The vision of an elegant sea crossing on a great ocean liner faded from the minds
of the men of the 4th Infantry Division as soon as they boarded the *Capetown Castle*.
By this stage of the war, ships like her were so busy carrying men back and forth
across the Atlantic that there was little time shoreside to ensure that the on-board
accommodations were entirely satisfactory or to remedy any defects. Recreation
facilities were minimal, which was a relief to the large numbers of men suffering
from seasickness for the first time in their lives. Magazines were freely available and
movies were shown. Every available space was occupied, including the holds. Officers
were allocated to cabins, but for the enlisted men it was a very rough crossing. Meals
were provided twice a day, but the standard and quantity of food left a great deal to
be desired in the opinion of all but the most seasick of men. The need to exercise
strict light discipline at night meant that men were not allowed on deck to smoke
during the night, in case the glow of a cigarette should help to give away the position
of the ship. At the same time portholes were blacked out and closed. Life was pretty
miserable and always tinged with the unhappy thought that at any time their ship
was vulnerable to enemy submarine attack. Training on board was minimal and
largely restricted to lectures and conferences of officers. Every day between 1000
and 1100, boat drill was held. Troops rehearsed how, in the event of an emergency,
they would observe ship's rules in getting to their assigned lifeboat station. By the
time the *Capetown Castle* docked in Liverpool after a 12-day crossing of the North
Atlantic, most of the men of the regiment had had their illusions about the elegance
of sea travel firmly crushed.

On arrival in England, the troops were received by Red Cross workers armed with
doughnuts and coffee. It was not until the early hours of January 30 that everyone
left the ship. The men were then loaded onto trains that would take them to their
destination in England. Only a handful of men in the regiment knew where this
was to be. The need for secrecy had been strictly observed. An advance detail under
Major Earl Edwards had set up a series of camps to house the regiment. All elements
of the regiment would locate to towns near the South Devon coast in preparation for
the Allied landings on the coast of France. The Third Battalion, as well as the Cannon and Anti-Tank companies, would go to the small town of South Brent, not far
from Ivybridge and the base of the First Battalion of the 116th Infantry. The Second
Battalion of the 22nd, Regimental Headquarters, and Service Company would be
based at the village of Denbury. The First Battalion of the regiment would be at
Newton Abbot, a small town and key rail junction that was already home to various
American units, including a hospital unit.

One of the major tasks of the officers of the regiment was to bring their men up to
a state of peak efficiency. The effects of a sea voyage and the process of settling into
new surroundings had to be combated. Thus, training resumed, and furloughs were
kept in very short supply to only the most deserving men. Accommodations and
food were the sources of much comment. The supply of coal was not sufficient to

keep the huts provided for the men truly warm, and food was always in short supply. Boredom was a constant problem and the threats to morale diverse. After reading one article in *Stars and Stripes* on April 8, 1944, Major General R. O. Barton wrote the to Supreme Headquarters, Allied Expeditionary Force, that he, and the rest of the 4th Infantry Division, were outraged that their role in the forthcoming landings was being publicly downplayed while the men of the 29th Infantry Division were being turned into the stars of the show.[6]

THE 507TH ARRIVES IN GREAT BRITAIN

Like the 22nd Infantry Regiment, the 507th Parachute Infantry Regiment was destined to spend only a few months in the United Kingdom before spearheading the invasion of Europe. In November 1943 the regiment loaded on the P&O liner SS *Strathnaver* in the port of New York. *Strathnaver* had lost most of her prewar grandeur by 1943. As usual on the transatlantic troopships, officers enjoyed a tolerable crossing while the enlisted men had to make do with poor and overcrowded accommodations. Seasickness, hunger, boat drill, boredom, and poor food were other features of the wartime transatlantic trooping experience not lost on the men of the regiment. At least one NCO resorted to stealing food from the galley.[7] A thriving black market built up between galley staff and paratroopers, with everything from bread to meat pies being available for the right price. Colonel Millet, the commanding officer of the regiment, had considerable differences with the colonel in charge of their transportation across the Atlantic. Seeing the impact of poor food on the morale and health of his men and on the discipline of the regiment, Millet decided to take action. He told Major Gordon Smith, the regimental supply officer, to use their supply of emergency rations to feed the troops adequately.

Other officers did what they could to improve life on board. With accommodations cramped, many men resorted to sleeping in the open on deck. It was cold, but at least it was well ventilated and spacious in comparison to the lower decks, where every corner was taken. Lying on a flat surface was felt preferable to the hammocks otherwise offered on the *Strathnaver*. In search of a quiet, flat spot, one GI encountered Captain John Verret, the regiment's Roman Catholic chaplain. The GI explained the problem to the chaplain, who ushered the GI into the chaplain's cabin and told him that he could sleep in the bathroom even though it was strictly against orders for enlisted men to sleep in officers' quarters. The chaplain advised that with a few cushions the bath would prove most comfortable. The GI was exhorted to keep out of sight except during boat drills and, if discovered, to maintain that he was the chaplain's altar boy. Verret would keep him supplied with food during the trip. When the GI explained that he was a Protestant, Father Verret told him not to worry and that until disembarkation he would be an honorary Catholic.

After two weeks at sea the SS *Strathnaver* docked in Liverpool. However, the regiment was quickly moved by train to Grenock on the river Clyde in Scotland. Just before Christmas the regiment was moved by ship across the Irish Sea to Belfast, Northern Ireland. The journey did not end here, and the regiment was transported by rail to Portrush. A seaside resort, Portrush had plenty of accommodations to spare during the war, especially during a particularly harsh winter. Large private houses, guest houses, and even hotels provided temporary accommodations for the regiment. For example, a guest house called Lisnavarna became home to the officers of the Third Battalion. Many of the rooms occupied by the men of the regiment had sea views. Portrush was a sizeable town, and passes were available to the cities of Coleraine and Belfast. A public bathhouse and shower on the seafront at Portrush was made available to American forces. Such features made a favorable impression on visiting troops. Unfortunately, the cold and rain of Portrush made an equally immediate and lasting impression. Field maneuvers and physical training were made still more unpleasant by the biting breeze that never seemed to relent. The coal allowance allotted to the men seemed inadequate to the task. At least training offered the chance to keep warm. Relations with the locals were largely good, and during Christmas in 1943 the men of the 507th went out of their way to redirect candy and other treats to the children of the town. This was in contrast to the experiences of GIs in other units, many of whom fell afoul of the sectarian divide. Some were violently anti-British in their attitudes and unafraid to show their republican sympathies. Others found themselves on the receiving end of threats from the Irish Republican Army. Catholics welcomed the American army since anything was better than the British. Protestants welcomed the American army as additional security from the disorderly Catholic masses.[8] However, the stay of the 507th at Portrush was not entirely without sectarian incident.

In order to celebrate Midnight Mass on the morning of December 25, Father Verret tried to find suitable premises. The local church did not hold Midnight Mass, as its blackout facilities were inadequate. Verret therefore approached the American Red Cross, which was using the hall of the local Protestant Orange order for dances and other events to entertain the troops. They were willing to help organize Midnight Mass, but the local Roman Catholic priest voiced his strong concerns at the sectarian reaction that would result from holding a Catholic mass in a hall of the Protestant Orange Order. Verret eventually sought guidance from the local Catholic bishop, who told him to do as he saw fit. Mass was duly held in the hall with a large congregation that included some locals. At the local level there was no problem. However, the matter was subsequently raised in the Northern Ireland Parliament, where William Lowry, the minister of home affairs, joked that "preparations were already under way to have the hall fumigated."[9] This apparent insult to both American troops and the Roman Catholic Church attracted press attention and that of the Vicar Delegate to U.S. forces in Northern Ireland. Lowry was forced to apologize. It was a significant reminder of the dangers of the sectarian divide and the capacity of visiting American units to unwittingly become embroiled in the religious struggles of Ireland.[10]

Like many other American units, the 507th organized a Christmas party for the benefit of local children. Throughout this time, the strength of the regiment continued to grow as additional jump-qualified personnel arrived at Portrush. The regiment received a late Christmas present on January 14 when it was notified that it was being attached to the 82nd Airborne Division, which had famously lead the assault on Sicily. The attachment to a crack division left few in any doubt that the 507th would be in the forefront of the next offensive in Europe.

On March 11, 1944, the regiment was transported across the Irish Sea to Scotland and then by train to Nottingham. They would be based on the Roclaveston Manor Estate at Tollerton, just outside the city. The 508th Parachute Infantry Regiment would be quartered at nearby Wollaton Hall. While the men from the 507th would sleep six to a tent, the officers would reside in the Tollerton Hall. By curious irony, the manor had been the seat of the Barry family, which could trace its ancestory back to a Norman knight who had left La Barre on the Cotentin Peninsula in France to campaign with William the Conqueror in 1066. The hall was a grand building set in five acres of garden with grand lawns and a lake. At its heart was a manor house that was probably constructed in the reign of Queen Elizabeth I.[11] Transformed in the eighteenth century, it appeared like a castle with battlements and crenellated roof line. It was an imposing and completely false structure. As General Gavin of the 82nd Airborne commented in his diary after visiting the 508th Parachute Infantry Regiment at Wollaton Hall and the 507th at Tollerton: "These are lovely sites, formerly castle grounds of some of the local rather small-bore royalty."[12]

Adjoining the hall, and connected by a crenellated wall, was the estate church of St. Peters. Able to accommodate no more than about 160 people, soldiers attending divine service (and by May 1944 the regiment was more than 2,000 strong) could look up on its interior walls to the coats of arms of the families of the manor. They could also look up to the gallery with fireplace, where above the congregation the squire's family could maintain their privacy and their warmth during services. The hall and the church were powerful reminders of a past society that had provided much of the impetus for the population growth of the American colonies. Nottinghamshire had been one of the great bastions of Puritanism, and from the country in the 1600s many men and women had made the journey to the Netherlands and the Americas.

At Tollerton training continued apace using Nottingham airfield and the nearby military airfields in Lincolnshire. Few doubted that the invasion was but weeks away. However, the process of training was disturbed by bad weather, which disrupted plans for mass practice jumps. In the end, the men of the regiment made only one day jump and one night jump during their time at Tollerton, and most of the training had to be concentrated on map reading, first aid, and small-unit tactics. The lack of jump practice caused some anxiety within the regiment and the division, but in practice it probably made little difference. Once out of the aircraft, the process of landing was largely a matter of physics. The problematic part came with the process of rolling up sticks, where the men at the ends of a serial of paratroops would progress towards its midpoint, picking up their fellow troopers until they all assembled at the midpoint. The process called for keen powers of observation on the part of all those concerned. At night the process became even more difficult.

The process of training for a parachute infantry regiment revolved around marches of varying length to maintain the physical fitness of troopers; combat exercises to rehearse the basics of combat; and lectures in a range of subjects, from map reading and first aid, to the dangers of gas and urban fighting, to sessions on unarmed combat and aircraft recognition. By March, training for the 507th was proceeding effectively. General Gavin could comment in his diary:

> BNs of the 507th and 508th jumped operation curveball at 1600 today. . .A well carried out exercise. It is refreshing to work with troops fresh from America, enthusiastic and anxious. They listen and hang on to every word and as far as I could observe try to do exactly as they are told. The battle hardened veterans of the 505th are by now a bit calloused. The 507 and 508 appear to lack the technical proficiency of the 505th but what they lack they more than make up for in their zeal and interest in doing the correct thing. They will do all right.[13]

That said, Gavin had his doubts over some of the leadership within the 507th. Gavin favored the removal of Colonel Millet, the regiment's commanding officer, and at least one of the battalion commanders. Gavin considered Millet "lazy, soft, indolent, lacking leadership necessary for combat."[14] With an alleged fondness for poker, ladies, and a well-stocked mess bar, some saw Millet as a hedonist. What was perhaps worse, for these alleged flaws were shared by many other officers in the parachute infantry regiments, was that Millet knew how to antagonize his fellow officers. Within the 507th, Millet weeded out a number of officers whom he did not approve of and then developed a fierce loyalty to the command team he slowly built up.[15] He was loved and hated in equal measure, but General Gavin remained bothered by an officer he saw as something of a maverick. On March 23 the 507th and 508th carried out a night drop that went perfectly to time and to target. Despite this, by the next morning neither regiment had dug in or properly organized for defense. The commanding officers of both regiments did not appear during the exercise. As Gavin noted in his diary:

> It worries me that they are not ready to take on the combat mission that General R[idgeway] is lining up for them. He believes they are. There is so much to be done. The officers are dogging. Col. Timmes [2nd] BN [507th] has the worse attitude that I have encountered in many a day, what to do? More and tougher training, chop off the worse heads, put the heat on where it will do the most good. Our combat commitment with these people is a worry.[16]

However, training exercises for American airborne units revealed that, no matter how detailed the plans, things could still go badly wrong. Exercise Eagle on the night of May 12–13 was rescheduled as a major practice for the airborne drop on D-Day. Some 800 C-47 troop carrying aircraft from the South 52nd and 53rd Troop Carrier Wings would be involved in the drops. Since the 82nd Airborne Division sustained so many men who had already made combat jumps over Sicily, its drop would be only a token effort. However, the jump by the 101st Airborne Division would be in full. Taking off around 11:00 PM on the night of May 12, the transport aircraft, flying in formation, navigated their way between a series of way points stretching from Wales to the south of England. The exercise began to run into major trouble when some of the transport aircraft got caught up in a German air raid approaching London. The flights of C-47s took avoiding action that in some cases set them on a collision course with other flights. The exercise descended into chaos as some troopers jumped too low, at too great an airspeed, or too far away from their target. The result was that paratroopers landed across southern England as far as nine miles away from their drop zones. Some 500 of them sustained injuries (thankfully, mostly minor). More seriously, two aircraft were lost in midair collisions, taking 14 men to their deaths. Exercise Eagle demonstrated several points that also had to be faced in the airborne drops over Normandy:

- The dangers of flying in tight formation
- The difficulties of close formation flying at night
- The likelihood that even a small mishap or element of non-navigation could spread the airborne drop over an area sufficiently large as to nullify the effectiveness of the units involved.

CHAPTER 4

Free Time, Crime, and the GI

Outside of training there was little for the average GI to do in wartime Great Britain. As one GI put it: "all we do is stay in camp, write letters and wash clothes."[1] Letter writing, the movies, local girls, and pubs offered the only distractions from the interminable wait to go into action and the weekly round of training. Letter writing to the folks at home was almost a daily ritual for many of the men, but censorship and the technology of the day placed strict limits on what could be communicated. The time taken for a letter to cross the Atlantic was considerable, but an alternative was the V-mail system. V-mail forms could be purchased at any army post office. On these, short letters could be written. The post office would then photograph the letters. The rolls of film would be dispatched, often flown across the Atlantic. The letters would be reproduced onto paper at the nearest major post office center to the delivery destination. Civilians could also, and were encouraged to, use V-mail to stay in contact. It meant that the delay between letter writing and delivery was reduced to around twelve days, but the letters were on the short side.

Self-censorship added another burden to the process of communication. GIs tended in their letters to minimize the dangers and hardships they faced. Their loved ones on the other side of the Atlantic also knew how to put an optimistic gloss on the difficulties of living in wartime America. There was also official censorship of letters. Officers read through the mail of their subordinates to ensure that information of military value could not find its way into the hands of the enemy. They would physically cut out or otherwise obliterate from the letters they scrutinized any fact or sentence with which they took issue. More serious breaches could result in disciplinary action. However, for most the censorship was not necessary. Even in the midst of battle, GIs knew that certain topics should not be mentioned. One study after D-Day, using over 60,000 pieces of mail as a sample, found that censorship violations were happening in only a small number of cases. The sample included mail from the 1st, 4th, 9th, 29th, and 30th infantry divisions, 2nd Armored, and the 82nd and 101st airborne divisions. Only 2.1 percent of officers' mail, and 1.3 percent of enlisted men's mail (1.4 percent overall), contained security violations.[2] GIs were acutely conscious of security, and only nine out of 828 cases merited anything other than the deletion from the mail of the offending section. There were strict limitations, private and official, on what a GI could say to the folks at home and how it could be said. On both sides the difficulties were usually hidden behind a brave face.

Even better than a letter from home was the package from home. As Sergeant Robert Slaughter of the 116th later recalled:

> The highlight of any day was mail call. Letters and packages from home brought smiles from those fortunate enough to get them, and it was a sad day when one failed to receive either. Boxes of goodies were shared by all in the barracks. Homemade specialities from the ethnic soldiers' moms were especially welcomed by the Southerner. Italian, Greek and Polish delicacies were deliciously different to the tastes of the unsophisticated hillbilly tongue. Our Yankee colleagues enjoyed the cakes, fudge and other non-perishables from our loved ones. Those packages kept many of us from starving.[3]

Understandably, homesickness remained a problem for the majority. Across the country, British people did their best to open their homes and make their visitors feel as welcome as possible. As a result, many GIs acquired what amounted to surrogate families. One particular expression of this came during December 1943 when the men of the 29th Infantry Division hosted a series of children's parties across West Devon and East Cornwall. More than 9,500 British and foreign refugee children were entertained at 40 Christmas parties hosted by the division. One local newspaper recorded:

> Tavistock Town Hall was yesterday festooned with red and green paper ribbons and there was also a large Christmas tree laden with fancy articles, interspersed with tinsel the occasion being the entertaining of 140 children of the Plymouth Road Junior Council School by members of the United States Army. The children were given presents of stuffed animals, picture books, knitting outfits and jigsaw puzzles. They also received stockings containing chewing gum and candy. The gifts were made by the American Red Cross, while the American Army gave all the food.[4]

Lady Astor, the Lady Mayoress of Plymouth and one of its local members of Parliament, attended one of the parties. With her own roots in Virginia, she had been particularly active in making the men of the 116th Infantry Regiment welcome in West Devon. Making a speech at one of the parties for two local Plymouth schools, she said: "All I have told Plymouth about the Americans has come true. There are no more generous people in God's world than the Americans unless it is the British."[5] Wandering around the party, eating ice cream out of a mess tin, she expressed the children's appreciation of the party by kissing Santa Claus, being played by a Jewish GI from Brooklyn.

The American Red Cross did its best to set up and run facilities and entertainment that would provide for the welfare of American soldiers overseas. American Red Cross clubs were set up across Great Britain, with the larger clubs in places such as London providing accommodations, food, coffee, and a venue for dances and other entertainment. They were run by American and British civilians—almost invariably female, which gave them an added attraction for American soldiers.

Moviegoing was one distraction embraced by many GIs. However, the majority found the experience not as fully satisfactory as it would have been in the United States. Cinemas in Britain were run down in comparison with their American counterparts and, although most featured American and British releases, some GIs found that unfamiliar British films were an acquired taste. One GI in the Quartermaster Corps complained: "I went to the movies Saturday and saw an English picture and it sure stank."[6] Showings of movies in camp offered a poor substitute to the real moviegoing experience, as the same GI testified: "they show the movies here in an empty mess hall and we all sit on the hard floor and boy does it get numb, but it is better than nothing. The pictures are about a year old."[7] Movies were both a distraction and a reminder of life stateside that only added to the homesickness of some. For those GIs stationed in the rural west of England, celluloid America appeared to be in a different time and space from the world that surrounded them.

Furloughs to London offered opportunities to see the sights and experience the big city and an English version of modernity. British Member of Parliament, Harold Nicolson showed GIs around the Palace of Westminster: "I had an appointment to conduct some American doughboys round the Palace of Westminster. In they slouched, chewing gum, conscious of their inferiority in training, equipment, breeding, culture, experience and history, determined in no circumstances to be either interested or impressed."[8] Interestingly, GIs also took furloughs as opportunities to visit other sites of cultural or historic interest. For men of the 507th at Tollerton, historic Nottingham was a magnet both for its history, made famous by Hollywood's depiction of Robin of Sherwood (Robin Hood), and for its girls and pubs. In the south of England, Stonehenge was a frequently visited landmark, and Plymouth with its American connections was similarly popular, but almost every town had its share of curious GIs. The *Western Gazette* recorded one aspect of the phenomenon in November 1943:

> The Mayor of Taunton (Alderman Harold Goodland) has informed a representative of this paper that quite a number of members of the United States Forces, whose homes are in Taunton Massachusetts, have visited the town, and that it has given the Mayoress and him great pleasure to see them. Some of them have come from long distances to spend their leave here.[9]

Also, baseball and football games offered an outlet for the excess energy of bored young men. Exhibition games, which often involved fund-raising for local charities, offered an excellent means to build bridges with local host communities.[10] On May 28, 1944, thousands of people came to the Notts County soccer ground in

Nottingham to watch two teams from the 82nd Airborne play an exhibition baseball game.[11] The 116th Infantry in particular achieved a considerable reputation for their skills on the baseball field. In 1942, when the regiment arrived in Britain, games of baseball were organized on an ad hoc basis. This rapidly evolved into games between companies, and ultimately games between the 116th Regiment and neighboring units. Colonel Canham, the regimental commander, could see the value of the games to his regiment's *esprit de corps*, and the men of the regimental team, known as the Plymouth Yankees, were relieved of all duties in order to train and practice. The Yankees played their games at the Plymouth Greyhound Stadium at Pennycross, in the Peverell district of the city. Baseball fields could be found in other towns and cities in the southwest, such as at Torquay, where a diamond was laid out in Torre Abbey Gardens. Perhaps the star of the 116th's team was pitcher Elmere Wright of Company A. He had pitched for Bedford High School, and scouts for major league teams had shown interest in him in the summer of 1941. Such was the proficiency of the Plymouth Yankees that in 1943 they were invited to play in the European Theater of Operations World Series. Held at the headquarters of the 8th Air Force at Bushy Park in London, the series was also contested by 20 teams from the U.S. Navy, Army, and Army Air Force. Teams consisted of fifteen men and one officer. In the final, the Plymouth Yankees beat the Fighter Command Thunderbolts by a score of 6–3. Their 1943 season record was 27–0.[12] Despite the team's success, none of its members who eventually returned to the United States in 1945 would ever play professional baseball in the major leagues.

Baseball was not the only thing at which the division's athletes excelled. The 29th's football team was similarly crowned ETO World Series champions at the end of an undefeated 1943 series. Likewise, the boxing and softball teams would be hailed as ETO World Series champions. The records of the basketball team was 16–1 in 1943 and 35–0 the following year.[13] The sporting success of the division reflected the thoroughness of the physical training it went through in preparation for D-Day.

For the majority of men, drinking in local British pubs was their principal local recreation. One even gave an interview on the subject to the *Western Evening Herald* in 1943:

> I suppose the Englishman's pet is the pub, and he feels that it is distinctive to his country. In some respects he has a right to be proud, for in few other lands will you find the wholehearted feeling of general good fellowship you have in the English pub. Here is meeting and singing and playing at darts such as you'll seldom see in America. But the States do have pubs. They are called taverns, or more familiarly "beer joints." In these you can guzzle beer or mixed drinks to your hearts content. . . . Here good fellows meet, slap each other on the back, tell funny stories, do business, or "sob" over their beers.[14]

The sense of Anglo-American comradeship which developed around the public house was quite remarkable. The Griffin Inn at Plumtree was placed off limits to the troopers of the 507th immediately after their arrival in the nearby village of Tollerton. It became a point of honor for some men from the regiment to frequent the pub, and it became a point of honor on the part of the locals to ensure that they were not surprised by passing military police. Locals would stand sentry duty to prevent the men of the 507th from being disturbed while on their excursion. The pub was a real meeting place for Americans and their British hosts, although overindulgence could sometimes mar the exchange.

Inevitably, drunken Americans found themselves involved in brawls with each other and with British troops. The antagonisms between British troops and their American counterparts was fed by German propaganda, which taunted the former that while they were busy fighting, the latter were enjoying all the comforts that England had to offer. Pay differentials, American self-confidence, and differences of culture and history made the relationship between the common soldiers of two allied nations somewhat problematic. Everything about the Americans seemed glamorous to a British populace suffering wartime shortages. As a small boy, John Keegan was struck by the difference in vehicles between the British and American armies:

> The British army's transport was a sad collection of underpowered makeshifts...The Americans traveled in magnificent, gleaming, olive-green, pressed steel, four wheel drive juggernauts, decked with what car salesmen would call optional extras of a sort never seen on their domestic equivalents—deep-treaded spare tyres, winches, towing cables, fire-extinguishers. There were towering GMC six-by-sixes, compact and powerful Dodge four-by-fours, and pilot fishing the rest...tiny and entrancing jeeps.[15]

On the individual level, the differences were even more striking. An American private earned more than four and a half times the pay of a British private. British junior officers were paid less than half their American counterparts. Alcohol was invariably the catalyst needed to turn national differences into individual conflicts. For example, in December 1943 four Royal Marines were convicted of seriously assaulting an American soldier on Union Street in Plymouth. The Royal Marines were drunk and the attack was unprovoked. The American soldier was attacked for being American, which did not sit well with the judge who sentenced the men to two months' imprisonment with hard labor.[16]

Perhaps surprisingly, American troops and Canadians also had their differences, whose resolution usually involved violence. A troubled regional information officer from the northwest of England commented in July 1942:

> It appears that wherever Canadians and Americans meet there is trouble. Two nice American boys walked into the YMCA lounge and started talking to two WAAF's. Three Canadians who knew these WAAF's came in and tried to pull the girls away from the Americans. One Canadian said "I'm the middle-weight champion of Vancouver," whereupon the Americans knocked him out.[17]

Brawls were not the only form of criminal activity with which GIs involved themselves. In January 1944 Sergeant G. Campbell of C Company, 116th Infantry, reported to the civilian police in Ivybridge that his greatcoat, torch, zippo lighter, and gloves had been stolen from the King's Arms Hotel.[18] The following month, First Lieutenant Anderson informed local British police that eight packets of cigarettes had been stolen from hut 26 at Uphill Camp. In April a member of B Company, 116th Infantry, was sentenced to five years' hard labor and a dishonorable discharge after using a firearm to wound another soldier at Uphill Camp following an argument. Similar incidents were happening at other American bases. One infantryman from the 22nd Infantry Regiment, stationed at Denbury in Devon, wrote:

> Never has there been so much restlessness among the men as now when the time for invasion draws near. There is greater danger of getting hurt by our own troops than by the enemy. In one outfit a private managed to get hold of a live round of ammunition. He loaded his rifle, went into where his 1st sergeant was sleeping and shot him between the eyes. Then he walked outside and said to a group of buddies, "You don't have to worry any more about the first sergeant, fellows, he's dead."[19]

Americans were also prominent in feeding the British black market for hard-to-get rationed goods. In October 1943 one soldier from a Quartermaster Unit stationed in Ivybridge was sentenced to six months' hard labor for supplying a local man with ten gallons of petrol. The local man was fined £5.00. In December 1943 at Newton Abbot, four men from neighboring Bovey Tracey were convicted and fined for receiving boots and uniform items that were the rightful property of the American army. They had been purchased second hand from "coloured members of the United States forces."[20]

American soldiers were also involved in the world of British crime since they constituted a rich potential market for the purchase of stolen goods. Wartime Britain, with its shortages of almost everything, had little to offer the wealthy GI, but markets were created for some things. Illicitly distilled alcohol was one item that could be peddled to GIs who could remember the days of Prohibition. Bicycles were another commodity that the GI craved and for which an illicit market emerged. The demand for bicycles was insatiable. As one author noted: "Immediately the 82nd arrived their first-off duty hours were spent purchasing bicycles in Oakham. The dealers sold out every week including replacement stocks which had to be drawn from suppliers all over the country."[21] Such demand created a lucrative market for those who could supply it by whatever means.

Facing the dangers of combat, many American infantry officers took a permissive line with their men. Committing a serious indiscretion, soldiers would often be given the opportunity to accept company punishment instead of a court-martial. The best officers knew when to turn a blind eye to the indiscretion of their men, or when to arrange their administrative priorities in such a way that the problem went away. Sergeant Edward M. Isbell of Company E, 507th Parachute Infantry Regiment, managed to miss the last bus back to Tollerton one night while on pass to Nottingham:

It was about 1 am and much too far to walk. I heard a jeep coming down the street, so I hid, knowing it would be the MPs. When the jeep came around the corner, I recognized the driver. He had been in our regiment at one time, but transferred to the MPs. I ran out and stopped him. I asked him if he would take me back to camp. "Sure, Isbell, get in," he said. He told me he liked being an MP and was glad he had transferred out of the 507th. I wasn't familiar with Nottingham so I didn't notice where we were going until he stopped in front of the MP station. He told me to get out, that I was going to spend the night inside. I couldn't believe he was going to arrest me. I was so mad I could have killed him. I started to jump out and run, but he pulled me back. Another MP came running out. I couldn't handle both of them, but I did get a few licks in before they carried me inside. As I was standing in front of a lieutenant who was filling out the report, the MP who brought me in came up beside me and grinned. I swung at him. Just then the lieutenant stood up and he got the blow. The lieutenant didn't seem to get mad at me, knowing that I hit him by mistake. The two MPs locked me up for the night. The next morning I was carried back to camp and turned over to 1st Sergeant Thomas. They told him I had been picked up after curfew and was charged with being in town after curfew and resisting arrest. They told him I had hit the officer in charge, but he was not going to press charges. The official charge would be sent to the 507th regimental headquarters for action. The next week we went out in the field for a few days. Since I was communication chief I was around our company commander, Captain Creek, most of the time. He didn't mention the trouble I was in until we started back to camp three days later. We were walking along when he asked me what kind of trouble I had gotten into in town. Before I could answer, he said: "Never mind, I have the report on my desk and it looked like a Sear's catalog. I'll look at it when we get back to camp." When we got back, our replacements had arrived from the States. Judging by the number, it appeared they expected us to have lots of casualties. Things were so snafu with trying to double-up to make room for them and getting ready to leave for the invasion, I don't think Captain Creek ever got the chance to read the charges. I didn't hear any more about it.[22]

For those Americans who did not have such an understanding man as their company commander, a court-martial could beckon after any wrongdoing. Held in public, these court-martials were there to dispense justice and to ensure that justice was seen to be done. They were held under American military jurisdiction and followed the pattern of American courts. This caught the attention of the British press on more than one occasion. After a court-martial at Paignton in Devon, one local journalist wrote:

It was with a shock that one realised that counsel really do, in true film fashion, leap to their feet and yell "I Object," to which the president of the court replies "Objection sustained" or "objection overruled." Counsel also paced about the court room sometimes spinning round on the witness with a particularly pertinent question.[23]

Criminal behavior by GIs was reported by the British press but not fully and openly. Many newspaper editors felt it their duty for the sake of Anglo-American relations to smooth over the problems. Nevertheless, enough news reports of American wrongdoing found their way into the press for a harmful impression of the impact of GIs on British life to emerge. Murder cases were especially harmful, and the British press was willing to report on the proceedings in some detail. In 1944 the *Exeter Express and Echo* reported on the murder of a crippled Colchester taxi driver by a black GI.[24] They also reported on the murder following an argument of an American sailor by a GI on a railway station platform.[25] Their respective sentences—death for Private Leatherberry, the black GI, and life imprisonment for Private Henry O. Battles, who had stabbed the sailor—were reported without further comment.

GIs could also find themselves before British courts testifying against criminal activity by British civilians. American troops had a particular attraction for professional prostitutes. Public air raid shelters, empty except during raids, provided a myriad of opportunities for prostitutes and their wealthy clientele. Two Portsmouth-based prostitutes were convicted of violating a secure area in Newton Abbot in May 1944. In court it was revealed that one had been convicted of prostitution in 1923 and had further convictions for larceny and shoplifting.[26] Brothels opened to cater for the lucrative trade in serving the sexual needs of the American armed forces. These brothels would sometimes be targets for police raids. For example, a brothel at Newlyn in Cornwall was under observation from October 11 to November 17, 1943, as American and British soldiers were seen to frequent the house at "all hours of the night." On November 14 the house was raided by police who discovered two women in the company of two men. Both women were married, with one husband a prisoner of war in Germany and the other serving overseas. The six-year-old son of one woman was on the premises during the raid, and was removed and sent to a remand home. Both women received two months in prison.[27] In June 1944 the *Somerset County Gazette* recorded a raid on a brothel in Taunton used primarily by American soldiers.[28] Professional prostitutes were just as happy to accommodate black troops as white. As Norman Longmate has recorded:

A Cornish newspaper reported in September 1944 a typical case where a married woman from Bude admitted "having spent three days in a camp," occupied by coloured troops, "sleeping in huts with soldiers during the night and removing herself to a wood during the day." She was sentenced to two months in jail and a younger girl with her was placed on probation for twelve months. An American officer revealed in court that "at least fifteen men had been court-martialled for absence from duty caused by the presence of [the] defendant and other women at the camp."[29]

Professional prostitutes were also used to lure wealthy Americans into situations where they could be robbed. These robberies would sometimes be at the initiative of an individual prostitute. She might, for example, lure a GI into an air raid shelter and relieve him of his trousers containing his wallet at the key moment. The trouser-less GI would have difficulty pursuing the lady who had taken his wallet. Other crimes involved GIs being lured into dark corners where they would be assaulted by male associates of the prostitute. Understandably, GIs were often reluctant to report such crimes. In 1942 the Metropolitan Police estimated that for every

prostitution-related larceny committed against an American serviceman that was
reported to them, another four or five were not.[30]

In London, Plymouth, and other major British cities, other forms of sexual entertainment were also available to young Americans. One young American sailor was a
visitor to the Barbican area of Plymouth in 1944:

> One night stands out. A huge red-headed Irishman was singing Irish ditties—a beautiful
> voice. Then a very tall, skinny, elderly gal started to dance and strip to the waist only.
> Obviously she had been of very large stature at one time, because her skin hung down
> in large folds—including the very very pendulous breasts. They came down to her
> WAIST! Well!—As she danced, she tosses the left breast over her right shoulder and then
> the right over the left shoulder while kicking her legs out in time with the music! The
> noise of cheering and singing was something. No animosity between anyone there![31]

For local British police forces, the heavy American presence in some areas made
their work almost impossible. The presence in the West End of London of large
numbers of American personnel from 1943 to 1945 sparked a growth in prostitution, which the Metropolitan Police Force struggled hard to contain. From June 1
to August 27, 1942, police based at the West End Central Station made 296 arrests
of prostitutes for soliciting clients.[32] British policemen relied heavily on the American military police and navy shore patrols to cope with the trouble generated by
American military forces. After a polite word to troublemakers, British police officers
would call in the military police so as to allow Americans to solve their own problems. The postwar history of Exeter City special constabulary noted that, with the
decline in the number of American troops in Britain following D-Day, there was "a
certain relaxation in the strain of police duties."[33]

Many GIs spent their free time chasing the large number of single women in wartime Britain. With the Americans' smart uniforms, comparative wealth, and an aura
of glamour and danger, most British women were only too happy to be pursued by
lonesome GIs. Even women police officers had their difficulties performing their
duties in the presence of GIs. One woman police officer, Joan Salhurst, who was in
Bristol, recalled:

> There were a lot of Americans on my division, both coloured and white.... They were a
> big attraction to the local girls and I had to make regular patrols to move them on. Also
> to identify the younger ones in order to notify their parents. The GI's found a "lady cop"
> very unusual and were always wanting to date me. I got very annoyed with one sentry
> who would persist in calling me 'Red'. When I remonstrated with him, he just said,
> "Ok, Ginger." So that was that! Another of their embarrassing tricks was for the officer
> to give an "Eyes right" (or left) as they passed me.[34]

The pursuit of British women by Americans almost inevitably led to allegations of
that British life was being debased. The sight of couples having sex in quiet corners
became very common and GIs sometimes made their contempt known. One GI
wrote home:

The women are far from beautiful and go for the Americans in a big way. Of course they make no secret of the fact that they would have their life's wish fulfilled if they could go to America with a GI. It has been stated and reiterated that the moral standard of our American girls has lowered somewhat because of the war and its encompassing problems. Well, if that's so, the moral standard among women in England has reached a new low in degradation. Or perhaps it's always been that way there, how would we know.[35]

American men were persistent in their pursuit of women, and almost inevitably this led to allegations of rape. The allegations were not always substantiated by subsequent inquiries. A British police officer investigating a complaint of rape made by a 14-year-old girl against a GI suspected that something was not right. He asked: "'Have you been raped before?' 'Oh yes,' came the reply. 'Often!'"[36] Despite the fact that prophylactics were freely available to American soldiers some 24,000 babies were born, out of wedlock to GI fathers during and after the war. At least 83 of these babies were born to mothers in Devon.[37] Obtaining paternity maintenance from a GI was next to impossible unless he was willing to admit to being the father. The sight of young women turning up at barracks in search of errant fathers to be was all too commonplace. One young woman found herself facing particular difficulties when trying to call on the Catholic Chaplain of a unit in barracks in Plymouth. Both she and her friend were members of a Roman Catholic youth organisation. Both were invited to tea by the Chaplain:

We arrived at the gate and asked the guard to direct us to Father S.... He said: "go away." Thinking he had not heard aright, we said again, "Please can you direct us to Father S.'s office?" "No," he said, and called another guard, both complete with bayonets, and said, "Beat it girls."...Nell told them we had been invited to supper. "That's a new one," they said. "Look, girls, we know what you're after. Clear off." We tried to protest but they jeered at us, walking away and carrying on with their patrol. I for one was nearly in tears so we went to the nearest telephone box. In a voice full of indignation I told Father S. what had happened. "Oh dear," he said, "we get so many girls in trouble demanding to see me that the guards have orders not to let them in. Come back to the gate and I'll be there." As I put the phone down I...heard him roaring with laughter.[38]

GIs considered that the British reserve highlighted in *Welcome to Britain* was somewhat exaggerated. A further side effect of the promiscuity of many GIs and their British partners was a sharp rise in venereal disease. Captain Francis Ware, doctor to Second Battalion of the 12th Infantry Regiment, later commented:

Several months spent in Southern England provided time for ample contact with all the problems of V.D. The chaplains talked to the men about the moral responsibilities to themselves and their families, recommending abstinence. The medical officers strongly emphasised the matter of prevention. Every man going on pass they advised—it was almost an order—to pick up condoms when he checked out, as the army was glad to provide them. In the event of sexual contact the orders were explicit and simple. Void as soon as possible and report to a prophylactic station. These were easily available and the MPs were scattered about town and could always direct a man to a station. Here he voided again, cleaned himself very thoroughly, and was injected with an Argyrol solution.[39]

The venereal disease and promiscuity that the American presence generated caused considerable concern in British social circles. Further tensions with British civilians arose over the use of U.S. military vehicles for:

> It was widely believed that GIs had ready access to military vehicles for pleasure purposes and many British civilians took exception to this. The U-Boat menace was at its height and merchant seamen were at great risk bringing petrol to Britain. However, although a certain amount of pleasure-riding undoubtedly took place, it was considered a serious offence by the Americans and punishment was correspondingly severe. Typically, at one court martial in Bristol a GI who crashed a jeep while out pleasure riding with a couple of girls was sentenced to four years imprisonment.[40]

Some of the women encountered by GIs were married women doing their best to give the Americans a warm welcome. Many of the Americans behaved impeccably towards them. Vincent Edward Baker, an artilleryman who would be attached to the 29th Infantry Division on D-Day, met one married lady at a dance at Addebury House near Oxford. The troops were entertained by a string orchestra and ladies from the surrounding area were invited. After the dance Baker took her home: "She and her parents invited me into their home in Oxford. I visited with them and truly enjoyed their company. Pauline's husband was flying for the RAF at the time. I never had the pleasure of meeting him but my respect was with him for what appeared to be an insurmountable task of keeping the Nazis from completely destroying England."[41]

Of course some of the liaisons between American men and British women ended in marriage. Such unions became a standard feature of many of the local newspapers in the southwest of England.[42] *Yank* magazine, however, reminded its readers in July 1942: "No military personnel on duty in any foreign country or possession may marry without the approval of the commanding officer."[43] One officer later recalled the process that would have to be followed: "We were directed to interview them together and explain to the girl that this man she was interested in marrying was going into combat and there was a good possibility that he might get seriously wounded or killed. And we wanted that fact brought very clearly to their attention."[44] To emphasize the point, the *Western Gazette* warned its readers in April 1944: "Many English girls are marrying American soldiers. Many more are seriously thinking about taking this step. It should be known, however, that no American soldier stationed here is allowed to marry a West Country girl without first obtaining the permission of his commanding officer."[45]

Occasionally British newspapers would record less happy outcomes for potential GI brides. In May 1944 a 17-year-old girl from a small village in Somerset appeared before a police court to ask permission to marry Sergeant Cruz Regis Carranza, age

26, of the American army. Having not attained the British age of consent of 18, her father objected to the marriage on the grounds that Carranza had lied to her. Carranza's promises that he owned orange and lemon plantations in California hid the reality that he was a simple fruit picker and had few means to support a family. The *Somerset County Gazette* recorded the fact that Carranza was of Mexican and Indian ancestry. Other factors in the case did not endear Carranza to the court. "The Chairman: 'I expect you know this little girl is expecting a child.' Carranza: 'Yes Sir.' Mr Elston [the girl's father] was then asked if he knew that his daughter and Sergt. Carranza had been courting. He replied that he was aware that it was going on to such an extent."[46] The father had approached Carranza's commanding officer, who had told her what to expect if she married him. Refusing to be put off from marrying Carranza either by his commanding officer or her father, the young woman had turned to the police court to obtain permission to marry against her father's will. In the end, the court sided with the father and permission to marry was refused. Race and perceptions about Carranza's behavior were clearly factors in the court's decision. Such events were comparatively rare occurrences. In total some 80,000 British women married American servicemen during the Second World War. In recognition of this facet of Anglo-American relations, and the impact of wartime restrictions on the ability of brides-to-be to find white gowns or material, the General Federation of Women's Clubs of the United States organized the dispatch of bridal gowns across the Atlantic. Once in England they would be hired out to brides at a cost of 10 shillings to cover the cleaning of the garment.[47]

Those GIs already romantically involved with women back in the United States spent much of their time worrying about how to sustain the relationship in the midst of a war of indefinite duration. German propaganda radio did its best to exacerbate these fears. Playing a mixture of swing music and ballads, Axis Sally asked listening GIs: "And what are your girls doing tonight fellows?—You really can't blame them for going out to have some fun, could you? Its all so empty back there now—better to go out for some drinks with that 4-F boy friend than to sit and wait forever."[48]

The boisterous antics of American GIs attracted considerable comments in some quarters of British society. Some newspapers in the South West were happy to report incidents of antisocial behavior on the part of American soldiers, while others were content to make only the vaguest references to American forces quartered in the locality. In May 1944 the behavior of American troops became an issue for Parliament and the press as Dennis Kendall, the Member of Parliament for Grantham, alleged in the House that so unruly were American troops that it was unsafe for women to walk about the town unaccompanied.[49] The Home Secretary, Herbert Morrison, responded that such allegations were "misconceived and rather mischievous."[50] Thanks to D-Day, the affair was quickly brushed aside, despite the fact that Kendall received extensive backing from civic leaders in Grantham.[51] Nevertheless the allegations were felt significant enough to be reported in the *New York Times*.

The British courts also responded to perceptions of moral degeneracy generated by the American presence. While they could not discipline American servicemen, they could deal with British civilians in contact with them. In particular, British courts took a harsh view on young British women associating with American soldiers. In March 1944 American police stopped a U.S. Army truck at Taunton. Driven by a black GI, the truck contained a woman and her underage daughter. The time was 1:30 AM, and they were returning from a dance at Martock. It was explained to the officer that the GI had merely offered the women a lift. The mother was eventually brought before Illminster juvenile court on March 28, where she was charged with "not exercising proper control" of her daughter. During the course of the trial it became very apparent that the daughter knew about "sex matters" and was routinely allowed to stay up late and mix with black GIs.[52] A juvenile court at Bridgwater in May 1944 sentenced a 15-year-old girl to three weeks in a Salvation Army home for associating with GIs, during which time "intimacy" had occurred.[53] The mother of the child blamed her husband, who was never around. It was explained that the girl had a mental age of 9.5 years but "was very fond of poetry." In June 1944 Taunton juvenile court heard the case of a 14-year-old maidservant who had had sex with a number of American service personnel—army as well as navy. She was remanded to a children's home. The following month another juvenile court heard the case of two girls, age 16 and 17, who had absconded from an approved school. They were found on Taunton station sleeping in a waiting room and in a drunken state.[54]

Such measures to control wayward teenagers may seem draconian. Approved schools offered a strict regimen to children of school age, which was designed to develop a sense of personal discipline. They were seen as a solution to failures of parenting. However, they did little to prevent such children from consorting with Americans. By 1943 health officials in Britain were alarmed at the number of children who were absconding from approved schools, soliciting American troops in the West End of London, and contributing to an explosion of venereal disease in wartime Britain. The use of physical restraints to prevent the girls from absconding was seriously discussed in 1943.[55] The role of the GI in this needs to be understood. They did not create the problem of wayward children, but they did offer a potential source of money for teenagers on the run from the authorities.

In recognition of the dangers to Anglo-American relations posed by the growing numbers of eager and anxious American troops in Great Britain the British government kept some of its files dealing with the problems caused by GIs secret for over 60 years after D-Day. Rather more usefully and immediately, Eisenhower issued an order in February 1944 directed to "Every American Serving under My Command." In it he listed the potential issues that might generate Anglo-American antagonism:

Improper use of motor transportation;

Drinking in public places;

Excessive drinking, at any time. In this connection, public drunkenness by an officer will invariably call for the sternest disciplinary action permissible;

Loud, profane or indecent language, especially in public;

Slovenliness in appearance;

Any discourtesy to civilians. I stress again the constant need for road courtesy on the part of all drivers of U.S. Army cars.

Eisenhower's order bore testimony to the fact that on a small cramped island under the tensions of wartime, unfortunate incidents could occur. By early 1944 a few too many of these incidents were reaching the ears of Allied high command and the press for comfort. Such was the crackdown on unauthorized use of U.S. Army vehicles that in late 1944 one U.S. Army Air Corps pilot found it easier to borrow a four-engined heavy bomber than a jeep in order to visit a friend at a nearby airfield.[56] However, a far more explosive issue than drunken American soldiers and the dangerous driving of jeeps threatened to sour Anglo-American relations.

CHAPTER 5

Segregation and Race

In addition to baseball, the GIs also imported with them some less desirable features of American society in the 1940s. American society in the South remained segregated between black and white, and the resulting tensions frequently erupted into violence. The summer of 1943 witnessed widespread race rioting across the United States. Los Angeles, Detroit, New York, and other cities witnessed serious disturbances, and in the South black troops in uniform, even in the midst of a war, were not spared racial abuse and violence. African-Americans remained second-class citizens, denied equal treatment in almost every sphere. The American army was similarly segregated, with African-Americans allowed to serve behind the lines but not at the front. Thus while the face of the assault regiments on D-Day would be predominantly white, that of the quartermaster service was much more representative of the racial diversity of the United States. By the end of October 1942 there were 12,000 African-American soldiers in the United Kingdom. By May 1944 it had risen to over 130,000.[1]

Separate, and usually inferior, facilities were made available for African-American troops by the Special Service Division of the U.S. Army. In late 1944, under the impact of the Ardennes offensive, segregation would begin to break down; but before D-Day, segregation remained the policy of the U.S. military. The policy of segregation found widespread support within the army. A survey completed in March 1943 revealed that 85 percent of white soldiers and 48 percent of black soldiers considered that segregation was a "good idea."[2]

Within the ranks of the British government there was an early recognition that the issue of segregation in the American army stationed in England was going to be a difficult one for it to face. On the one hand, some members of the government were just as racist in their views as any fine Southern gentleman. On the other hand, the needs of the multicultural and multiethnic British Empire meant that any official support for a policy of segregation was out of the question. In 1942 the issue of government

42

policy towards the American color bar caused a flurry of discussion. As memorandums flowed back and forth in the higher levels of British government, the implicit racism of the upper levels of British society was very evident. A paper by the Home Secretary in October 1942 did not pull its punches.

> I am fully conscious that a difficult social problem might be created if there were a substantial number of cases of sex relations between white women and coloured troops and the procreation of half-caste children.... There is no doubt that respectable English girls may not realise that if they show to coloured men from the United States the same friendliness as they commonly show to our Service men the coloured man from America is likely to misunderstand their intentions and their character; and the creation of such misunderstanding is unfair to him and may be dangerous to the girls.[3]

Eventually the government settled on a policy of asking the British people to accept the American practice of segregation, while not endorsing it officially. The British government was not going to be involved in the provision of separate facilities for white and black troops, but if the American army chose to do this, then that was its affair. Likewise, the British would not endorse any policy that might have repercussions throughout the empire. Instead the British people would be asked to be careful, tactful, and respectful.

In practice it was a policy that many British people could not follow. Incidents of racial violence and discrimination between black and white Americans became so common place that many people felt forced to take sides, usually with the black GI. British disapproval became even more evident when white GIs were involved in violence against some of the empire's citizens of color, who had flocked to Britain in her hour of need in 1940. One incident to attract widespread public attention came on June 23, 1943, when Sergeant Walrond, a West Indian serving as an air gunner in the Royal Air Force, was assaulted by a sergeant in the American army. The incident took place at a dance and was sparked by Sergeant Walrond's invitation to a white woman to dance with him. A journalist by profession, Walrond took the matter up with the British Colonial Office:

> I came to this country from the British West Indies as a Volunteer for Air Crew Duties under the protection of the British Government, and I demand as far as is humanly possible that I get that protection and its corresponding consideration. I therefore request strongly that the incident referred to, be thoroughly investigated and taken up by the Colonial Office and the people concerned punished. I also request that action be taken to ensure the non-recurrence of such an affair as this either with myself or other coloured people in this country. As a newspaper journalist I have in every way criticised this horror of civilisation—(supposed civilisation to me). I have never been trained to think in terms of nations or races and I had hoped that four years of war would have at least have taught the world this lesson. But the long standing underlying prejudice for coloured people despite their value, ability or achievement still remains to rear its ugly head, and leaves a most distasteful gap to be bridged. To say time will remove these ills, is not good enough. The Government, I have assured myself can do a great deal towards it and must.

Is it fair, is it just, to ask me to risk my life nightly over enemy territory when behind me
I have left something as treacherous to humanity as any "ism."[4]

Before Walrond could take his campaign any further, he was posted as missing in
action over enemy territory. However, a British newspaper, the *Sunday Pictorial*, got
hold of the story and published it under banner headlines that read "What are we
Going to do About This—This Man was a Hero—He died that the Empire Might
Live."[5] The attitudes of white GIs were firmly on the public agenda, even if they
did not register at the political level.

Within British society, there was continued outrage at the treatment of the
African-American and at the way in which the racial politics of the American South
were allowed to intrude into British life. This was despite attempts by some white
GIs to turn British civilians against African-Americans. This included the deliberate
spreading of stories, such as the story that African-Americans had their monkey tails
tucked into their trousers.[6] To a certain extent British civilians had been prepared for
the repercussions of the racial politics of the American South. Louis MacNeice commented on the issue in his pamphlet *Meet the US Army*: "It must be remembered . . .
that while the Negroes form a very large section (one in twelve) of the American
nation, they are in the unique position of being descended from slaves; this memory
of slavery, being still fresh retains a psychological hold both on the Negroes themselves and on many of their white fellow-citizens."[7] MacNeice was, however, ada-
mant that "any American Negro who comes to Britain must be treated by us on a
basis of absolute equality."[8] Despite the prevailing attitude in British society that
racial bigotry could not be tolerated, attitudes born out of empire died hard for most
British civilians. While overt racism was the preserve of a minority of British civilians, covert racism was widespread. Some thought that the best way to limit the tensions in Britain generated by segregation was for the American military to limit the
number of African-Americans coming to Great Britain. Indeed, concerns about the
potential for racial violence led to a certain reluctance to deploy black units for service in the United Kingdom.[9] In the westcountry, the presence of large numbers of
troops from Virginia and Maryland in and around Plymouth was one of the factors
that counted against the deployment of black troops in the port.

The policy of segregation was to cause considerable problems for Eisenhower's
Supreme Headquarters, Allied Expeditionary Force. An order of July 16, 1942,
revealed the difficulties and contradictions arising out of segregation. Overt discrimination was to be averted, but it would be left up to local commanders as to how they
would square this policy with maintenance of the army's policy of racial segregation:

1. The presence of Negro troops in this Theater will present a variety of problems that can
   only be solved by constant and close supervision of Commanding Officers. It is the
   desire of this Headquarters that discrimination against the Negro troops be sedulously
   avoided. So far as London and other cities and leave areas where both Negro and White
   soldiers come on pass and furlough, it would be a practical impossibility to arrange for
   segregation so far as welfare and recreation facilities are concerned. . . .

2. A more difficult problem will exist in the vicinity of camps where both White and Negro soldiers are stationed, particularly with reference to dances and other social activities. This Headquarters will not attempt to issue and detailed instructions. Local Commanding Officers will be expected to use their own best judgement in avoiding discrimination due to race, but at the same time minimizing causes of friction between White and Coloured Troops.[10]

To a large extent the attitude of British civilians did not matter to white American soldiers. The sight of a white woman accompanied by a black GI was a sure-fire flashpoint, and the fact that many of these women were also married caused further offense to conservative whites. Racial antagonism went beyond race. The scale of dating between white British women and black GIs was remarkable, and many GIs must have wondered what was happening to stateside sweethearts in their absence. While white GIs found it easier to target African-Americans wearing the same uniform as themselves, rather than challenge the behavior of adulterous British women, many British civilians shared the prejudices against married women consorting with black GIs. Their behavior represented a threat to family and society irrespective of the color of their boyfriends. For example, five women were brought before Newton Abbot magistrates in April–May 1944, charged with violating security of protected areas in and around the town. All five were married and were in the process of seeing black boyfriends. They were publicly named and shamed and the local newspaper was not above revealing details such as "Chartres was a married woman, whose husband was serving abroad, and she had two children, aged 7 and 4."[11]

Trouble between black and white troops from Launceston to Torbay to Bristol and beyond was endemic. Usually this took the form of scuffles, but occasionally more serious violence erupted. Despite attempts to prevent black and white troops coming into conflict by limiting access to civilian facilities at closing time, drunken troops of both races could find themselves in the same street, resulting in trouble. This would have to be brought under control by the white-helmeted military police, referred to by the troops as "snowdrops." The snowdrops tended to respond to any problem rather more forcefully than the local constabulary, with the result that trouble sometimes escalated to even more serious levels. This certainly happened at Launceston on September 23, 1943, when harsh treatment by snowdrops caused a group of black GIs to arm themselves and return to the scene of an earlier incident in the town center. Two American military policemen were wounded before the incident came to an end. The public were informed in October that 21 arrests had followed, although the press did not report the outcome of the court-martial proceedings.[12]

Some towns were particularly prone to racial violence. Ivybridge at night had some of the features of a Western frontier town in the 19th century. Mortarman Randolph Ginman from Company D, 116th Infantry Regiment, had one memorable duty in late 1943:

During either November or December of 1943, I was picked to go on MP Duty—I weighed 195 lbs. at the time—at the dance hall in Ivybridge. Although this wasn't emphasised on the home front, the dance hall rules were that whites and blacks would alternate using the hall to dance with the English girls. This came about after a company of black engineers moved in at the opposite end of town... Anyway, that night I reported to the MP Station in the Center of Ivybridge and a regular MP and I started our tour of duty at 6pm when the black engineers were coming in for their night on the town. All was going well until around 9pm when a fight broke out between two of the black engineers over some of the English girls. It seemed like all of them wanted to get into the act and they started swinging. My MP partner and I were caught right in the center of this melee. But before we really had time to react, their First Sergeant jumped up on one of the tables and started blowing his whistle as loud as he could. As soon as it quieted down a little, he hollered out to all of them, "Any of you that start another fight will not get another pass to this dance hall as long as we're stationed here." Those magic words did the trick. The remainder of the night was a breeze.[13]

Another Company D man on MP duty, Sergeant John Slaughter, was caught up in another burst of violence that threatened to have even more serious consequences:

While we were away on an exercise, black troops moved into Ivybridge. Everyone knew that Ivybridge belonged to the 1st Battalion, 116th. The village simply could not support any more troops. Acrimony led to fighting between the newcomers and the battalion. One of the men found his girlfriend had been with one of the new arrivals, and it soon became apparent that the troops had to be separated. Every other night was off-limits for one race or the other, and, to make matters worse, when the blacks were in town the military policemen were whites, and vice versa. The trouble got worse, and there were several stabbings. One of our mortar platoon sergeants was caught leaving camp with a submachine gun, heading for town and intending to "clean the place out." I was selected for MP duty one night and paired with a soldier from one of the rifle companies. After the pubs had closed that night a mob of black soldiers, fortified by beer, came up the street shouting obscenities and acting belligerent. If was beginning to look ugly, and my partner and I backed into a doorway. One of the men, a rather large sergeant, was carrying a pistol. I called for him to drop his weapon. He hesitated, and I fired my carbine into the ground at his feet. He dropped the pistol and the crowd dispersed. This temporarily ended the crisis, but the problem persisted until we finally moved from Ivybridge to the assembly area in Dorset.[14]

In the Midlands, the 82nd Airborne Division around Nottingham and Leicester was involved in some particularly nasty incidents of racial intolerance. While the *Leicester Mercury* was happy to feature photographs of black GIs touring the city, General Gavin of the 82nd Airborne was less pleased with the reception accorded to African-Americans.[15] He recorded his thoughts in his diary:

Several near riots in town last night. English people, especially the lower classes, do not discriminate in any way. In fact they prefer the company of colored troops. The colored troops have been in this community for almost a year and they are well intrenched. Many are living with local English women. With the advent of the white troops frays and minor unpleasant encounters have occurred in the local pubs and dance halls. American whites resent very much seeing a white woman in the company of a colored soldier. Here they almost see them in bed with them. Last night the 505th had its officer patrols armed. The negroes resented this alleging that the white officers intended to get them. A group of negroes broke into an arms storeroom secured arms stole a truck and headed for town. They were intercepted on the way by one of their own officers and taken back to camp thus avoiding what might have been a disastrous situation. Today I had conferences with...anyone...interested. Placed Leicester off limits until further orders, had all unit CO's make a shakedown for weapons and talk to their men person- ally. Now is no time to settle our racial problem. The attitude of the British is in many respects difficult to understand. Their treatment of colonials is deplorable yet they entirely mishandle the colored problem. They inflame it and run, yelling all the while, this is no way to do things in a democracy. Visited our packing sheds in Cottesmore. They will have chutes ready for the BN tests and the jump school. This colored problem took most of the damn day.[16]

There were several repercussions from the ongoing racial tension in Leicester. One of the most dramatic was the removal of Lieutenant Colonel Herbert Batcheller from command of the 505th Parachute Infantry Regiment. In response to trouble in Leicester on February 28, he announced to his regiment that everyone would be allowed on pass to Leicester. Majority opinion in the regiment was that their com- manding officer was giving them a chance to settle scores. That night the trouble escalated, and it took strong intervention from divisional officers over several nights to calm the city. On March 21, following an inquiry, Batcheller was relieved of his command. However, there was recognition that Batcheller was a good officer, and he was sent to the 508th Parachute Infantry Regiment. Like the 507th, the 508th had arrived in Nottingham after shipping out from the United States. Batcheller would serve as a battalion commander in the 508th and would be killed in action on D-Day. Despite prompt and ongoing action by Gavin, racial trouble continued to be a feature of the 82nd Airborne's stay in the English Midlands.

The level of racially generated violence generated by American troops resulted in the development of widespread segregation across Britain. Within the U.S. military, separate facilities were provided for white and black soldiers. To prevent conflict, the idea of separate facilities was extended to the civilian world. This was managed in dif- ferent ways. At Newton Abbot, black troops were allowed into town on certain days, white troops on others. At Buckfastleigh, black troops frequented some pubs and the whites other establishments. In Exeter, American authorities chose to use the River Exe as the line of segregation. White troops were given free reign in the city center and areas north of the river, while black troops were kept in the suburbs on the south side of the river. With one bridge over the river the Exe made an easily defensible boundary for the military police to control.[17] The extent to which the policy of seg- regation helped to control the level of racial violence is highly questionable and, in the circumstances of a war being fought for liberty, some wondered just how far democratic values would be tarnished by the mechanics of winning it. Many GIs were deeply alarmed by 1944 at the extent of the racial violence taking place in towns across England. One GI of the 22nd Infantry Regiment wrote:

Conditions in town are worse than ever. It is hardly safe to walk on the streets at night even in the company of three or four others. Last night in Torquay a quartet of white soldiers was cornered by fifteen colored and beaten up in the dark. It happens that they indiscriminately picked on four of impeccable reputation who never get into trouble. While it is true that whites are generally the provokers, it is not doing the Negro cause any good when they jump whites at random. The matter has reached major proportions of national scandal which America may not live down for years.[18]

While the levels of racial violence were worrying, there were instances when British public opinion was instrumental in changing the attitudes of the American army. In May 1944 a black driver was sentenced for raping a woman near Bath. The court-martial trial was told that one night he knocked on her door after becoming lost. After asking her for directions, the man then raped her. He alleged that he had twice previously had sex with the woman, who charged him £1.00 on both occasions. On the date of the alleged rape, she had demanded £2.00 with the threat that she would make allegations against him unless he paid. The court-martial trial found him guilty and sentenced him to death. A British newspaper got hold of the story and organized a petition. Some 20,000 signatures were collected and sent to General Eisenhower.[19] He set aside the conviction because of insufficient evidence. In planning for a successful invasion of Europe, the supreme headquarters had to fight on military, political, and social fronts.

CHAPTER 6

Amphibious Training

In addition to general training designed to ensure that troops were up to the highest physical standards, the 22nd and 116th infantry regiments received specific amphibious training in England to supplement their training stateside. The training in England was particularly interesting, because by 1943 the nature of the task facing an invading Allied army on the shores of France was already evident. With the Germans investing heavily in coastal defenses, it was clear that Allied efforts to cut through them would require equal investment, precision, ingenuity, and bravery. It called for a vision of how to employ infantry regiments, assault engineers, amphibious Duplex Drive (DD) Sherman tanks, and other weapons of war:

> The first waves would consist of two battalions from the regiments, landing in a column of companies, with the third battalion coming in behind. Assault teams would cover every inch of beach, firing M-1s, .30-caliber machine guns, BARs, bazookas, 60mm mortars, and flamethrowers. Ahead of the assault teams would be DD tanks, Navy underwater demolition teams, and Army engineers. Each assault team and the supporting units had specific tasks to perform, all geared to opening the exits. As the infantry suppressed whatever fire the Germans could bring to bear the demolition teams would blow the obstacles and mark the paths through them with flags, so that as the tide came in the coxswains would know where it was safe to go. Next would come the following waves of landing craft, bringing in reinforcements on a tight, strict schedule designed to put firepower ranging from M-1s to 105mm howitzers into the battle exactly when needed, plus more tanks, trucks, jeeps, medical units, traffic-control people, headquarters, communication units—all the physical support and administrative control required by two overstrength divisions of infantry conducting an all out offensive.[1]

This was the way in which the U.S. Army planners envisaged their forces would land on the coast of France and force a way inland. Aerial bombardment, an intense naval barrage, and amphibious Sherman medium tanks would allow the infantry to engage the few surviving enemy positions with heavy weapons. The Atlantic Wall, a network of fixed positions and extensive beach defenses designed to prevent an Allied landing and stretching along the length of the Atlantic coasts of Belgium and France, were the boast of the German newsreels in 1943 and 1944. To counter the defenses the Allied armies would land at low tide to avoid the beach obstacles, whose placings were predicated on the basis of a landing at high tide. A high-tide landing would give the assaulting troops the shortest distance of beach to cross. A landing at low tide would leave them fully exposed to enemy fire on the beach, but it would avoid the obstacles, many of which had been mined. However, the U.S. Army had confidence in the assault doctrine it had developed to overcome German defenses. It would call for the initial waves of infantry to work in particular and unaccustomed ways. This, and the need to practice "green troops" of regiments like the 116th Infantry, called for extensive rehearsal and training. As the U.S. Army steadily built up its forces under the Bolero plan, it was forced to survey existing training areas and to survey new sites on which it might practice landing on the shores of France.

In July 1943 a U.S. Army Assault Training Center was set up in North Devon. Utilizing the extensive beaches available in the Woolacombe area, it would provide training and a space to hold exercises for the regimental combat teams to test and develop assault techniques. The center would be staffed by a team who would oversee the training. As well as infantry assault training, the center would train antitank, engineer, communications, supply, and medical units that would follow up the landings after enemy fire had been largely suppressed. Much of this training would involve learning the secrets of embarkation/disembarkation, including the preparation of vehicles for landing and subsequent use. Tank crews would also rehearse the techniques for deep wading and practice coordinated fire with infantry units.

Before the training could begin, the Assault Training Center had to be carefully prepared. The U.S. Army wanted Woolacombe and the other villages near the beaches to be evacuated, but the British government would not allow this. Locals and GIs would coexist with Woolacombe like an armed camp. Land had to be acquired from local farmers, and the 112th Engineer Regiment was brought in to construct facilities, erect quonset huts for accommodations, and put in the necessary infrastructure to cope with the influx of hundreds of young men. Drains and roads were improved, and headquarters were established in the Woolacombe Bay Hotel.

The influx of American troops into the area around Woolacombe was not universally welcomed. The Cotton family, originally from Boston, Massachusetts, had moved to Instow in North Devon from London in 1940. Richard Cotton was managing director of British Rola Ltd., and when the factory relocated from London to rural North Devon, so did he, his wife, grown-up daughters, and son who was still at school. In 1943, fearing for both her community and daughters, Mrs. Mary Cotton wrote:

> Hundreds of Americans have taken over Woolacombe sands and cliffs as training ground for an assault course. The headquarters is adjacent to Mr Tomsette's factory, and the fields are full of tanks, "ducks," and jeeps. The confusion and explosion noises

Tank landing, Assault Training Center, Woolacombe (Olin Dows collection, Franklin D. Roosevelt Presidential Library)

of almost...constant manoeuvres are turning Woolacombe into a nightmare for residents and evacuees. Martha has had a lot of nice young officers...They take her and Alix to the dances—those fabulous dinner-dances of an American Army HQ where the food is like ambrosia to people so long on rations...The swaggering, boisterous antics of thousands of GI's bewilders Devonians. In the pubs the American soldier treats the English beer and whiskey-soda like soda fountain or milk-bar drinks.[2]

With the establishment of the Assault Training Center, the engineers set about constructing dummy enemy positions, including concrete pillboxes. On these targets, the infantry assault teams would practice. Each infantry assault team consisted of 30 men (eight riflemen, a four-man demolition team, a four-man bangalore torpedo team, a four-man mortar section, a four-man machine gun team, a four-man bazooka team, and a four-man flamethrower team). Each team was heavily armed with a variety of weapons to give it the capacity to deal with a range of enemy threats. Bangalore torpedoes would cut through enemy barbed wire, while suppressing fire was laid down by the riflemen and machine gun teams. Enemy troops out of line of sight would be attacked with mortar fire while bazookas, flamethrowers, and demolition charges dealt with fortified enemy positions. The assault doctrine called for

Men of 116th Infantry Regiment practicing disembarkation from ship, Assault Training Center, Woolacombe (Olin Dows collection, Franklin D. Roosevelt Presidential Library)

much rehearsal and practice. Separate areas of the Assault Training Center were set aside for training on a variety of weapons, and a special frame was constructed using steel scaffolding poles and scramble nets on which troops could practice clambering down the sides of a ship and getting into the LCAs (Landing Craft Assault) waiting for them below. On a typical day in almost every area of the Assault Training Center, from Saunton Sands to Morte Hoe, visitors could see different aspects of assault techniques being practiced and refined. Some onlookers found it tremendously exhilarating:

> Amphibious Landing Manoeuvres became the background to every day life in Woolacombe. There were aircraft flying overhead, machine gun fire, mortars going off, smoke screens and landing craft of all sizes coming ashore in mock invasion most days with tanks and half-tracks moving about the sands and hinterland behind the dunes. Everything was very much for real and, of course, there were hundreds of American troops in full kit scurrying about all over the place...By and large the Americans were immensely generous, very friendly and helpful to the communities where they were billeted.[3]

Inevitably casualties resulted from the live firing practice and assault training. On one occasion, twelve tank crewmen and two landing craft crewmen were killed when

Men of 116th Infantry Regiment practicing disembarkation from landing craft, Assault Training Center, Woolacombe (Olin Dows collection, Franklin D. Roosevelt Presidential Library)

three landing craft overturned in the surf. On another occasion, a similar disaster overtook a convoy of ducks. It is probable that at least 30 Americans were killed at the Assault Training Center during its short life. Training accidents would happen elsewhere across the southwest of England.[4]

No authoritative or even approximate figure can be determined for the number of training fatalities suffered by U.S. forces based in Britain during the Second World War. What is certain is that such a figure would be remarkably high. When examined at regimental or battalion level, training accidents are reported as a daily fact of military life. Oral evidence highlights the realistic nature of the training and a wide awareness of accidents. Some incidents even made the British press despite wartime censorship: "Residents of a Southern town were alarmed by a violent explosion in the district on Monday morning. Twenty-nine United States soldiers were killed and eight injured when explosives were accidentally set off during training activities...It is stated that six of the men killed came from one street in their home town."[5]

Three regiments of the 4th Infantry Division (8th, 12th, and 22nd), three regiments of the 29th Division (115th, 116th, and 175th) and three regiments of the 28th Division (109th, 110th, and 112th) would pass through the center between 1943 and 1944. The first unit to go through the center in September 1943 was the

Men of 116th Infantry Regiment practicing disembarkation from landing craft, Assault Training Center, Woolacombe (Olin Dows collection, Franklin D. Roosevelt Presidential Library)

116th Infantry Regiment. Traveling by truck convoy from West Devon, the advance guard arrived at the center on Sunday, September 12. The advance guard would act as assistant instructors to the Regimental Combat Team, which arrived on Monday, September 20. Their course lasted three weeks and concluded with a full assault landing against an "enemy" beach. The Regimental Combat Team of the 116th Infantry Regiment returned to the center for a refresher course from May 20 to 29, 1944.

At every stage the training was recorded. Over 100,000 feet of film were shot by a film unit under a Lieutenant Ries. Some of the footage was released for public consumption, but most of it was used to analyze particular aspects of the training. The Woolacombe Bay Hotel had its own cinema, which was used to show recreational and training films. Local children were particularly impressed by the development:

> As children, one aspect of the arrival of the army in the village was Saturday Morning Film Shows which the soldiers put on for the local boys and girls. These were held in the Ballroom of the Woolacombe Bay Hotel which had been converted into a cinema for showing military training films to the troops. The rear of the hall had seating on a raised wooden ramp which helped convey the feeling one was in a real cinema! There were all the usual cartoons of the times: Mickey Mouse, Donald Duck...cowboy films and Laurel & Hardy. Later in the war, I seem to remember going to the Bungalow Cafe

Men of 116th Infantry relaxing on the beach, Assault Training Center, Woolacombe (Olin Dows collection, Franklin D. Roosevelt Presidential Library)

(now the "Red Barn") which was in use as a cinema. Around 1943, a huge aircraft hangar was erected on the seafront green, about opposite Rock Field Road. Here the American soldiers presented weekly cinema shows of the top Hollywood Entertainment Films, many in technicolor, which locals and troops were welcome to attend; there was a modest entrance fee, something like a shilling.[6]

The U.S. Army invested heavily in the Assault Training Center and the assault doctrine it helped to develop for the invasion of France. However, even before June 1944 there were signs that all might not go according to a highly complex plan. While the 29th Infantry Division was inexperienced, the 1st Infantry Division, alongside whom it would land on Omaha Beach, had seen action in North Africa and the Mediterranean. Only select elements of the division were to pass through the Assault Training Center. Some of the veterans of the 1st Infantry Division reacted badly to the Center's training regime:

Most of the veteran dogfaces thought it was mostly B.S., this constant assault on dummy emplacements by men who had been through the real thing several times. One day, when [Lieutenant] Dowling was out visiting the troops in the field, he came upon one of the rifle platoons sitting behind a high dune on the beach. The instructor Lieutenant had the riflemen clustered around a small fire, which they kept going by shooting flamethrower charges into the ground. Two men were posted atop the dunes as outposts, to

116th Infantry Regiment bazooka training, Assault Training Center, Woolacombe (Olin Dows collection, Franklin D. Roosevelt Presidential Library)

warn of visits by high-ranking officers; the rest of the troops just huddled round the fire, smoking and waiting for lunch to be brought up. No wonder: their Assault Training Center instructor was a brand-new second Lieutenant who had never been in combat. When the dogfaces started telling him about their Sicilian and African experiences, the Lieutenant really had to shut up.[7]

Like the infantry, the training of the combat demolition units, which David Howarth has described as "hurried and incomplete," was marred by problems and a lack of experience.[8] It was hard to keep pace with the ongoing development of the anti-invasion defenses on the beaches, and demolition techniques continued to evolve with the ingenuity of the defenses they were designed to overcome. The techniques taught by the Assault Training Center were in late 1943 and early 1944 put to the test in a series of large practice landings codenamed Duck (December 31, 1943, to January 2, 1944), Fox (March 10–12, 1944), Muskrat (March 24–27, 1944), Beaver (March 29–31, 1944), Tiger (April 27–29, 1944), and Fabius (May 3–6, 1944). These landings made use, among other areas, of Slapton Sands, a section of the South Devon Coast that had been requisitioned in 1943 for use as an Assault Training Area. With wide sandy beaches and a freshwater lake behind, Slapton Sands resembled what would be Utah Beach and the inundated area behind it. Thirty thousand areas of farmland and small villages would be requisitioned. As local historian Grace Bradbeer noted:

> Slapton and Blackpool Sands, in company with all south-coast beaches, had been shut off to the public ever since the beginning of the war and given protection in case of possible landings. There were mines, masses of barbed wire and notices everywhere, while any little fishing boat, even a dinghy, could only put to sea if granted a permit. The forlorn appearance of Slapton Sands was already aggravated by the damage done to the hotel which, right on the sands, had been evacuated in 1939 at the outbreak of war. A local black-and-white farm dog, named Pincher, had succeeded in crawling under the barrier one day, had trodden on a mine and blown up a part of the building as well as himself. That lovely stretch of coastline was indeed looking shabby and neglected.[9]

Locals living inside the requisitioned area were given short notice to leave their homes. Many would never return. Some 3,000 people were given six weeks to leave their homes, their farms, and their businesses. Local churches were cleared of their valuables, while efforts were made to protect those items and monuments that could not be moved.[10] The scale of destruction that would be visited on the local area around Slapton, the scene of repeated military exercises, would unfortunately exceed the worst fears of the families who were forced to evacuate it.

During the exercises, certain problems repeatedly became manifest, including the tendency of troops to bunch together on the beach, the difficulties of coordinated all-arms assault, the difficulty of navigating landing craft, and the difficulty of protecting the assault forces from enemy attack. Deaths and other serious injuries accompanied the training, as artillery rounds fell short and troops fell victim to accidents. In the Adjutant General's files at the National Archives and Records Administration II building in College Park, Maryland, are preserved the records of the pre-invasion exercises. Among records are reports from the medical detachments which had to deal with a wave of real as well as simulated casualties. For example, during Exercise Fox at Slapton, the 53rd Medical Battalion dealt with 15 real casualties, including two dead, two wounded, four injured, five sick and two gassed as a result of carbon monoxide poisoning.[11] Casualties in training were an accepted feature of military life.

Most tragically of all, during Exercise Tiger on April 28, 1944, three LSTs (Landing Ship Tank) out of an eight-ship convoy were torpedoed by German E-Boats from the Fifth and Ninth Schnelboot Flotillas. The flower class corvette HMS *Azalea* had been assigned to protect the convoy, but at the time of the attack she was 15 miles away. LSTs 507 and 531, "loaded with [an estimated] 749 Army and 282 Navy personnel," were sunk.[12] Lieutenant Eugene Eckstam was on LST 507 when it was torpedoed:

> The torpedo hit amidships starboard in the auxiliary engine room, knocking out all electric and water power. We sat and burned. A few casualties came into the wardroom for care and, since there was ample help, I checked below decks aft to be sure no one required medical attention there. All men in accessible areas had gone topside. The tank

deck was a different matter. As I opened the hatch, I found myself looking into a raging inferno which pushed me back. It was impossible to enter. The screams and cries of those many Army troops in there still haunt me. Navy regulations call for dogging the hatches to preserve the integrity of the ship, and that's what I did. Until the fire got so hot we were forced to leave the ship at 0230, we watched the most spectacular fireworks ever. Gas cans and ammunition exploding and the enormous fire blazing only a few yards away are sights forever etched in my memory. Ship's company wore life jackets, but the medics and Army personnel had been issued inflatable belts. We were told only to release the snaps and squeeze the handles to inflate. Climbing down a cargo net, I settled into the 42 degree F. water, gradually getting lower as the life belt rose up to my arm pits. The soldiers that jumped or dove in with full packs did not do well. Most were found with their heads in the water and their feet in the air, top heavy from not putting the belts around their chests before inflating them. Instructions in their correct use had never been given.[13]

As hundreds of men entered the water, the American officer commanding the gun batteries on the coast at Portland instructed his men not to fire at any E-boats for fear of killing Americans in the water. Some 290 men were later picked out of the water. William Smith was a signalman on British motor launch 303, which was sent out to rescue survivors and recover the dead. He remembered:

On arrival we found hundreds of dead US soldiers floating and bobbing around. Their body movements were being accentuated by a heavy swell. They were fully clad with steel helmets firmly fastened. A large proportion had badly burnt faces and hands and from a distance we initially mistook them for colored troops. Having passed through burning oil-covered sea it would seem a fair number had suffocated and in their death throes had drawn their legs up to their May West life jackets, causing them to hunch up with rigor mortis. We pulled them in with boat hooks and set them on the boat sides, along the rails, with their faces facing outboard; we loaded about fifty or so per boat and returned to Portland. The action of placing the bodies facing outwards was to avoid the crew having to look at the damaged and grotesque faces. However, this served little purpose as the next boat alongside had done the same and we could easily see the awful visage on those boats. [Back at Portland] American ambulances manned by colored GIs were waiting to load the bodies and at first they attempted to carry two on a stretcher but that did not work, as the gangplanks were too narrow and encumbered with safety rails. . . . We did two trips that day and it was a very subdued crew that evening with the added warning that it was a complete hush-hush affair and under no conditions were the day's events to be discussed outside the ship, or reported in letters home.[14]

One landing ship, LST 289, eventually returned to Dartmouth despite the scale of the damage inflicted on her. Four of her crew were dead and nine missing as a torpedo wrecked the crews quarters and steering gear.[15] Some 749 Americans lost their lives as a result of Exercise Tiger. Higher estimates of the number of casualties (up to 948) may well incorporate numbers killed in other training accidents. It was a worrying warning of the possible casualty levels in the invasion yet to come. Cause for concern was also generated by the fact that the protection for the convoy had broken down as a result of Anglo-American misunderstandings. The 4th Infantry Division would lose more men on Exercise Tiger than they would in the eventual assault on Utah Beach.

In the aftermath of Exercise Tiger, considerable efforts were put into recovering the dead. Allied naval units recovered as many as possible from the sea. Many bodies were stacked on Castletown Pier in Portland Naval Dockyard. The task of recovering the bodies was as grim as could be imagined. Royal Navy leading telegraphist Nigel Creswell served on a motor torpedo boat involved in the operation to recover the bodies:

> On a bright, sunny late spring morning I saw us approach what looked like an outdoor swimming pool, but there were hundreds of bodies in the water and they were all dead. I was not quite 21 and had seen the odd dead body, but nothing to what we saw before us. . . . I remember examining two or three of the bodies that had been brought on board. Their Army denim uniforms had the button crimped to the material so that the buttons could not be removed. I remember two of the dog-tags had "Rome City, New York."[16]

Others were recovered from the beaches of southwest England. The dog tags of the dead were collected until at last General Eisenhower and the Supreme Headquarters Allied Expeditionary Force (SHAEF) were certain that 20 missing officers, with a security clearance that meant that they knew key details of the invasion plan, were accounted for. Until Allied intelligence could be certain that the Germans had neither time nor opportunity to take key men out of the water, the D-Day invasion plan was imperilled.

Exercise Tiger was a rehearsal for the landings on Utah Beach. Hard on its heels came Fabius, from April 27 to May 6. In the light of Exercise Tiger, the public relations department at SHAEF drew up a news plan covering how it would respond publicly to any successful attack against units involved in the four phases of Fabius, which would see landings along the south coast of England from Slapton in Devon to Littlehampton in Sussex.[17] Fortunately Fabius, involving landings supported by aircraft, passed without major incident.

The exercises also served to demonstrate that certain regiments and their battalions could be expected to perform better than others when it came to an actual landing in France. The 116th Infantry outperformed its fellow regiments within the division. The chief umpire for Exercise Duck rated the regiment's assault on the beach at Slapton as "very good," and the umpire assigned to monitor the regiment noted the quality of its staff work and the aggressiveness of the regiment.[18] The assistant to the division chaplain, who was acting as an observer, recorded his thoughts:

> I attended the exercise of the 116th Inf. Regiment as an observer. To me it was a great show. The morale of the men was excellent and they have every confidence in the ability of their leaders . . . The protection laid down by the heavy guns was amazing. The way the Infantry Regiment took to the beach would defy any enemy.[19]

Other regiments performed less well. The Second Battalion of the 175th Infantry Regiment failed to impress the lieutenant colonel who was its monitor. He identified failings at almost every level, from poor staff work to the landing itself. The tendency of troops to bunch together and afford an easy target to a potential enemy was a feature of their assault. Lieutenant Colonel Partin concluded rather gloomily that "there was a basic lack of knowledge of or disregard of the elements of basic soldiering" and that "an actual assault by the same troops against a determined enemy of the strength assumed would have failed with heavy casualties."[20] The assault section of the exercise had been a complete disaster, with one umpire noting on the performance of the 2nd Battalion, 175th Infantry Regiment:

> It took nearly three hours for assault sections to cross the beach, considerably bunched, and exposed to enemy fire. No fire was placed on enemy positions and there was a general lack of initiative or any sort of a plan. Finally, with utter disregard of enemy positions, troops moved laterally across the beach to Slapton Bridge and some infiltrated to Strete Gate. Lack of adequate planning and forceful leadership was evident. Had this been an actual operation, it is extremely doubtful if many men would have left the beach alive.[21]

The proficiency of the 116th Infantry Regiment ensured that it would be entrusted with the task of forcing the enemy's line on D-Day.

However, throughout the assault units that would carry the attack on D-Day, there was recognition that exercises and training, no matter how good, fell short of the realities of combat. Major General Gerhardt, commanding officer of the 29th Infantry Division, warned his senior officers in his review of one exercise: "This is another one of the series, and there is one we won't come back from.... We hit the beach, and then fight for our lives. That means that you should maintain a chain of command, you should maintain control of your units, you should see that things happen right and nothing wrong. It is your responsibility to your platoons, company and battalion, and on up the line."[22] For Gerhardt, training was no substitute for effective and bold leadership.

On May 26 the Assault Training Center was disbanded. Some 22,500 men had gone through it in 1943 and early 1944. Now they waited in secure areas near their ports of embarkation for Eisenhower, supreme commander of Allied forces in Europe, to give the go-ahead for the assault.

CHAPTER 7

The Waiting Enemy

The nervousness of American troops awaiting the coming battle in May 1944 was mirrored on the other side of the English Channel. Along the coast of Europe, from the south of France to the furthest regions of Norway, the German occupation forces defending Hitler's Europe stood waiting for a battle that they knew was inevitable. While the German public was told in propaganda broadcasts that the western coasts of their empire was defended by the powerful fortifications of the Atlantic Wall, those closer to the front knew the realities of the military situation. There was little possibility of defense in depth, and for the most part the invasion would have to be stopped at the waterline. Failure to do so would result in the formation of an Allied bridgehead in France, which the German army would not be able to contain in the long run. A successful landing on the European continent would cause the collapse of the German war effort, already burdened by fighting a three-front war in Russia, in Italy, and above Germany's cities. With Allied superiority in the air, and with only limited reserves available on the coast of France, it was unlikely that bold counterattacks could destroy a bridgehead once formed. Either Allied forces had to be stopped on the beaches, or Germany would lose the war.

The German army by 1944 was in many ways a shadow of the former self that had smashed through Poland, the Low Countries, and Russia. The war in Russia was bleeding the German army white; while the need to protect the territories gained in 1940–41 led to geographical overstretch. To address the problem, the German army had taken into its ranks thousands of people from the conquered lands in the East, such as Poland. Many were volunteers who knew that a lack of eagerness in volunteering would end in only one outcome. They were channelled into particular divisions. With experienced German officers at their head, it was believed that they could at least play a valuable role in defense. The offense would be left to the regular army divisions that contained the highest numbers of ethnic Germans and to the Waffen SS. The number of ground troops in Western Europe was augmented by combing out surplus men from the Luftwaffe and using men from the navy to man some coastal artillery positions. On paper, at least, there were significant questions about the homogeneity of the forces that would face the Allied invasion in 1944. In practice, however, the veterans of the campaigns in France and Russia knew a great deal about fighting, as well as how to motivate the non-Germans pressed into service in the German army.

Transport and equipment would, however, remain a critical issue for the German army. Much of the German army remained reliant on horse transport, and while German industry was capable of turning out fine weapons, there were not enough of them to address the military needs of the Nazi state. Captured material, from heavy guns to tanks to mortars to light transport, was evident across the German army. The logistical problems that this inevitably caused were self-evident. The German army found it increasingly difficult to respond to Allied armies equipped with a seemingly unstoppable flow of material from American factories.

The situation in Normandy exemplified the condition of the German army in 1944. One of the principal units expected to counter an Allied landing in either Brittany or Normandy was the 30th Schnell (fast) Brigade. Based at Coutances on the Eastern side of the Cotentin Peninsula, its fast status derived from the French-made bicycles that were its principal source of transport. The 716th Infantry Division defending Omaha Beach was made up of 50 percent non-Germans whose allegiance to the cause of the Fatherland was questionable. Most of the division was engaged in manning defensive positions along the beach, and its reserves were not considered likely to be able to counterattack effectively. Meanwhile, the 352nd Infantry Division, based some 20 miles inland, was regarded as one of the better units of the German army in the west. Most of its officers had seen service on the Russian front, and it was considered that the division would be able to make effective counterattacks by the afternoon of D-Day. Elsewhere, sections of the Cotentin Peninsula were defended by the 91st Luftlande Division based at La Haye du Puits. A Luftwaffe division, it was supplied with obsolescent French tanks, but it was backed by the Sixth Parachute Regiment under Colonel Baron Freidrich von der Heydte, whose headquarters were at Carentan. The 3,500 men of the regiment would be among the most effective enemy units the Allies would face in Normandy. With the German army in the west it really was a case of make-do and mend in the construction and equipment of divisions.

Discipline and zeal could make up for many of the shortcomings. For example in October 1943 Hitler decided to raise a new SS Panzer Grenadier Division, the 17th SS Gotz von Berlichingen, at Thouars in mid-France. With a cadre of experienced NCOs and officers, many of its recruits would be ethnic Germans from the east. The division was ordered to complete its basic training by February 15, 1944, and more advanced training within the following two months. Critically short of equipment (particularly trucks), and with its training disrupted by the resistance, the division would nevertheless play a key role in trying to contain the advance beyond the Allied beachhead in Normandy. What it lacked in terms of equipment and training, it would make up for in determination and ideological zeal. This was ruthlessly instilled into the men of the division during the training period. The training was highly realistic, and the use of live ammunition resulted in numerous fatal casualties. Relations with the local French population were pleasant and mutually beneficial, and any indiscipline by SS troopers was firmly addressed. When two SS NCOs got drunk and rang the church bells in the town of Mirabeau, they were forced to apologize to the local parish priest. Orders reaching the division in late 1943 and early 1944 constantly emphasized the dangers from the civilian population, especially in the aftermath of the anticipated invasion. In February 1944 Generalfeldmarschall Sperrle gave the Division specific orders about fighting terrorists:

a. Any soldier moving outside of his secure military quarters without a firearm shall be punished, with no regard for mitigating circumstances...

b. If a troop is the target of any aggression whatever, whether on the march, in billet or anything of that kind, the commander is required to take immediate independent countermeasures on his own authority. These include:

- Immediately answering fire! If in so doing bystanders are hit, this is unfortunate, but entirely the fault of the terrorists.

- Immediately setting up roadblocks around the place where the offence was committed and arresting all civilians standing in the vicinity regardless of who or what they are.

- Immediately setting fire to houses from which the fire came....[1]

Sperrle concluded his order with a reassurance that "over harsh measures cannot be grounds for punishment." Psychologically, the Gotz von Berlichingen Division was being speedily and effectively trained for total war against the Allied invasion forces, and from June 1944 until the end of the war they would fight with a tenacity that would repeatedly see the division decimated to the point at which it would have to be rebuilt from a low establishment. The men of the Gotz von Berlichingen Division believed in their cause every bit as much as the Allied troops who would oppose them in Normandy. They were equally determined to defend their cause and equally proud of their division as any American, British, or Canadian soldier.

The army would receive very limited support from the Luftwaffe, with the skies increasingly dominated by Anglo-American fighters. In the end, the Luftwaffe would mount around only 100 sorties before darkness on D-Day. This is a considerably higher number than the impression that would register on the popular consciousness, but hopelessly small given the scale of the Allied effort. Seventy of the sorties would be by single-seat fighters, which would lead the British Air Ministry to comment that the German effort in the air on D-Day was "barely perceptible."[2] To some extent this dominance was countered by the impressive performance of German anti-aircraft units, but they could be of only limited use against the invasion fleet. The German navy posed a more significant threat thanks to its motor-torpedo boats, submarines, and coastal artillery. Since 1943 Germany had been developing a midget submarine arm under Vice-Admiral Hellmuth Heye that, it was hoped, could make effective attacks against an invasion fleet in the English Channel. In 1944, however, the fleet was not quite ready for large-scale operational use. The burden of defense would fall most heavily on the German army.

To make up for the inadequacies of the German army in the west, the military hierarchy resorted to a vast building program to develop defenses that could significantly assist the defenders. Batteries of heavy guns were constructed that could cover likely landing zones along the European coast. Heavy guns captured in the defeat of France in 1940 were put to good use in specially developed concrete casemates, which could resist bombing and naval bombardments. They were often sited so that they could provide mutual covering fire. They were also protected by machine gun bunkers, mortar pits, and defensive positions for industry. Along the coastal zone, "resistance nests" were situated along vulnerable beaches. Machine guns, mortars, and medium guns were emplaced inside concrete fortifications defended by infantry, mines, and automatic flamethrowers. Again, careful thought was evident in the development of interlocking fields of fire and emplacement of positions so that guns could fire across broad sections of beach.

In front of the resistance nests, and the infantry positions that supported them along the coast, stood another layer of the Atlantic Wall. Naval mines and beach obstacles along the coast of Europe threatened to take a heavy toll on an invasion fleet. They varied in depth and construction, but the most vulnerable beaches were heavily protected. In Normandy, for example, "Element C" formed an initial layer of obstruction. This consisted of an iron-framed, gate-like structure, topped with a teller mine. Its purpose was to physically prevent enemy landing craft from getting their troops ashore. Behind this was a layer of "Rommel's asparagus," logs driven into the sand that pointed out to sea. At the seaward end of the log was lashed a teller mine, or shell, which could destroy an unlucky landing craft. A final layer of obstruction, about 130 yards from shore, came in the form of hedgehogs. Made out of steel rails or angle iron, three or more 5–6 foot lengths were joined together at their centers to make an obstacle that could damage landing craft and stop tanks. A British War Office memorandum on the "Tactical Problems of an Invasion of North West Europe" set out for its readers the obstacles an invading army would face:

a. In general, there are two or more continuous belts of wire along all open beaches, usually sited between high water mark and the back of the beach. In addition, all strong points are wired, belts varying in depth between thirty yards and two hundred yards according to the importance of the strong point. Beach exits, particularly gulleys in cliffs, are often barred by a dense wire entanglement. The use of anti-personnel and anti-tank mines is now general along the coasts of FRANCE, BELGIUM, and HOLLAND. The former are normally found round the perimeter of defended localities and at infantry exits from beaches; the latter at AFV exits from beaches, in open country behind beaches and road junctions and road defiles up to five miles inland. (For details of types of minefields and their sitting, see Apppendix "A.")

b. Of the various types of beach obstacles employed, walls, anti-tank ditches, dragons teeth, concrete pillars, rail pyramids, wire knife rests, the re-inforced concrete or brick wall are the commonest types. Walls block streets leading from a beach or harbor, and roads on the outskirts of towns on the landward side, also well-defined exits from open beaches. Road blocks of this type together with existing buildings often form a continuous obstacle along the entire sea-front of a town.

c. Anti-tank ditches are sometimes found in front of beach strong points of all types, on the seaward side of anti-tank or sea walls along the front of towns, and surrounding strong points containing RDF and other wireless installations. Continuous anti-tank ditches are sometimes found on the landward side of strongly defended ports. Steel fence obstacle ("Element C") along stretches of open beach is becoming more common.

d. An outstanding feature of the defensive system is the concrete protection provided for troops defending these obstacles. Strong points abound in pillboxes and shelters flush with or nearly flush with the ground and constructed of reinforced concrete at least three feet and sometimes six feet thick. Pillboxes within strong points are linked up by highly developed trench systems, sometimes running underground.[3]

Beyond the beachhead, German mobile forces lay in readiness to respond to any attack, but such was the nature of the German high command, with Hitler exercising his dominance over his generals, that problems of coordination would inevitably arise in the event of invasion. The army commander in the west, von Rundstedt, did not have his full forces under his control. The panzer divisions, which were expected to play a key role in staging a counterattack against any landing, were under Hitler's personal control. Such was Hitler's authority and the fear that he generated that von Rundstedt would have to request the Fuhrer's permission to authorize their movement.

It was little wonder that Field Marshall Rommel, who oversaw the development of the Atlantic Wall and German preparations for the invasion, was less than sanguine about his chances of stopping any Allied landing. All he could do was wait and hope to respond appropriately. Few could argue with his credentials:

> He had great experience in mobile warfare with armoured forces. He also had recent experience—in contrast to the other generals—with the greatly improved Allied tanks, and particularly their anti-tank weapons, and he knew what it meant to fight without an adequate air force. He did not think movements at night impossible, but he expected them to be too slow to be decisive, particularly with the short nights of summer. Moreover, he visualized the political as well as the military side of the war. He knew that there was no hope of winning, but hoped that the war could be brought to a tolerable end. Any kind of beach-head in the West would mean a third front, because it would be impossible to get the Allies out again even if they suffered a set-back in the battle with armoured forces. He was sure that, with their superiority, they would break out sooner or later, with disastrous results for the Eastern Front, too. So he looked for a way to defeat the landing on the beach, and to win a respite which could be exploited politically.[4]

To overcome the German resistance Allied generals intended to play to their strengths and the enemy's weaknesses. The numerical superiority of Allied forces would be exploited to the full. Landings would be made on four beaches on the coast of Normandy and one on the Cotentin Peninsula. American forces would land on beaches codenamed Utah on the Cotentin Peninsula and Omaha on the coast of Normandy. The British and Canadians would land at three other beaches (Gold, Sword, and Juno) on the coast of Normandy. The size of the resulting beachhead would make it difficult to contain. The nature of the terrain beyond Normandy enhanced the chances of a successful defense of the beachhead in the event of a strong enemy counterattack. The lack of a sizeable port on the invasion coast would be alleviated by the use of technology. Two artificial harbors would be constructed off Omaha and Gold beaches. They would serve to bring in the badly needed men and equipment to expand the beachhead until a major port could be captured and brought into operation.

Before the landings, paratroops would be landed to cover the flanks of the beachhead. The American 101st and 82nd airborne divisions would cover the western flank formed by Utah Beach; and the British 6th Airborne Division would cover Sword Beach, which formed the eastern flank of the landings. Regiments like the 507th Parachute Infantry Regiment would play a pivotal role in preventing or delaying the reinforcement of German forces defending the bridgehead. They would also play a vital role in capturing key strategic points that would facilitate a speedy advance beyond the beachhead. The paratroopers would land several hours before the main amphibious landings. That meant landing in the dark, which would inevitably have severe consequences for unit organization and effectiveness. Originally the 101st Airborne Division was scheduled to land just behind Utah Beach to seize the exits, which would allow for a speedy advance. The 82nd Airborne was to be dropped further inland to allow American troops to cut off the Cotentin Peninsula from the rest of France. Fears about the length of time it might take for troops from the beachhead to link up with the 82nd led to a late change in the landing plan. The change saw the landing zones for the division shifted further eastward to ensure that a linkup could be effected within 24 hours of the landings.

During the landings, Allied military strength would be used to its full. With Royal Air Force and U.S. Army Air Force dominating the skies, airpower would be used to disrupt German supply lines and to target coastal defense installations. The French railroad network would be disrupted by Allied medium and heavy bombers. This would prevent use of the rail network to bring German armored units from the interior to the coast. Allied fighter bombers would later ensure that use of the road network was heavily curtailed, and it remained a dangerous proposition for any unit forced to try it. The French resistance would add to the transport problems facing the German military as it struggled to contain the beachhead.

The landings would be preceded by heavy naval bombardment of German coastal defenses. It was not anticipated that the German navy or air force would be able to offer anything other than token resistance to the invasion force. Although Allied planners recognized the quality of construction of the German coastal defenses, it was anticipated that such was the firepower of the invasion fleet, with rocket firing landing craft, cruisers, battleships, and destroyers, that most enemy heavy weapons could be neutralized. Infantry landings would be supported by tanks, some of which had amphibious capabilities. Artillery would be landed as soon as the beaches were secure.

Despite the wealth of firepower, it was recognized that it would still be left to the infantry to seize and occupy enemy territory. The leading infantry units, such as the 22nd and 116th infantry regiments, had been trained in assault techniques at Woolacombe and Slapton Sands and were to be issued with the equipment to deal with blockhouses, gun positions, and machine gun nests.

Allied planners believed in the superiority of the invasion force over its opposition on the beaches. However, they also recognized the professionalism of the German military. Victory would not come easy, and it would be at a price. It might take only small misfortune, oversight, faulty intelligence, or human error to turn superiority and expected victory into a defeat. With an amphibious landing, defeat could prove spectacularly bloody and costly. On all sides there was a recognition that the stakes were very high indeed. So much was at stake that in 1943 Allied leaders preferred to sanction the invasion of Sicily and Italy, even though it delayed the invasion of France by diverting resources to the Mediterranean. British Prime Minister Winston S. Churchill played a key role in framing Allied strategy. At the start of 1943 Washington hoped for an invasion of Western Europe. Churchill considered it too risky.[5] The invasion of Italy was a less risky venture than a crosschannel attack. Some have argued that by delaying the invasion a key opportunity was missed. With Hitler shaken by defeat at Stalingrad, and the German army heavily engaged on the Eastern front with the Battle of Kursk, an invasion of France in 1943 was a comparatively easier prospect than it was to be a year later. In early 1944, as Allied photoreconnaissance revealed German preparations to meet the invasion, some felt that the delay in launching the invasion was likely to prove very costly indeed. The speed and ingenuity with which the defenses were being constructed was the cause of considerable alarm. If the Germans were given the time to develop their fortifications in depth, a direct assault on the coast of Europe might become an impossible undertaking. Every week the invasion was delayed gave the Germans more time to construct their defenses. In June 1944 the long prelude to D-Day was over. The day anticipated by thousands of soldiers was almost at hand. The moment of decision had arrived.

CHAPTER 8

Preinvasion Movements

In May 1944 Allied units across the south of England began final preparations for the great assault. This would involve moving into sealed camps, the issuing of new equipment, and detailed briefings. The final destination of the invasion force, Normandy in France, would be left until the last possible moment. The process was deeply traumatic, especially for men who had English girlfriends. Movement orders allowed little time for goodbyes or thoughts on the imminent campaign.

116TH INFANTRY REGIMENT

In late May the 116th Infantry Regiment moved to Blandford in Dorset in preparation for loading onto the ships that would carry them across the English Channel. Leaving their "homes" in West Devon brought moments of reflection and fears for what was to come. Captain Cawthon of the Second Battalion later wrote:

> The 2nd Battalion gave Bridestowe Camp a final raking and brushing, turned over all excess toilet articles over to a nearby orphanage—soap was a scarce and valued wartime item in Britain—and left the moors. Watching the trucks pass out of the camp gate, I was impressed that the battalion was at its peak, as ready as an outfit can be. Its people, many of whom I knew by name, looked hard and fit; trucks, weapons, carriers and jeeps, in dull olive drab, were spotless—and moved at careful sixty yard intervals. I was not aware of it, but we were never to look exactly that way again. Battle turned sleekness to a weary, worn look; after D-Day, the company [would become]...a kaleidoscope of changing faces.[1]

Once in Dorset, everyone was confined to camp and civilians were excluded from the assembly areas. The high command was determined to prevent any leakage of information of potential use to the enemy. The troops were given new equipment, given the best quality food, and briefed about their mission using models and photographs. At least one officer, Taylor Fellers, who had trained with 29th Rangers, considered the mission to be tantamount to suicide and told his commanding officer as much. The briefing that the troops received extended to estimates of the number of pillboxes that they would encounter on their landing beaches. The men of the 116th Infantry were told that only two out of the 21 pillboxes covering the beaches at Vierville on Omaha Beach would be manned. Moreover, they were told that those two pillboxes would be manned by Poles and Russians of the Ost Battalions forcibly recruited by the Germans in the East. The whole process left none of the GIs under any illusions as to the dangers they were about to face. Sergeant Robert Slaughter remembered:

> We were incarcerated behind barbed wire and MPs made sure that no one entered or left camp. No soldier inside the compound was allowed to talk to anyone outside; he could suffer the possibility of getting shot. This was serious business. Brand new equipment was issued, and the new weapons had to be test fired and zeroed in on the firing range. Unlimited amounts of ammo were given to each of us for practice firing. Bayonets and combat knives were honed to a keen edge. Steak and pork chops with all of the trimmings, topped off with lemon meringue pie, were items on a typical menu, and it was all-you-can-eat. This caused one of the "wags" to say, "They're fattening us up for the kill."[2]

Discipline seemed to relax a little and the officers became friendlier. Some confided their fears about the forthcoming battle in trusted noncommissioned officers.

On June 4 the troops loaded onto ships in Weymouth. A pleasant seaside resort, Weymouth was one of the smaller ports to be used to load the invasion force. An eight-year-old farmer's daughter, Anne Emmings, was witness to the troop trains arriving in Weymouth. She witnessed American troops throwing their British coins towards passersby in the street. She did not understand that where they were going, the Americans would not need shillings and pence. Nor could she understand her father's reactions in not letting her pick the cash up.[3] Elsewhere in other loading ports, children witnessed similar scenes of generosity that they did not fully understand. Norma Churchward was a six-year-old living in Torquay in June 1944 as the process of embarkation began: "We stood outside on the pavement frantically waving and shouting to all these young men, many of whom had become our friends during the previous weeks. They all waved back and smiled, and as they passed by showered us with goodies—sweets, chocolates and especially wrapped sugar lumps. It was the sugar lumps I remember most of all!"[4] Across the southwest of England an army was divesting itself of the things that it would no longer need, or that it did not feel able to carry into combat.

Unfortunately, for the troops on the boats D-Day, originally scheduled for June 5, would not come until a day later. Poor weather in the English Channel forced a postponement of the operation until June 6. Even then, Eisenhower was informed, the weather would be less than helpful resulting in rough seas off the invasion beaches. Faced with the choice of an extended delay to the operation to ensure the right combination of moon and tide, Eisenhower on June 5 opted to launch the invasion the following day. He knew that he was taking a huge gamble with the lives of the men he commanded and possibly with Allied chances of victory in Europe.

On the ships, confidence was high despite the postponement. Many were just glad to be away from Dartmoor. The battle for which they had trained over many months was finally about to begin. As E. P. Hoyt has written: "In those last few hours before the invasion many of the older men had written letters, while some of the more bloodthirsty of the younger troops had sharpened their bayonets and looked to their other weapons."[5] Within hours the first waves would be clambering down the sides of the troop transports into their LCAs (Landing Craft Assault) to make the journey to the beach. Brigadier General Norman Cota, assistant commander of the 29th Infantry Division, called his staff together for the last time at 1400 in the ward room of the USS *Charles Carroll*. Cota counselled:

> This is different from any of the other exercises that you've had so far...The little discrepancies that we tried to put right on Slapton Sands are going to be magnified and are going to give way to incidents that you might at first view as chaotic. The air and naval bombardment and the artillery support are reassuring. But you are going to find confusion. The landing craft aren't going in on schedule, and people are going to be landed in the wrong place. Some won't be landed at all. The enemy will try, and will have some success, in preventing our gaining "lodgement." But we must improvise, carry on, not lose our heads.[6]

Despite Cota's warnings, the intelligence briefings had been so precise that nothing seemed open to chance. Allied superiority in material appeared so overwhelming that nothing could stand in the way of the invasion force. However, the intelligence briefings received by the troops were based on information that was several months out of date. From March 1944 onwards, detailed observation of the beaches had declined, from a high point in December 1943–January 1944, out of fear that the Germans would divine the intentions of the Allied high command.[7] In order to create the necessary cover, detailed reconnaissance of other beaches away from Normandy continued. On June 6 Allied forces, who continued to derive detailed intelligence from German signals intercepts, did not have the benefit of the most up-to-date intelligence derived from direct observation of the beaches.

22ND INFANTRY REGIMENT

As part of the process of amphibious training, the men of the 22nd had on several occasions practiced loading their gear and moving down to the points of embarkation at Plymouth, Torquay, Dartmouth, and Brixham. To support the invasion fleets that would depart from British shores in June 1944, the American corps of engineers had spent the previous two years building new roads to carry invasion traffic to the points of embarkation. The corps had also been very active in augmenting the number of potential loading points in and around the ports. So called "hards" were constructed at as many points as possible on the English coast. Using rock and cement, they provided a gentle and stable gradient across a foreshore that would allow a landing ship to beach itself for the purpose of loading vehicles at high tide. The "hards" massively augmented the loading dock facilities available along England's south coast.

Plymouth was one of England's greatest naval ports, from which Sir Francis Drake had sailed in 1588 to engage the Spanish Armada. A fine natural anchorage, it was the primary port for the launching of Force U against Utah Beach. In 1943 it had become home to a U.S. Navy Advanced Amphibious Base with its headquarters at Queen Anne's Battery. Capable of handling every aspect of landing craft service, repair, and provisioning, the base comprised shore facilities with out stations at Saltash, Calstock, and Manadon Field, providing everything from hospital facilities to hull repairs. The initial complement of sailors grew from 296 in 1943 to more than 21,000 in early 1944. Plymouth could handle almost any kind of maritime activity, and the port would see the loading of more than 36,000 men and more than 60,000 tons of cargo during the opening phases of the D-Day operation.

To the east of Plymouth lay the smaller ports of Torquay and Brixham. The latter, a major fishing port, had become home to the Belgian fishing fleet as it fled the German occupation in 1940. The corps of engineers had spent considerable time in preparing Torquay and Brixham to handle the loading of tanks and other military

Antiaircraft gun guarding Plymouth Sound (Olin Dows collection, Franklin D. Roosevelt Presidential Library)

equipment. Dartmouth, like Plymouth, had connections to the Royal Navy, since it contained the Britannia Royal Naval College for the Training of Officers. Set on the river Dart, Dartmouth provided a useful anchorage for many of the smaller assault vessels that would support the Allied landings. In 1943 an advance party of 150 American sailors had begun construction of U.S. Navy Advanced Amphibious Base 114 at Sandridge Park near Dartmouth to support the fleet of landing craft that would operate from the river Dart. The base expanded rapidly until in December 1943 it moved into Britannia Royal Naval College. The base supported the growing numbers of landing craft that assembled in preparation for D-Day. So packed with vessels was the river Dart in May 1944 that some locals claimed that there was no longer any need to use the ferry to cross the river—one could simply walk from one ship's deck to another until one reached the other side.

On May 18 the 22nd Infantry Regiment decamped from South Brent, Newton Abbot, and Denbury and headed to specially prepared invasion camps near the ports of embarkation. Accommodations were in the form of tents and, like the 116th Infantry, all contact with the outside world came to an end. The nature of the task faced by the troops was explained by officers using sand tables and other visual aids. On June 2 the troops began to load. Travelling through the towns and villages en route to the port, some of the English onlookers sensed that this was not another rehearsal. Norbonne Gatling, who served with divisional headquarters, recorded in his diary: "We had a pleasant ride through the bright English countryside, and many people lined the streets of the villages as we passed. They seemed to sense that this might be the real thing, and not merely another problem such as we had gone through twice already."[8]

The Third Battalion, embarking at the small fishing port of Torquay, was bombed during the night of June 2–3 but there were no casualties. Extra equipment and rations were issued to the troops as they boarded, including escape maps. By the afternoon of June 3 the invasion force was ready to sail. Margaret Blackwell, a member of the Women's Royal Navy at Dartmouth, saw the first transport depart:

> At about mid-day it started. A very large LST ground her way out of the harbour. She had been one of those anchored, tied on to the old rusty iron buoy just outside our office window. She weighed anchor, and later, out she went, slowly at first, then gradually gathering speed. Some of the boys waved to us as they went, but not the usual wave of greeting, this was a goodbye wave. We waved back desperately with our handkerchiefs, from behind the bars of our office windows. We couldn't speak—one of the girls was crying. And from then on it was one continual stream of landing ships, roaring down the river and out to sea. They never ceased all the afternoon and evening and on into the night. It is incredible that one river could ever hold so many ships.[9]

Force U, destined for Utah Beach, would consist of "30,000 men and 3,500 vehicles on 4 troop transport ships and over 200 large landing craft."[10] The departure of such a large force provided early warning to people in the invasion ports such as Plymouth and Brixham that the invasion was imminent.

507TH PARACHUTE INFANTRY REGIMENT

In the third week of May 1944 the 507th Parachute Infantry Regiment prepared to move to the airfields from which it would take off for the assault on France. On May 20 the regiment assembled on the parade ground at Tollerton. "Sharpen your jump knives" was the instruction given to the men of the regiment by its commanding officer. It was the most succinct way of communicating to the men that the invasion was at hand. Knives, bayonets, and all manner of bladed weapons were sent to Nottingham for sharpening. They were duly returned sharpened by a local firm, which refused to accept payment for the work.

The process of final preparation was accompanied by a farewell barbecue and dance at Tollerton Hall. The frenetic nature of the farewell was recorded by one 19-year-old girl who had been to similar social events at the hall on previous occasions:

We girls had been to the usual Tuesday dance and were invited to the barbecue, with buses laid on to take us, but not (this time) with Red Cross escorts. Off we went on the Saturday afternoon. It was fine but cloudy; this turned to heavy rain. There was food laid on, BUT also unlimited alcohol. Most of the troops were drunk when we arrived. I remember my own escort turned up partly drunk. Then we found that the camp was full of all the local prostitutes and after a time the whole thing degenerated into a free-for-all with each man trying to get a girl, any girl, into his tent. . . The buses had been sent away by the troops and the whole camp had girls of a decent standard trying to stick together to get out. . . We were well into the country, several miles from town—while taxi-loads of tarts poured in. I literally fought my way out of that camp with a girl friend ad we were fortunate enough to be a seen by a paratrooper who had known us on happier occasions. He grabbed a taxi and paid for it to take us home. I remember lying in bed safe at home and shaking with terror all that summer night. Even now it seems like a scene from some bizarre film.[11]

The Second and Third battalions moved to Barkston Heath airfield, the First Battalion to Fulbeck, and the Pathfinders, who would spearhead the assault, to North Witham in Lincolnshire.[12] Almost at the same time, a decision was taken to alter the Airborne assault plan. The 82nd Airborne would drop closer to the invasion beaches instead of further west on the Cotentin Peninsula. It was a recognition that, with strong German forces in the vicinity, the 82nd might find itself in difficult circumstances unless relief forces could reach its landing areas relatively quickly. The divisional staff were thus forced to redraw their own plans, which had been developed with meticulous care. As General Gavin recorded in his diary on May 27: "Meeting of the regt COs at which time the new situation was outlined to them. Lots of work. These damn changes. Complete sets of plans, terrain memory classes, plastic models, all wasted."[13]

Wired into secured compounds on the airfields, and closely supervised by the military police, the men of the 507th were not permitted to have contact with the outside world. The regimental counterintelligence plan laid down six rules to ensure that the hastily revised plans for the coming assault did not leak out:

a. 24 hour perimeter of interior guard will be maintained to insure against ingress or egress of unauthorized personnel.

b. Ingress and egress *on official business only.*

c. Ingress or egress from present camp only by pass, dated and signed by Base Commander...

d. Passes will include a physical description of holder, purpose of his visit in or out of the base, time authorized for him to be in or out of the base.

e. Commanders and staff officers from higher headquarters will be admitted without pass if they carry a Bigot-Neptune Classification card, provided their identity has been established.[14]

In the secure compound the missions of each battalion were carefully explained using photographs and terrain models. The intelligence briefing drawn up by Dickerson, the regimental intelligence officer, was remarkable for its accuracy and appreciation of the situation. It opened with an overview of the strategic situation in the west:

The strong German Army which once rolled mercilessly over small and quite unprepared European countries has for sometime now been retreating. This once mighty military machine has spent itself to a point where in no sector is the German on the offensive. The German General Staff is well informed relative to the status of the war at present but is determined to prevent a complete defeat by fighting a defensive war indefinitely if need be in the hopes the Allies will agree to peace terms less harsh than unconditional surrender with the result being Germany would be able to retain her Army an in a few years plunge the world into another World War.... The enemy has found it difficult to maintain the strength of his divisions. In order to maintain the number of his divisions he has increased the percentage of foreigners (Poles, Czechs, etc.) and prisoners of war serving in combat units. In many units, particularly static divisions, AA, and Coastal Artillery, this may run as high as 33.3%.[15]

For most men of the regiment, waiting in wired-in compounds, boredom and apprehension mixed with excitement. Some, though, were more aware of the developing tension than others. Edward M. Isbell of Company E had a friend who had gone ahead of him to prepare the enclosure at Barkston-Heath:

Chuck went to the marshalling area a week before we did to set up a sand table for our company. It covered the area where our mission was to take place. Chuck was very good at this. The table showed the town and bridges we were to capture and where the German positions were located. Photographs of our drop zone were taken each day. It was changed several times because the Germans were flooding all the open fields and placing poles with barbed wire strung between them in anticipation of our arrival. I couldn't believe how Chuck's personality had changed from the last time I saw him. His bunk was covered with candy, chewing gum. (goodies that were given to us by the Red Cross and others). He must not have slept in days and had lost weight. It was obvious that he had not used his bunk. He told me to take anything I wanted—that he wasn't going to need it. I couldn't get him to talk about anything. All he seemed to want to do was look at the sand table. He just wasn't himself. He had been studying our mission for days. I'm sure he could see what the Germans had in store for us better than we could. We all knew our chance of being a casualty was very high. Even if we survived our mission, our lives still depended on the beach landings being successful. Chuck knew that many of us wouldn't make it back and that this might be the last time our original company would be together after several years of living together through the hardships of airborne training.[16]

On June 4 ammunition was issued to each man along with escape kits and invasion francs. Passwords were issued along with an American flag that was to be sown onto the right shoulder of their uniforms.[17] The men were also instructed about the handling of enemy prisoners. The intelligence officer for the 507th stressed the importance of prisoners as sources of good intelligence. They were to be treated carefully and handled according to their rank and potential usefulness. This was not perhaps a universal imperative.

In at least two American airborne units, official sanction was given to a policy of not taking prisoners after the landing. At one briefing for the 501st Parachute Infantry Regiment (101st Airborne Division), troopers were told that they would not be taking prisoners for the first 24 hours of the operation. In the 508th Parachute Infantry Regiment (82nd Airborne), one pathfinder was ordered not to take prisoners for the first nine days of the campaign.[18] The logic was simple. Behind enemy lines, outnumbered and lightly equipped paratroops could not encumber themselves with the additional burden of prisoners.[19] Such burdens were best avoided. The suggestion drew protests from the chaplains attached to the 501st, who appealed to their bretheren not to follow such cold, hard military logic. Disarm prisoners and remove their boots to prevent escape, but avoid killing them, was the advice the chaplains gave to their flocks. The advice was undoubtedly sound theologically. It was also sound legally. An order or suggestion not to take prisoners amounted to a violation of the laws of war and threatened to bring a moral equivalence between Allied forces and the evil they were fighting. The instruction, if obeyed, would amount to a war crime.

That such orders were given may shock many readers, and its significance needs to be understood in full. The murder of German prisoners of war by Allied forces has been hinted at since 1945. Carlo D'Este's *Decision in Normandy*, published in 1983, suggested that the battle was down to infantrymen who gave each other little quarter.[20] In his book *Overlord*, published in 1984, Max Hastings revealed that he had met scores of men who knew about or who had participated in the murder of prisoners in the heat of battle and under the impact of watching their friends die. He went on to suggest that some Allied units executed prisoners routinely.[21] The link between individuals taking the decision to kill and how whole units came to shoot prisoners routinely is not explained by Hastings, and the reader is left with two conclusions as to how a general policy of not taking prisoners might come into effect. It might be arrived at the by the emergence of a consensus from below—individual soldiers observing, emulating, and perhaps discussing each other's behavior. Alternatively it might be arrived at by an order from above—a senior officer taking a calculated decision about the enemy and their treatment after capture. The consensus from below is perhaps understandable on a human level. The order from above creates an entirely different situation. In the aftermath of the Normandy campaign, it was alleged that some Nazi atrocities had been a response to reports of Allied units killing German prisoners of war. Since 1945 there has been an unwillingness to accept that, at least on a regimental level, such orders might have been given. In the 82nd Airborne an order not to take prisoners was perhaps more understandable than in other units.

Events during the landings in Sicily in July 1943 perhaps formed an important backdrop to the instruction and the expectations of the paratroops as they contemplated dropping into Normandy. Private Michael A. Scambelluri had entered the folklore of the 82nd Airborne Division as a result of his experiences at the opening of the Sicily campaign. He was captured by Italian troops as he struggled free from his parachute. During his interrogation, Scambelluri began to speak to his captors in Italian. His family had left Italy for a new life in the United States when Scambelluri was a small boy. His interrogators, however, regarded Scambelluri as a traitor rather than as an enemy combatant entitled to fair treatment under the Geneva Convention. One of the two Italian soldiers drew a pistol and shot Scambelluri repeatedly in the stomach. They then threw grenades at Scambelluri. Remarkably, he survived and was found by fellow troopers from the 505th Parachute Infantry Regiment. He explained what had happened to him. Their outrage was such that when an Italian soldier was captured, he was paraded before the badly injured man. Scambelluri identified him as one of the men who had tried to kill him. Scambelluri's fellow troopers then forced the man to dig his own grave, then they executed him. A second Italian soldier was then brought before Scambelluri. Although he could not identify him as the second of his attempted murderers it was clear that he was part of the force that had captured Scambelluri. One of the troopers from the 505th executed him on the grounds that he was at least guilty of failing to stop the attempted murder of Scambelluri. At that point, the killings stopped. Scambelluri was evacuated to a British hospital ship and even managed to survive its sinking to reach the hospital. *Stars and Stripes,* the soldier's newspaper, featured Scambelluri's story. Scambelluri became more than just a badly injured soldier. Described as "Iron Mike," he became a potent symbol of the airborne elite.[22] His experiences, and perhaps the actions of his comrades, became a key element in the mythos of the airborne. The story of Scambelluri and several other men during the Sicily campaign meant that few members of the Allied paratroop forces were under any illusions in June 1944 as to the harshness of the treatment they might expect to receive from the enemy. Offering a defeated enemy quarter while behind the lines was a luxury that some units felt that they could not afford. In some, illegal orders were given before the invasion at least verbally.

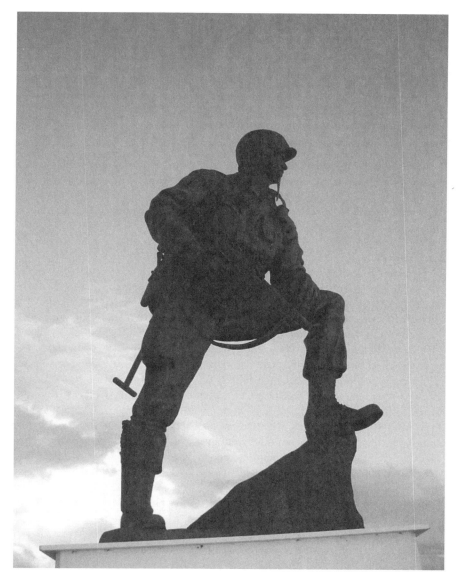

Iron Mike Statue at La Fiere, Normandy (Picture taken by author)

While such orders in paratroop units in June 1944 were perhaps understandable, evidence suggests that some of those units that would spearhead the seaborne assault were also operating under similar instructions and that men did obey them. After D-Day, one GI in the 22nd Infantry Regiment wrote in his journal about American troops retaliating against German atrocities:

In retaliation many "Huns" are treated in kind. In one instance, a paratrooper offered to relieve an MP of thirty prisoners. He marched them to a field hidden from observers, lined them up, opened fire with his Tommy gun and annihilated them to a man. But even before there was a feeling of retaliation for German atrocities, our troops landed in France with the intention to take no prisoners at least for the first few days. The briefing preceding D-Day. . . made clear that we would be at a disadvantage to encumber ourselves with prisoners while trying to secure a beachhead. About the second day, however, an order was issued rescinding this understanding.[23]

The GI was keeping his journal in contravention of orders, and in the period around June 6 few men were willing to commit to paper the nature of the instructions they had received regarding prisoners.. Written revelations about a no-prisoner policy were hardly likely to be welcomed back home, even if they escaped the attention of the censor. In the aftermath of the war, many thought that it was best to maintain a discreet silence on the issue. The American army, however, has admitted that at least on one occasion during World War II, orders for the murder of prisoners were be issued at the regimental level. During the Ardennes offensive in December 1944, the headquarters of the 328th Infantry Regiment issued orders that "no SS troops or paratroopers will be taken but will be shot on sight." The official army history of the campaign notes the order and hints that oral orders to the same effect were given in other regiments. It does, however, suggest that there is "no evidence" that the order was obeyed.[24] The caveat is a little disingenuous. The plain fact is that, in the clearest terms, an American regiment was instructed to carry out murder. There is every likelihood that men did act on them, and that similar orders were given to other regiments charged with similar tasks. We can only guess at the number of such orders given in the European Theater, but what the American army admits to in its history of the Ardennes offensive was probably an ingrained feature of life for an infantry regiment. At certain times, and in response to stimuli such as the behavior of the enemy and the task at hand, soldiers were encouraged not to take prisoners. The massacre of American prisoners at Malmedy in December 1944 was the stimulus that led to the order in the 328th Infantry Regiment. German forces were felt to have violated the codes by which the infantryman was fighting in Europe. A violation could be addressed only by counterviolation to regain what amounted to a live-and-let-live system. What was perhaps surprising is that in Normandy and elsewhere, a considerable number of men ignored whatever instructions they had been given regarding prisoners. In the midst of battle, and under the severest provocations, large numbers of prisoners were taken and American GIs were not above risking their lives for men who they identified as fellow human beings even if they wore the colors of the enemy.

In Normandy in 1944, American soldiers were to behave no better, and no worse, than they had in the wars against the Plains Indians and in World War 1. Revelations about the behavior of American troops in Korea, Vietnam, and Iraq have caused considerable disquiet in American society, but the reaction rests on the assumption that the GI in World War II behaved with saint-like restraint in the midst of mass murder.

In war, no matter how righteous the cause, bad things happen, and it is men who commit them and have to grapple with the consequences. There are few right choices to be made; only wrong, death-inducing, choices to be avoided. For some of the men in preparing to land on the beaches on Normandy and by parachute, taking prisoners was a wrong, death-inducing choice that they would opt to avoid. Equally, some regarded it as their Christian duty to offer quarter and protection to a defeated enemy even if they meant endangering their own lives. The majority of men would follow a line between the expediency of a survival situation and their consciences and upbringing. They were neither saints nor sinners.

While it is hard to think about guilt or innocence in relation to the men who would land in occupied Europe on June 6, the guilt of those officers who might issue commands about prisoners is rather less problematic. The implications of such orders and practices are disturbing indeed. After the war, German soldiers would be put on trial for issuing or obeying similar orders. What is equally disturbing is the question of how far up the chain of command might go in terms of awareness and involvement in the issuing of illegal orders. In units belonging to three out of the five American assault divisions deployed on D-Day, no-prisoner orders appear to have been given. It is therefore difficult to typify this as an isolated problem, or to come up with an easy-to-accept explanation of how such a situation might be determined.

Undoubtedly many men were wrestling with dark thoughts in early June 1944. The postponement of D-Day from June 5 to 6, 1944, as a result of poor weather, caused considerable concern within the 507th. It gave men longer to think about what lay ahead. The postponement came on top of a late switch of the division's drop zones to points closer to the invasion beaches. The paratroopers sensed that they would be landing right on top of the enemy, and the struggle to escape from their parachutes would be a race against death for many. Without the quick-release harnesses provided to British paratroopers, their American brothers would rely on the knife to get free from their parachutes as quickly as possible. The instruction "sharpen your jump knives" was sound advice as much as it was a call to the aggressive spirit of the regiment.

Just after midnight on June 6, the C-47 transports carrying the 507th and other parachute infantry regiments destined for Normandy began to take off from their airfields. Among many British civilians, unaware of the drama about to unfold, there was a growing feeling that the invasion had been postponed indefinitely. Sydney Race recorded in his diary on the morning of the invasion: "Coming home last night I wondered—it was so cold & windy—why the invasion had been so long delayed, & whether, after all, there might not be something in the theory held by a surprisingly large number of people that there would be no overseas invasion at all."[25] Sydney Race did not realize it, but the invasion was already well under way.

CHAPTER 9

Launching the Invasion

Leading the assault on Hitler's Fortress Europe on June 6 would be the paratroop pathfinders. Jumping in advance of the main body of their regiments, they would mark the drop zones which had been selected for the two American airborne divisions, the 82nd and 101st, which would be dropped on the Cotentin Peninsula to protect the western flank of the Allied invasion of Normandy. The eastern flank of the invasion would be protected by British airborne forces. The 101st was given the job of securing the roads leading back from Utah Beach at the base of the Cotentin Peninsula. To counter the invasion threat, the Germans had flooded the low-lying land behind the beaches so that the roads leading back from the beach represented the only safe way to move inland. If the 101st Airborne could not seize the landward end of the roads, then the invasion force would be contained on the beach and left at the mercy of the heavy German batteries at places like Crisbecq and Azeville. The 82nd, and with it the 507th Parachute Infantry Regiment, were given the job of seizing the key points on the routes, particularly St. Mere Eglise, which led from Utah Beach towards the west coast of the Cotentin Peninsula.

Much of the plan depended on the accuracy of the airdrops that would place the different paratroop units in the positions where they could assemble and move onto their various objectives. To ensure this accuracy and to encounter the effects of a night drop, the pathfinders were issued with the latest locator technology called Eureka. A lightweight portable transmitter with telescopic aerials, Eureka could broadcast on five frequencies. These would be received by a leading transport aircraft fitted with a special receiver called Rebecca. Eureka could thus act as a homing beacon for a flight of aircraft. To support the Eureka-Rebecca system, the pathfinders were also issued with beacon lights. Visible from the air the lights would be switched on as soon as the pathfinders heard the noise of approaching aircraft.

The pathfinders of the 82nd Airborne Division operated with varying rates of success on June 5–6. Unfortunately, the pathfinders of the 507th met with considerable difficulties. Dropping near the manor at La Fiere on the Merderet River in the early hours of June 6, one group was overwhelmed by the enemy as they struggled with their equipment. A second group landing at 2:17 AM suffered losses in both men and equipment.[1] Of the 51 men assigned to pathfinder role for the 507th on June 6, 35 became casualties or were captured. Nevertheless, two of the Eureka sets were operational before the aircraft carrying the main body of the regiment arrived over the drop zone four miles northwest of the key route center of St. Mere Eglise, to the West of the Merderet River and its swamps.

A little after 2:30 AM the first of 117 C-47 transports carrying the 507th arrived over drop zone T. Their departure from England had been an emotional event:

> Before we left to board the planes on the evening of the 5th, Captain Creek gave us a talk, wishing us the best of luck and ended with an outstanding prayer. I can never forget that evening as we walked to the planes. The cooks in our regiment were not going into combat, but they were lined up on both sides of the road, presenting arms, with tear-filled eyes as we passed through. Even though they were non-jumpers, we thought as much of them as we did of each other. They were very special to us. We were always kidding them about the food they prepared even though most of the time it was very good. I know it was hard for them to see us go.[2]

By 2:30 AM (the men of the 507th were among the last to drop), the crews manning the antiaircraft defenses of the Cotentin Peninsula were well awake and anxiously seeking out targets.

The airdrop of the 507th turned into chaos as antiaircraft fire combined with a fog bank over the coast of the Cotentin Peninsula to break up the formations of C-47s carrying the regiment. Some pilots took evasive action, some climbed above the fog bank, some dived below, many exceeded the required maximum airspeed for safe parachute jumping. The formations broke up and began to disgorge their precious cargoes over locations at which the crews of the C-47s guessed and hoped were right. The result was that the men of the 507th began to float to earth across a wide section of the Cotentin Peninsula. Instead of landing on a tight drop zone, well prepared by pathfinders, the paratroopers came down up to 20 miles from each other. The 507th was to be the most misdropped Allied unit on D-Day, and their problems were only just beginning. The Germans had made the most of the natural defenses of the Cotentin Peninsula. The Merderet and Douvre rivers had been managed in such a way as to turn their low-lying flood plains into a great marsh. Usually the marsh was a seasonal feature of the landscape. In winter, the low-lying valleys flooded as the drainage ditches crisscrossing the landscape overflowed with water. Thanks to the Germans, the marsh no longer dried out in summer. The result would be that some of the heavily laden paratroops would drown in a marsh that they did not expect to find. In the postwar period, the official histories were open in their condemnation of the failure of intelligence to discern the danger:

> Intimations of this situation should not have been wholly unknown to the airborne forces. The sheet maps published by Company B, 660th Engineers (Second Edition of

April 1944) rather clearly defined the limits of the inundations though it was done in terms of classic under-statement—"ground probably soft." But what had further confused the issue was that detailed study of the most recent air photographs of this terrain—taken within a few days of the invasion—did not reveal the marsh, though what false trick of photography was responsible for that mischance must go unknown. All that is certain is that the men felt sure the marsh was not there.[3]

The inundation was not necessarily that deep—less than five feet deep in most places—but struggling with the weight of equipment and a parachute canopy that would not collapse proved beyond the capacity of many troopers. Don Reiland of Company G was one of the men caught by the marsh:

> On a backward oscillation I plunged into about four feet of water in a field flooded by the Germans. I was being dragged backwards underwater by my chute. Parachutes often have an uncanny way of remaining full with air and dragging you without mercy. Every time I struggled to my feet . . . the chute would jerk me under again. My rifle pushed up under my neck and I could not reach down to the knife strapped to my boot. Desperately I reached into my collar pocket and pulled out my switch blade knife and frantically cut my harness to freedom.[4]

Reiland's experiences were far from unique. Lieutenant Colonel Charles Timmes, commanding the second battalion, spent 20 minutes almost being drowned by his parachute before he came to rest on the embankment of a drainage channel. Some men, like Reiland, struggled free of their chutes and found dry land only to listen to the cries of drowning comrades further out in the marsh. The marshes were alive with the sound of splashes, gunfire, and cries for help. Some men landed on the coast of the Cotentin Peninsula only to hear the splashes as their comrades landed in the seas beyond.

Landing in the marsh caused considerable disorientation, which only added to the confusion caused by the misdrops. Paratroops landed all over the Cotentin, and in the gloom they looked around for the fellow members of their stick, their regiment, their division, or any friendly face. Approximately 150 men from the 507th rallied on the drop zone under Lieutenant Colonels Ostberg and Maloney, where they encountered General Gavin. The regiment as a whole was in a parlous state:

> The 507 Regiment was in a bad way. The drop had left its elements so badly scattered that for three days thereafter the Regiment remained uncollected. The regimental drop zone was about 1000 yards north of Amfreville and a little to the south east of Gourbesville. Not a single stick from the 507 landed on the drop zone, though one pathfinder team, which had arrived in advance of the Regiment, made it . . . The one officer and 3 men of the successful team maintained the signal on the Drop Zone from 0220 to 0300, by which time all of the assault sections had passed over. The signal appears to have been of little benefit. Many of the sticks came down between the drop zone and the Merderet and most of the men landed in the marsh.[5]

The men of the regiment began to assemble around certain features in the landscape such as the railway embankment, carrying the main line to Cherbourg, which ran around the edge of the marsh. The bridge across the Merderet River at La Fiere formed another rally point, as did the parish church at Graignes to the southeast of the town of Carentan. Towering over the surrounding marshes, the church was easily visible against the night sky for those men landing in the marsh. During this critical period of disorientation, the first contacts were made between Americans and French civilians. A warm reception was received by many as wet paratroopers were invited to warm themselves by fires and offered homemade apple brandy, food, and hot milk. For most, the prospect of liberation was a joyous event. The German occupation forces had antagonized the civilian population throughout France. Most had escaped outright violence from the German military and Gestapo. However, low-level thievery by German troops ready to take without compensation what they wanted in the form of eggs, milk, and other goods had upset many civilians whose attitude towards the German authorities might otherwise have been ambivalent.

For most members of the 507th, the night of June 5–6 would be spent trying to organize themselves into larger groups, work out where they were, and decide on the course of action to take from daybreak. The regiment would fight D-Day not as an organized military formation but as a series of groups pursuing different objectives. Some groups would find themselves pursing the objectives of other elements of the 82nd Airborne Division. Others landed so far beyond the drop zones that they were cut off from their objectives and would have to come up with their own. What

Marshes of the Merderet River. Graignes old church and memorial are on the hilltop to the left of the picture. (Picture taken by author.)

was truly remarkable was that all would contribute to the key strategic objective of the airborne divisions—securing their own areas and attempting to control the approaches towards the beaches. The airborne units would form a protective shield for the landing beaches, which would hinder the development of any counterattack from German units inland from the coast.

By a curious irony, German inundation of the marshes of the Merderet and the Douvre River would help the 507th and the other airborne units achieve their strategic objective. The marsh would protect the western flank of the landings if the groups of paratroopers could control the handful of crossings across the Merderet and Douvre at places like La Fiere, Chef du Pont, and Port de Planques. From the early hours of June 6, the 507th would be involved in a disorganized fight it did not expect—a battle for the control of the marshes of the Douvre and Merderet rivers. The different groups of the regiment fought their battles while the 116th and 22nd infantry regiments fought for control of Omaha and Utah beaches.

THE 116TH INFANTRY REGIMENT ON OMAHA BEACH

On June 6 the 116th Infantry Regiment was given the task of assaulting part of the coast of Normandy codenamed Omaha by Allied planners. The 29th and 1st infantry divisions had the job of capturing Omaha Beach, while to the west the U.S. 4th Infantry Division would land on Utah Beach. As a defensive position Omaha Beach stood out from the rest, even though they were all protected by a network of beach obstacles designed to prevent a landing. What made Omaha Beach special was the natural environment. The beach was cut by deep runnels, which meant that a landing craft could ground only to disgorge its troops into deep water. Omaha Beach is also swept by powerful currents, making small boat operation difficult and wading ashore with heavy equipment next to impossible.

On the beach, the assaulting force would face heavy enemy fire and numerous obstacles before it could reach a shingle bank where it could take cover. Beyond this lay a patch of marshy ground at the foot of the rise to the land above. The ground above the high water mark was mined. In books one sees references to the sand dunes that confronted the troops on Omaha Beach. Stephen Ambrose refers to them as "bluffs." Most visitors to the beach refer to them as cliffs. This seems to be a rather more useful term to use in connection with what nature had placed in the way of two American infantry divisions in 1944. They weren't sheer, but they weren't that far from it, although nature had softened the visual impact of the scarp with the addition of a covering of vegetation. Five valleys, or draws, provided a more gentle egress from the beach. Unsurprisingly, in 1944 these were the most heavily defended sections of beach. The American military knew that the task it faced on Omaha Beach would be a difficult one, but there was a belief in the prowess of the American army. If this bordered on overconfidence, then there could be no doubt that the assault against Omaha Beach was necessary. If Omaha Beach could not be secured, then there would be a dangerous gap between Utah Beach to the west and the Anglo-Canadian beaches to the east. If American forces landing on Utah Beach could be isolated and eliminated, the whole invasion might fail. If the Allies were to secure a large enough bridgehead on the coast of Normandy, then Omaha Beach would have to be taken. Moreover, concerns about the difficulties of securing Omaha Beach lay alongside a host of other nightmares in the minds of Allied planners, secret German weapons, gas attack against the beachheads, and submarine attack being just three. For example, on Utah Beach the U.S. 4th Infantry Division faced fewer natural obstacles on landing, but would have to negotiate a flooded area behind the beach as it tried to move inland. If U.S. airborne forces could not seize the causeways that ran through the flooded area, then the advance of the 4th Infantry Division might stall on the beach.

The 116th Infantry Regiment's assault on Omaha Beach was led by Companies A, E, F, and G. At 0400 they loaded into their assault craft and began to head towards the beach. Each man was heavily laden—worryingly so. Sergeant Gilbert Gray Murdoch of A Company:

> Every man had his OD uniform [made of cloth specially treated to prevent penetration by gas]. Over this we wore a special landing [assault] jacket, with four huge pockets in the front, and two huge pockets in the front, and two huge pockets in the back. As a rifleman I had my normal allotment of M1 ammo, sixty rounds plus three bandoleers around my neck, three fragmentation grenades, one smoke grenade, one phosphorus grenade. Each of us had a quarter pound of TNT (for blowing foxholes we were told!). We carried one set of K rations, a breakfast, dinner, and supper, and three D-bars. On the back we had the rations, raincoat, and what was called a paratroop packet which was a pouch holding a syrette of morphine and a tourniquet. This was for our own immediate use...Over this jacket we had a navy-type lifesaving belt, the type with two tubes that are inflated by the breaking of two capsules. Around the neck and under the jacket went the one inch band of the amphibious gas mask...In my pockets in the front of the jacket I had my blanks to be used in propelling my antitank grenades. Under my left arm hung the antitank grenades in a web bag.[6]

Within 90 minutes, well before they were due to land, it was apparent that things were going wrong. Allied bombers had been due to pound the beaches to soften up the enemy and to cut through their wire. By and large, however, most of the bombs fell inland away from the beach, its defenders, and their positions. Specially adapted Sherman medium tanks (DD), which could swim with the addition of a canvas screen and propellers, were supposed to support the landing. However, as the tanks descended the ramps of their landing craft and entered the sea, a distressing number simply sank. Preinvasion planning had assumed near-perfect weather conditions for the assault. Other tanks were lost when, in their attempt to navigate toward particular landmarks, they slowly came broadside to the waves. The tanks' canvas screens were inadequate given the state of the sea on June 6. With the wind at force four to five, only four of the tanks would eventually reach their destination.[7] Even the assault by the infantry landing craft began to unravel at an early stage. Each company was due to land opposite the German positions that they were supposed to eliminate. However, in the prevailing sea conditions, and with navigation dependent on such landmarks as church steeples by which the coxswain could navigate, the careful plans for landing soon dissolved. As the official historian of U.S. Naval Operations in the Second World War put it:

> Had you been in a helicopter when day broke, around 0515, you would have seen something very different from the neat diagrams in operation plans which show all boats steaming along their prescribed lanes and hitting precisely at H- hour 0630. You would have assumed that something was wrong and you would have been right.[8]

Most of the 116th Infantry Regiment in the first wave would not hit their assigned sector of beach. To some men in the first assault wave, the situation seemed strangely unreal as they headed for the beach. Cecil Breedin, one of the medics in Company A later recounted:

> I looked over the top of the end of that boat and I said. . . "We're going into another God Damn dry landing, dry run, Slapton Sands." Or I didn't somebody else did and I looked up over and I said "It sure as hell looks like it" and just then a machine gun burst hit the front of that boat and I said "They didn't shoot that straight at us when we were going into Slapton Sands."[9]

Company A landed on Dog Green sector of Omaha Beach adjacent to the Vierville draw. Companies F and E were supposed to come ashore opposite the draw at Les Moulins. Company G would come ashore in the gap between Vierville and Les Moulins. In fact, G landed on top of F, and Company E came ashore a quarter of a mile east of its assigned landing zone at Les Moulins. The men from Company E would find themselves fighting alongside soldiers of the 16th Infantry Regiment, spearheading the 1st Infantry Division's landing. Company A was effectively isolated, and the assigned tasks of each company rendered meaningless, by the currents and poor navigation.

Forty minutes before the assault craft reached the beach, the naval bombardment of German shore positions began:

> At 0550 [the battleship] *Texas* began to work over enemy positions on top of the Western side of the road [up from the beach at Vierville] with her secondary battery, which was shortly aided by the 4.7-inch guns of LCG-424. Destroyer *McCook* shot at pillboxes and anti-tank guns on the other side of the road. *Texas* fired 190 rounds, and both PC-568 and LCT-464 joined in; but the volume here and elsewhere was not enough to attain the desired results, because not enough time was allowed for the bombardment—the army did not wish it to start before daylight.[10]

The army's desire to give the Germans the barest minimum of warning that a landing was underway meant that many enemy positions remained intact as the first landing craft hit the beach.

Already the Americans' numbers had been thinned by enemy artillery, rough seas, and enemy mines placed on many of the obstacles designed to prevent a beach landing. Those troops whose landing craft succumbed to the sea or enemy fire short of the beach found themselves in a particularly difficult position. The subsequent waves of landing craft would pass men desperately trying to keep their heads above the waves. Life preservers had been distributed to the troops in massive numbers so that not only they, but also their equipment, would have a chance of staying afloat. In practice, however, the troops were carrying such a weight of equipment that once in deep water they had to abandon most of it in order to give their preservers a chance to do their job. PFC John Barnes of A Company was a flamethrower's assistant. Carrying his equipment, pack and rifle, together with the flamethrower's pack, and rifle, his LCA was swamped by a large wave:

> Suddenly a swirl of water wrapped around my ankles and the front of the craft dipped down. The water quickly reached our waists, and we shouted to the other boats on our sides. They waved in return. The boat fell away below me, and I squeezed the CO_2 tubes in my life belt. Just as I did the buckle broke and it popped away. I turned to grab the man behind me. I was going under. I climbed on his back and pulled myself up in a panic. Our heads bobbed up above the water. We could still see some other boats moving off to the shore. I grabbed a rifle wrapped in a floatation belt, then a flamethrower that was floating around with two belts wrapped around it. I hugged it tight, but still seemed to be going down. I was unable to keep my head above the surface with all the equipment I was carrying. I tried to pull the release straps on my assault jacket, but I couldn't move. Others shouted at me. Then Lieutenant Gearing grabbed my jacket and, using his bayonet, cut the straps. Some of the others helped release me from the weight. I was all right now I could swim. We counted heads. One was missing; Padley our radio operator, who had a big SCR-300 radio on his back. No one saw him come up.[11]

With at least 5 percent of the 200 landing craft in the first wave foundering, Barnes's experience was by no means extraordinary.

Once on the beach, the first wave found itself heavily engaged by the German defenses, which had survived the initial naval bombardment. Wet, seasick, and scared, the troops tried to cross a beach swept by machine gun and mortar fire. Although the antilanding defenses on the beach gave them some cover, entire squads were mowed down before they could reach the relative safety of a shingle bank at the high water mark. Private Dantin of Company A came ashore and was immediately wounded as he scrambled through the surf:

> "Help," he shouted. There was no one to hear. Everyone around him had been killed or wounded. It was every man for himself. He could not get up, overloaded by his equipment. Then he remembered his father's trench knife, inside his legging. Dantin got it out and cut the laces of the heavy combat jacket [loaded with rations and ammunition] until it fell off. Then he could get up.[12]

Most of the soldiers that reached the relative protection of the seawall were in no fit state to attack the enemy positions on the heights above them. The careful plans for a coordinated assault against fixed enemy positions using bangalore torpedoes, machine guns, bazookas, mortars, and flamethrowers had gone to the bottom of the channel along with the bulky equipment needed to deliver it.

Company A was reduced to tatters during the landing. Stephen Ambrose estimates that 60 percent of the 200 or so men in the company came from Bedford, Virginia, and that "only a couple of dozen survived, and virtually all of them were wounded."[13] Within minutes of landing, the company had been reduced to one officer, Lieutenant E. Ray Nance, who had landed with Company B, and he had been wounded. June 6 would be a black day for Bedford in particular and the U.S. Army in general.

Companies E, F, and G were in better shape than A but had still sustained casualties, which took them out of the battle as an effective fighting force. The second (B and H companies) and third waves (C, K, I, and M companies) came onto the beach at 0710 and 0720. They too began to suffer the same treatment that had met the first assault wave. PFC John Amendola landed with H Company: "Two of the men from my section got down behind a tetrahedron to escape the bullets. An artillery shell hit the tetrahedron and drove the steel back into their bodies. I tried to prize the steel loose from the men but couldn't do it. Then I figured they were dead, anyway."[14]

Amendola's H Company lost many men to machine gun fire from the German resistance nest at the village of Les Moulins, which sat astride the next draw to Vierville-sur-Mer, the regiment's other principal landing objective. As the tide began to come in, Amendola noticed that a straight line of bodies was forming along the high-water mark: "They looked like Madam Tussaud's. Like wax. None of it seemed real. I felt like I was seeing some kind of show."[15]

Twenty minutes after the landing of B and H companies, the regimental command landed. They were confronted with a disaster mounting in scale and tragedy. Lieutenant J. T. Shea, aide-de-camp to Brigadier Norman Cota, second-in-command of the 29th Infantry Division, later recorded his experiences on coming ashore to a beach still under heavy enemy fire: "Although the leading elements of the assault had been on the beach for approximately an hour, none had progressed farther than the sea wall at the inland border of the beach. [They] were clustered under the wall, pinned down by machine-gun fire, and the enemy was beginning to bring effective mortar fire to bear on those hidden behind the wall."[16] The landings were in complete chaos, and there were at least two incidents of landing craft coxswains being persuaded to take their boats into shore by threats of violence. For example, as Company B was making its run in to the beach, the coxswain of the LCA carrying the Commanding Officer, Captain Ettore Zappacosta, shouted "We can't go in there. We can't see the landmarks." Mistaking the coxswain's reluctance to land at the wrong spot for cowardice Zappacosta reacted forcefully pulling out his pistol: "By God, you'll take this boat straight in." The coxswain was forced to comply, and within minutes of landing Zappacosta was dead along with 90 percent of the men who landed with him. Army historian S. L. A. Marshall, who would later interview many of the survivors of the 116th Infantry Regiment while still in the field, would later comment that Zappacosta's insistence on being landed then and there amounted to a "fools order."[17] On other parts of the beach, British coxswains did their best to land American troops in positions where they would at least have a chance of engaging the enemy. Zappacosta, and some other American officers, sometimes mistook this for cowardice, or as a variation to plan from which there could be no variance.

Some of the Royal Navy ratings manning the landing craft were to pay a high price for putting American troops ashore. In one of the third-wave boats carrying Company D, an argument broke out between the Royal Navy crew and Sergeant Phil Hale, section leader and ranking noncommissioned officer. Seeing how badly the first two waves were being mauled, the Royal Navy crew told Hale that it might be best if they disembarked in deep water. Hale argued that they had to go in all the way because of the weight of equipment that each man carried. "Reluctantly they said they'd try."[18] They tried to move away from the Vierville draw where they were supposed to land and towards a section "that looked fairly open." Landing in a foot of water, four of the 30-man section were hit, but the rest made it onto the sand. Giving first aid to a wounded man, Randolph Ginman paused long enough to notice "Both of the English sailors lay draped over the side of our landing craft and they too had been killed by machine gun fire." Ginman was to spend the next four hours inching up the beach towards the safety of the seawall.

On landing, Company D had commanding officer Captain Walter O. Schilling. George Kobe was in Schilling's boat:

> We were getting closer to the shore…We could see up ahead what was going on. Company A had hit the beach first and then Company B. Things didn't seem too bad from where we were, and Captain Shilling said, "See, I told you it was going to be easy." But when we went in, they threw everything at us. The Germans scored a direct hit on us and an 88 shell hit us, tearing off the ramp and knocking off both steel doors. Captain Shilling was hit and killed instantly by the steel door. The whole front of the LC was knocked off, and the other door hit our platoon sergeant and knocked his left eye out. I jumped into the water and the LC washed right over me, and my assault jacket hooked onto a jagged part and the waves flipped me around like a rag doll. The only way to get out was to get out of the jacket so I tossed my carbine away and slid out of my jacket and made my way to shore.[19]

The amphibious DUKWs, amphibious trucks, together with their precious cargoes of heavy weapons and supplies, were also faring badly. Sergeant William Otlowski was with the cannon company of the 116th Infantry Regiment on D-Day. His DUKW was loaded with a 105-mm cannon, 90 rounds of ammunition, and 10 men. It drove straight off the ramp of the landing craft and into trouble:

> When I got my men on the DUKW and tried to get off the ramp, the rough water put us on the up side as we were almost off the ramp and it hit our rudder and bent it…The coxswain running the thing, the navy boy, decided to shut off the motor, which was a mistake because when you shut off the engine you shut off the pumps and it started to fill with water, and what happened was, we sank.[20]

The same fate befell most of the DUKWs assigned to the regiment.

PFC Harry Parley, who had come ashore with Company E carrying a flame-thrower, found himself reflecting, amidst the carnage, that it was a very long way from what they had been trained to expect:

> Along the beach, I could see burning wreckage and equipment, damaged landing craft, and of course, men trying to come off the beach. The enormity of our situation came as I realized that we had landed in the wrong beach sector, and that many of the people around me were from other units and were strangers to me. What's more, the terrain before us was not what I had been trained to encounter.[21]

Everywhere one looked, there were scenes of agony and death. Many of the men of the 116th Infantry Regiment had known each other for months, and in many cases for years. Harold Baumgarten of Company B was badly wounded as he landed, but from the relative safety of the seawall he could see his comparative fortune:

> I saw Sergeant Draper and Vargos and all of Company A dying in the water to my left. It was ultra sad for me because these men who had landed a little before me in Company A were my friends that I had trained with...There was no medical aid available at this time, and many had bled to death and many drowned.[22]

By 0730, approximately one hour after the first landings, small groups of men were making a determined effort to get inland. Led by elements of Company C, with support from 5th Rangers, soldiers from the First and Third battalions eventually managed to scale the heights between Les Moulins and Vierville. Further to the east, another group of men managed to ascend the heights and engage enemy positions. Slowly the enemy line began to crumble as more and more men came ashore. These included men from the 111th Field Artillery Battalion, which was supposed to provide fire support to the 116th Infantry Regiment. Eleven of its 12 howitzers went to the bottom of the channel as their DUKWs foundered or were hit by enemy fire. "To hell with our artillery mission, we're infantry now!" was the cry of Lieutenant Colonel Thornton Mullins, commanding officer of the 111th Field Artillery Battalion. Mullins's infantry reached shore at 0830, picking up weapons from the dead to join in the assault against Les Moulins. Mullins would not survive the day, but his men would help to widen the breach in the German line and to bring effective pressure against the German defenses still protecting the draw.

At Vierville the arrival of a tank made a decisive impact. It had taken Randolph Ginman of Company D four hours to reach the seawall after landing.[23] Shortly after reaching it the tank came down the beach towards the Vierville draw. The tank proceeded to put several rounds into the gun emplacement and machine gun nest at the mouth of the draw. No longer pinned down, Ginman and his mortar section were asked to fire against another machine gun nest. Having lost most of their equipment Ginman's section had to work hard to assemble just one mortar and fire against the enemy position. Just after they had done so, Brigadier General Cota and Colonel Canham appeared to lead them up through the draw.

By midday the tide of battle on Omaha Beach was turning, and by nightfall the bridgehead, while precarious, was at least established. As he waited for evacuation, Harold Baumgarten of Company B surveyed the scene around him: "It looked like the beach was littered with the refuse of a wrecked ship that were the dead bodies of what once was the proud, tough, and the well-trained combat infantrymen of the 1st Battalion of the 116th Infantry."[24] The 116th had won its place in history, but the cost had been high.

After D-Day many people reflected on the events of the day. Most of that reflection took place on a personal, rather than an official governmental basis. The war had to be fought to a successful conclusion, and there would be other black days for the American army—from the fighting in the Bocage of Normandy, to the icy hells of the Hurtgen Wald and the Ardennes. As time went by, respect for the veterans of D-Day muted debate on the rights and wrongs of Allied planning. By the 1990s the principal focus of academic and public attention was on the need to understand the veterans' experience. Analysis and criticism were very much secondary impulses to remembrance.

Stephen Spielberg's *Saving Private Ryan* laid bare some of the failures that led to the slaughter on Omaha Beach. Indeed, in the press pack for *Saving Private Ryan,* the director described the landings as "a complete foul-up: from the expeditionary forces, to the reconnaissance forces, to the saturation bombing that missed most of its primary targets. Given that, I didn't want to glamorize what had happened, so I tried to be as brutally honest as I could."[25] In the opening section of a film about the role of the individual in war, Spielberg probably was as honest as he could be, but the rest of the film and its principal themes of sacrifice, the need to remember the past, and patriotism, overlay the depiction of military failure. Indeed, failure was a necessary part of the patriotic sacrifice that lay at the heart of the consensus narrative of the landings on Omaha Beach. Failure maximized the scale of the achievement of the soldiers who eventually climbed the bluffs, and failure maximized the patriotic and disciplined nature of their struggle to defeat a cruel and efficient enemy. While a few conservatives attacked the film, the majority regarded it as an affirmation of American values, of the American past, and of the American present. The film became what Alison Landsberg has described as "prosthetic memory" for the American psyche, a shared experience so powerful as to contribute to the sense of what it is to be an American.[26] The film serves as a validation of Jean Baudrillard's warnings of the power of the simulation because of "the desert of the real."[27] What his theory means in relation to the landings on Omaha Beach is that *Saving Private Ryan* is a powerful film partly because our understanding and image of such a significant event is severely deficient in a number of ways. The mishaps of Ford and Capa were part of the desertification of the real, as Spielberg, and indeed Dows, present us with different and differently powerful simulations of the real. With the deficiency of the real, the history of the landings on Omaha Beach has been turned into a mythic event for social, and perhaps political, reasons.

However, long before Spielberg, some had questioned the wisdom of the army's assault tactics against Omaha Beach. Back in the 1950s Samuel Eliot Morison, rear admiral and one of America's finest historians, had completed the official history of *United States Naval Operations in World War II*. In volume XI of his multivolume work, he turned his attention to the invasion of Europe. His writing was surprisingly emotional and revealed something of the navy's disgust with the army over the landings. On point after point, his language was scathing: "One of the persistent myths about Omaha is the story that all the trouble was created because a first-line tough German division just happened to have been sent there for a tactical exercise when our troops landed. This yarn makes a good cover for faulty intelligence, but there is nothing to it."[28] Both the 716th and 352nd divisions had been allocated to this section of the Atlantic Wall after a reorganization of the German line in mid-March 1944. In Morison's view it wasn't due to bad luck that the assault squads were faced with different opponents from the ones they had been expecting; it was a result of Allied failure. This was a word that later few would dare use in writing about the landings. For Morison the "faulty intelligence" was just one of a string of failures at every step in the operation. The positioning of the German gun positions "so cunningly... [dug] into the bluffs as to enfilade the entire length of beach, and gunfire...resulted in [a further] failure to observe them on reconnaissance photos."[29] Morison's language reveals his anger. Reflecting on the events of June 6, he felt mistakes had been made and he wasn't afraid to say so in unvarnished words.

More recently, American academic and former soldier Adrian Lewis has argued that the plan, which was an uneasy compromise between British Mediterranean and American Pacific doctrines of amphibious warfare, could have produced disasters on the other landing beaches if their defenses had been as formidable as those on Omaha Beach.[30] He has argued persuasively that the blame cannot be put on U.S. Army planning; rather, it was a failure of inter-Allied collaboration and staff work. If the landings had been made at night or preceded by a lengthier bombardment, the carnage on Omaha Beach could have been reduced.

For the survivors of the 116th Infantry Regiment, reflecting on the events of D-Day would continue long after the war had ended. One of those members of the regiment who would record his thoughts was Major Sidney Bingham, commanding officer of the Second Battalion. On D-Day he found himself surrounded by the dead and dying, unable to exercise effective control over leaderless companies that had sustained heavy casualties. His later analysis of D-Day was pithy and to the point. Seasickness, he argued, took a heavy toll on the troops, reducing their morale and combat effectiveness before the landing. He was convinced that if the Germans had attempted to launch a counterattack against the survivors of the first assault waves huddled together against the shingle bank, the result would have been their annihilation. In Bingham's eyes, the greatest single error committed on D-Day was the overloading of the troops: "The individual loads carried were in my view greatly excessive, hindered mobility, and in some cases caused death by drowning."[31] Few of his fellow members of the regiment would have dissented from Bingham's analysis. However, it must be remembered why the men of the 116th Infantry Regiment were carrying such great loads.

The tactical doctrine employed by the U.S. Army on D-Day had envisaged the assault units working in a particular and very precise way. Aerial bombardment, naval gunfire, and DD Sherman tanks were supposed to neutralize much of the enemy's defensive firepower, leaving the assault units to deal with any remaining positions and begin the process of clearing the beach. Infantry units rely on two factors for their success: firepower and maneuverability. On June 6 the assault units would sacrifice maneuverability for the firepower necessary to deal with the few enemy positions not dealt with by bombs, naval units, shells and 75-mm rounds from the DD tanks. In the end, most of the DD tanks would never reach the beach, and the bombardment from ship and aircraft would prove surprisingly ineffective. The tactical doctrine employed by the generals on D-Day could not survive such a catastrophic failure. The 116th Infantry Regiment found itself trying to do a job for which it was not adequately prepared.

Amid the carnage of the landings, there were clues as to the tactical doctrine that might have been more successfully employed on June 6. Each company was supposed to come ashore directly in front of some of the most heavily defended German positions. Those boats that did so suffered the heaviest casualties. The boats that came ashore out of position, between the enemy pillboxes, sustained fewer casualties. Greater importance could have been given to getting ashore safely, rather than getting ashore in a position to engage the enemy as quickly as possible.

The wisdom of sending out in the first waves small assault squads on which the Germans could concentrate their fire was also drawn into question by the greater success experienced by later waves, which saw larger numbers landing on the beach. Enemy gunners found themselves unable to concentrate their fire on the large number of targets, and the defenses were slowly swamped by the weight of numbers.

Some of the assault units found that they received less enemy attention as a result of grass fires, which had been started by the firing. The greater success that those assault units that came ashore at such points had in getting to the shingle bank serves as a reminder of the importance of visibility in war. Allied planners considered that a night landing, or one supported by the use of smoke, would negate the potential of Allied naval gunnery. Thus the troops had to land in conditions of clear visibility that in the end served the interests of the defending forces rather than the attackers.

In the process of getting ashore, and to a position of relative safety, most troops instinctively realized the flawed nature of the tactical doctrine that they were being asked to serve, and they made appropriate responses. Heavy equipment was dropped, cut away, or lost as infantrymen tried to increase their mobility. However, such was their degree of shock at the ferocity of the German fire, and the apparent impossibility of the role they had been expected to fulfill, that once in a position of relative safety, few were eager to move. The initial plan had failed and, with the death on the beach of so many officers and senior NCOs, reorganization was next to impossible. Rigid thinking produces rigid results. On June 6 it would take a little while for the men of the 116th Infantry Regiment to gather their breath, wits, and courage and to think outside the demands of Allied planners.

When they did so, it was usually up to the initiative of a junior officer here, a sergeant there, together with the odd private. They knew that mobility had to be restored. They had to get in land using fire and maneuver. Their tactical doctrine was based on improvisation, flexibility, and infiltration. Their primary goal was to get off the beach, and at first they engaged only those targets that stood in the way of this objective. A relatively small number of men found their way to the top of the cliffs at Omaha Beach, but once they had done so the primary advantage of the enemy was negated. German positions found themselves under threat from the flanks and rear as well as the front. The defenders began to react accordingly, resulting in a lessening of fire against the beach, which in turn allowed more men to scale the heights. Thus the effect of the first few men finding a way up the beach became exponential. The battle of the Omaha beachhead would be won by troops whose bravery, tactical sense, and combat skill exceeded the wisdom of the plan they had been called on to execute.

Inevitably the question must be, "Could the flaws in the plan not have been foreseen"? "Probably not" must be the answer. Amphibious warfare was still in its early stages in 1944 and despite earlier landings and victories, the Allies were extremely wary of a dangerous opponent. However, certain officers in the 29th Division, such as General Norman Cota, expressed their concerns, and what happened on Omaha Beach had some interesting historical parallels with which Allied military planners should have been fully familiar.

On the first day of the Somme offensive in 1916, the British army was so convinced of the power of the artillery barrage that it was able to mount that British troops were told to expect little in the way of opposition. The German wire was to be swept away by the lengthy preparatory barrage and the German soldiery rendered dead or incapable by the most concentrated bombardment in history. British troops were told to walk, rather than run, towards the enemy lines to ensure proper co-ordination with the artillery barrage that would lift in stages. In any case, the troops were so heavily laden with the equipment with which they were to guard newly won positions that running over the shell-pocked terrain was impossible. Each man carried 60 pounds or more of equipment. In the end, the British were surprised at the ineffectiveness of their bombardment. The Germans had dug deep bunkers into the soil of the Somme, and much of the wire in front of their trenches survived intact. The result was the slaughter of thousands of British soldiers who could do no more than walk to their deaths in the name of a deeply flawed tactical doctrine. Some 60,000 British infantrymen died or were wounded on that day. By comparison, the scale of the suffering on Omaha Beach was light, but the mistakes were similar. Overconfidence in the effectiveness of the bombardment meant that the infantrymen, carrying 60-pound loads, were robbed of their maneuverability.

By the end of the First World War, a war carved into the minds of the officers who in the 1940s would have to make the key decisions, the difficulties of assaulting heavily fortified and defended positions had been thoroughly thought through. In the spring offensive of 1918 that would come close to winning the war for them, the Germans made effective use of specialist storm troops. They would lead the assault, moving as quickly and as far as possible, and infiltrate the British lines, leaving pockets of heavy resistance to follow-up units. Their primary goal was to dislocate the defenses and to force a general retreat. This they managed spectacularly, bringing the Allies to the brink of defeat before the Allies could reconsolidate their lines. German storm troop tactics called for flexibility, initiative, and independent thinking to be exercised by even the most junior ranks. Storm troops were selected and trained on exactly that basis. In many ways they were the equivalent of the U.S. Army's Rangers. It is perhaps significant to the tactics that eventually won the day on Omaha Beach on June 6 that the 116th Infantry Regiment had been strengthened by the reincorporation of men from the 29th Ranger Battalion, and by the men of the 2nd Rangers who landed alongside them.

If history provides certain instructive parallels with which to assess the landings on Omaha Beach, then comparisons can also be made with British army tactics on D-Day. By 1918 the British army's assault doctrine rested heavily on the tank as a means of piercing the enemy line. In the interwar period they unlearned most of the lessons learned at great cost at the end of the First World War. The Germans reminded them of the significance of the tank in modern warfare in 1940. For D-Day they developed a range of specialist armored vehicles, based on American and British types, that could clear minefields, act as mobile flamethrowers, bridge gaps, and dispose of enemy bunkers. In effect, the British used armor and technology to do part of the job assigned to the U.S. infantry on June 6. Significantly the British "funnies" were offered to the American army for D-Day, but General Omar Bradley rejected their use.[32] His boys did not need such things.

While hindsight is wonderful, and comparison difficult, two things are certain:

1. American tactical doctrine on June 6 called for a degree of precision that one could not expect in war. There was too little slack built into the plan, too great a level of expectation, and too great a level of rigidity in thinking. Level after level of the plan, from the effects of aerial bombardment to the landing positions of individual companies, went wrong. Given the command-and-control technology of the day, Bradley and his command could see, by 0730, that all was not proceeding to plan, but their understanding was based on direct observation and limited amounts of information from the shore. There was nothing they could do to influence events as they unfolded.

2. What saved the landing at Omaha Beach was the ordinary soldier, from the level of colonel downwards, who could collect his wits, appeal to his buddies and come up with Plan "B." It was a victory for the ordinary "Joe."

While the American military did not hold a formal inquest into the landings at Omaha Beach on June 6, it certainly tried to learn the lessons of that day. The men of the 116th Infantry Regiment and others were interviewed to construct as detailed as possible a picture of the events on Omaha Beach. Even before the end of the war the message of that day was clear, as featured in the army's digest of *Combat Lessons Learned,* circulated so that troops from one battle area could learn lessons from other units. In 1945 it reproduced a section of an after-action report drawn up by an officer of the 1st Infantry Division that had landed alongside the 29th on D-Day. In unequivocal terms, it stated:

> Leading Assault waves should pass through the beach defenses as quickly as possible in order to get inland in depth. The mission of mopping-up beach defenses should be assigned to support waves. The first objective of the assault, after the beach is crossed, must be seizure of the terrain from which [the] enemy can observe the beach. After this has been accomplished the destruction of the enemy rather than the capture of territory is the prime consideration.[33]

At the cost of 3,000 American lives, the lessons of Omaha Beach had been learned.

THE 22ND INFANTRY REGIMENT ON UTAH BEACH

While things were going badly wrong on Omaha Beach things were substantially different to the west on Utah Beach, the other American landing zone. Although seven of the landing craft carrying the first wave of the 4th Infantry Division were lost on the run into the beach, opposing fire was mercifully light. Some 865 vessels in twelve convoys from nine different sortie points had come together to form Force U.[34] Strong currents and navigation failures combined to place the first wave of Force U some 2,000 yards to the south of their intended landing point. Thus the men of the 4th Division came ashore on a weakly defended sector. They were also well supported by DD tanks, which proved far more seaworthy than off Omaha Beach. The 4th Infantry Division quickly had control of the beach, and the engineers began to clear the obstacles on it. Mercifully, the obstacles on Utah Beach were thinner than on Omaha Beach. Tom Treanor, a war correspondent with the *Los Angeles Times,* came ashore on Utah Beach early on D-Day. He found a pleasantly surprising scene. He later wrote:

> I stepped ashore on France, walking up a beach where men were moving casually about carrying equipment inshore. Up the coast a few hundred yards, German shells were pounding in regularly but in our area it was peacefully busy. "How did you make out?" I asked one of the men. "It was reasonably soft," he said. "The Germans had some machine-gun posts and some high velocity guns on the palisades which made it a little hot at first. They waited until the landing craft dropped their ramps and then they opened up on them while the men were still inside. In a few cases we took heavy casualties, but then the navy went to work on the German guns and it wasn't long before they were quiet." The general lack of fortifications at this point was astonishing. The barbed wire consisted of four single strands, such as we use at home to fence in cattle. A man could get through by pushing down on one wire and lifting up another, providing they weren't booby-trapped. The engineers and beach battalions had blown gaps in the wire through which we could drive vehicles. A few dead lay about and some wounded were here and there on stretchers, awaiting transfer to ships at sea. All the way down the broad beach as far as I could see, men, jeeps, bulldozers and other equipment were moving about like ants. A few columns of black greasy smoke marked equipment which had

been hit by shell fire and set afire. The German shelling continued up and down the beach but had so far not reached the area in which I was walking.[35]

The establishment of the Utah bridgehead had cost mercifully few casualties, but men in the units like the 22nd and 8th infantry regiments, who had borne the cost of the landings on Utah Beach, would not quite remember it this way. For them Utah Beach held its own share of terrors and memories. Colonel Arthur S. Teague, commanding the Third Battalion, later recounted:

> I started on up the beach wall and ran into more troops and they said Lt. Tolles had been shot. On my way there, I passed along a number of baby tanks which had electrical wiring and were loaded with TNT. Some troops wanted to fire into one and I told them to stop that action, and I posted guards on it. I went on around this little firing trench marked by barbed wire and sandy beach grass. Near this firing trench I went behind a sand dune into an open place and found Lt. Tolles lying on his side near another wounded man. I asked him what happened and he said he saw a white flag and he tried to get them to surrender and someone had fired on him. I immediately sent someone back to notify a doctor to get him out of this place. I went further up and ran into members of his platoon who had stopped and were having quite a little rifle fire back and forth. I saw what was happening as they moved along. My German interpreter was with me. We ran and hollered to them and he yelled to the enemy in German. I ran on top of the sand dune. There I picked up an M-1 rifle and called to our men to get going. We went forward and suddenly encountered direct fire. I saw two Germans wounded. About seventeen of them raised up from different places around and started running across the beach. Pvt. Meis yelled at them in German. I questioned them and asked them where their mines were and about the number of Germans. They said they didn't know...I told them they did know and that they would go with us. I then started a skirmish line up the beach. They went about fifty yards up the beach and yelled, "Mine!" They started showing us paths we could take to get out of there. I had seen Lt. Burton and Sgt. McGee wounded by mines along the beach. We moved on down the beach and picked up about 40 more Germans. Where they came from I do not know; evidently troops ran them out. They came with their hands up and ran down the beach.[36]

Teague's story brings home the horror of Utah Beach and the fighting in Normandy: the use of a white flag to lure men out into the open; prisoners used as human mine detectors; and the steady stream of casualties from enemy fire and mines. The events on Utah Beach were less dramatic and deadly than on Omaha Beach, but strip away the comparative element and the bloody nature of the 22nd Infantry Regiment's task can properly be appreciated. Nor was the securing of the beach necessarily the end of their problems. Behind the beach lay a flooded area crossed by five causeways, the western ends of which the men of the 101st Airborne Division were supposed to have captured. The priority for the 4th Infantry Division was to drive inland across the causeways and relieve the paratroopers inland. A second objective was to eliminate the heavy artillery fire landing on the beach. Much of this was coming from German heavy batteries to the north of the landing zone. Housed in substantial concrete casemates, the guns could fire on the beach and into the concentration of ships offshore. Casualties on the beach mounted steadily, and at sea the USS *Corry* came under heavy fire from the German naval battery at St. Marcouf. Bracketed by fire from the battery, the destroyer ran onto a mine while trying to maneuver. Of the *Corry*'s 294-man crew, 13 would perish as she sank at 7:35 AM. Something would have to be done to silence the batteries.

That task was entrusted to the 22nd Infantry Regiment. The third battalion of the regiment landed with the initial assault wave along with the 8th Infantry Regiment. The task of the third battalion was to expand the landing zone by advancing northward up the beach, reducing German beach defenses in the process. Tanks would support the advance and attacks on strongpoints. This was no easy task as the flooding of the rear areas limited the scope for flanking attacks.

The first and second battalions landed some 210 minutes after the Third Battalion. It would fall to them to cross the flooded areas, advance inland, and neutralize the German heavy batteries at Crisbecq and Azeville.[37] These were formidable fortifications, as William S. Boice, one of the regimental chaplains recorded in his history of the 22nd. The Azeville battery, operated by 2/1261 Coastal Artillery Regiment, consisted of four 155-mm French-made Schneider guns under the command of Leutnant Kattnig. The Crisbecq battery, operated by the navy gunners under the command of Oberleutnant Walter Ohmsen, held four Czech-made Skoda 210-mm guns batteries. However, the dangers of these strong points did not end there:

> The fortress of Crisbeq had not been completed by the Germans, but it was the most formidable arrangement of pillboxes on Utah Beach. This fortress of concrete and steel, carefully camouflaged, was connected with surrounding fortresses by partially finished underground passageways. It was an excellent observation point and it was a constant source of information, by means of a deeply laid underground cable to the German defences and command at Cherbourg.[38]

The concrete of these emplacements was typically six to seven feet thick, reinforced with 0.5-inch-thick steel reinforcing rods spaced every nine inches horizontally and vertically. The roof slabs for the emplacements were as much as 12 feet thick. Throughout the standard of construction was very high. The casemates at Crisbecq were state-of-the-art defensive positions.

The fortress at Azeville was similarly formidable and could coordinate its fire with that at Crisbecq to good effect. Unsurprisingly, the advance of the 22nd Infantry Regiment proved considerably more difficult than the initial assault landing, and by the evening of June 6 the Regimental Command post was having considerable difficulty in locating the First Battalion. Within the command post, the officer charged with maintaining the signal log reflected on the regiment's first taste of action: "All of us got our first taste of what combat looks like after an assault. There were several German corpses laying [*sic*] around—some were blown inside out almost. . . . On the way up [to where the Regimental Command Post would be established] we met some paratroopers with about 25 prisoners with them. They didn't look much like Hitler's front line troops. They looked much more like a home guard or something. They were members of the 919th Inf. Regt."[39]

CHAPTER 10

The Battle for the Marshes

LA FIERE

Daybreak on June 6 saw several parties of paratroopers from the 82nd Airborne Division converging on the manor house at La Fiere. A stone-built farmhouse with turret, the manor house controlled the eastern end of a causeway and road across the Merderet River. At the other end of the causeway was the hamlet of Cauquigny with its small Roman Catholic Church. Among the groups converging on La Fiere was Captain Floyd "Ben" Scwartzwalder, commander of G Company, 507th Parachute Infantry Regiment. Finding himself on the wrong side of the marsh from the regimental objective at Amfreville, he rapidly began to gather men. Leading a party of 45 men, Schwarzwalder followed the tracks of the railroad that linked St. Mere Eglise to Cherbourg. He knew that if he was to pursue the regiment's objectives, he would have to cross the Merderet River, and the nearest point at which this could be done was at La Fiere. By 0800 groups of Americans from the 507th, 505th, and 508th parachute infantry regiments were converging on the manor house at La Fiere and were engaging the 28 German soldiers who had been sent there on June 5 to protect it and the vital crossing. Gaining control of the crossing had been assigned in the invasion plans to Company A of the 505th. However, like Schwartzwalder's group, several other parties had concluded that they would have to ensure control of the crossing in order to complete their objectives. Thus Scwartzwalder's party from the 507th, which had grown to 80 strong by the time of their arrival at La Fiere, joined Company A of the 505th in the attack on the manor house. The manor house was an incredibly strong defensive point. Stone-built Norman houses could be turned into veritable castles with machine guns and a little ingenuity from the defenders. The manor house took considerable punishment from small-arms fire and bazookas before a sergeant from the 508th could gain entry to the ground floor of the manor house. Firing up through the ceiling above him, he compelled the remaining defenders to surrender. The French owner and his family then emerged from the wine cellar. The fight at La Fiere had been intense and the 507th had incurred several casualties, but it was only a precursor of what was to come. As General Gavin set up his command post just up the road from the manor, developments elsewhere would serve to turn La Fiere into perhaps the most intensely fought-over piece of territory in Normandy.

THE TIMMES GROUP

Lieutenant Colonel Charles Timmes, commanding the Second Battalion of the 507th Parachute Infantry Regiment, had landed in the Merderet marshes near the regimental objective of the village of Amfreville. Moving along the edges of the marsh, he had gathered 10 men, and at 0400 he picked up another 10 from two gliders that landed in the vicinity. Forced to make a withdrawal after being engaged by an enemy machine gun, the group eventually entered the village of Cauquigny, which controlled the western end of the crossing to La Fiere. The village controlling the vital causeway was undefended; but instead of holding the position, Timmes and his group pressed on towards Amfreville. The strength of the group was augmented by another 30 troopers from Company D. The decision to march on Amfreville was motivated by the fact that Timmes could hear firing coming from that direction.

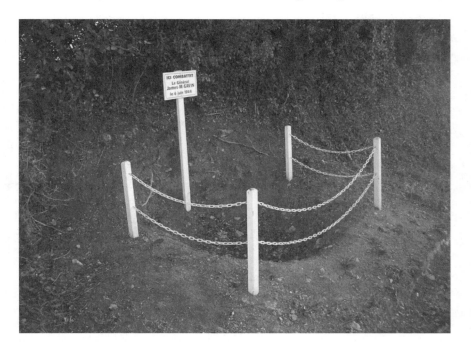

General Gavin's preserved foxhole at La Fiere, Normandy (Picture taken by author)

He assumed that other elements of the regiment were engaged around the village. They moved out of Cauquigny across open farmland. En route they encountered another lost party from the 507th, but instead of joining the Timmes group they were determined to march on to their own objective. Approaching Amfreville, the Timmes group began to receive a growing volume of fire from the village. Timmes realized that the gunfire he had heard earlier was directed at him and his group. The undisciplined attempt by the enemy to engage him at long distance had prevented the Americans from wandering into what otherwise might have been a trap.

Timmes decided his best option was to retire towards Cauquigny. As he did, some of the Amfreville garrison pursued them. At 0930 Timmes decided to hold a position in an orchard next to the marsh, which might provide them with a means of escape if the enemy made a concerted attack. They were about a mile away from Cauquigny and in a good position to attempt to reach the western edge of the causeway from La Fiere. However, the position began to attract a growing volume of enemy fire. Finding themselves besieged in their position, Timmes decided to stay where he was.

Within 90 minutes or so of being besieged in the orchard, Timmes began to wrestle with thoughts of what he should do next. Capturing Amfreville was clearly beyond his means. Leaving the orchard would result in his force sustaining moderate casualties. He decided, instead, to dispatch a force of 10 men under Lieutenant Levy to gain control of Cauquigny and the western end of the causeway to La Fiere. Levy's force found Cauquigny empty of the enemy. They did, however, encounter a force of 20 men from D Company of the 507th Parachute Infantry Regiment. Under the command of Lieutenant Kormylo, they had set up a position overlooking the village and causeway. The bulk of Kormylo's group was sent to join Timmes in the orchard. Thus around noon, little more than a dozen men began to dig in at Cauquigny with its vital causeway.

The main problem was that Timmes, Levy, and others did not anticipate an enemy attack in force to seize Cauquigny. With a church and a handful of houses, the village did not seem to be the kind of real estate that the enemy would highly prize. The failure to grasp the strategic importance of Cauquigny showed how long it took for many to come to terms with the geography of a battlefield that was radically different from that promised in preinvasion briefings. At least chance served to build up the forces at Cauquigny, as 39 men from the 508th Parachute Infantry Regiment marched into the village. One of the officers with the 508th party was convinced of the importance of holding Cauquigny, so they were added to the defense of the village. Shortly thereafter, the defenders of Cauquigny witnessed an attack against the German forces holding the Manor of La Fiere, which dominated the other end of the causeway. An exchange of orange signals from both ends of the causeway indicated that American forces were in control of the vital crossing. However, along the causeway were a number of weapon pits containing enemy troops. Seeing that both ends of the causeway were in American hands, the Germans on the causeway put up only a token resistance before surrendering. Captain Ben Schwartzwalder and a large party of paratroops from the 507th crossed from La Fiere to Cauquigny. Reasoning that the fight for the causeway was over, he set out to capture the regiment's original objective of Amfreville. In the process, he would relieve Timmes in the orchard. The majority of the men from the 508th who had augmented the defenses of Cauquigny went with Schwartzwalder's force.

Almost as soon as Schwartzwalder's men were out of sight, the defenders of Cauquigny found themselves under heavy attack. Shell fire preceded the arrival of Renault tanks (which in 1940 had been part of the French army until captured by the Germans). They were supported by infantry. In a short-lived but intense fight, a bazooka put one tank out of action and gammon grenades two more. However, the disparity in force sizes meant that Levy had to withdraw, which he did in the direction of Timmes. This unfortunately left exposed several squads of American paratroopers coming across the causeway from La Fiere to reinforce Cauquigny. As S. L. A. Marshall recorded:

> The two leading squads had already reached firm ground and turned south along the shore preparatory to digging in when the blow fell. It caught them unaware, but the squads that followed fared far worse. The tank artillery shelled the causeway behind them, thereby cutting off their line of retreat; the enemy machine guns, banding against the twisting road, forbade any movement to the right. It was too late to advance, retreat or deploy. The men broke to the left and individually tried to wade, crawl and swim back through the marsh. But Germans and their weapons were thick on the western bank and were flailing the marsh with fire before the Americans had time to vanish into the rushes and reeds. Many of the fugitives were shot dead while wading in the muck next the west shore; more of them, wounded, struggled on, only to die by drowning in the river; if any escaped, report was not made of it.[1]

Levy and Schwartzwalder arrived at the orchard occupied by Timmes and his force. Instead of marching off towards Amfreville, they found themselves trapped in the orchard by a growing volume of enemy fire. The 175 men in the orchard were under attack from the same enemy push that had ousted Levy from Cauquigny. Here they would remain for another three days until developments elsewhere released the pressure on the defenders. As well as drawing off enemy forces that could have been used elsewhere, the Timmes group also prevented the Germans from using a ford, in the form of an underwater causeway, across the marsh. It would take until June 8 for the trapped Americans to discover it and begin to bring reinforcements across from the other side of the Merderet River. While the loss of Cauquigny was a blow that would prove costly to regain, the defenders of "Timmes's Orchard" prevented the Germans from using their greater knowledge of the marsh to potentially devastating effect against American forces on the east bank of the Merderet River.

THE BATTLE FOR CHEF-DU-PONT

When Captain Roy Creek landed in the swamps near La Fiere on June 6, he immediately faced the same difficulties that faced every other member of the 507th that night. He landed in deep water, and when he was able to free himself Captain

Creek could only locate one man from his stick, the Merderet serving to sever it in two. Meeting up with a larger party of Americans, Creek was placed under the command of Lieutenant Colonel Edwin Ostberg, commanding officer of the First Battalion of the 507th. Crossing through the swamps under enemy sniper fire, Ostberg and his force reached La Fiere after Levy's forces had occupied Cauquigny. Reporting to General Gavin at La Fiere, Ostberg and his force were ordered to seize the crossing of the Merderet, to the south of La Fiere, at Chef-du-Pont. Lieutenant Colonel Maloney was put in overall charge of the operation. The force he commanded was about 100 strong and armed only with sidearms and three machine guns. By 10:00 AM they had reached the railway station at Chef-du-Pont and had not encountered any enemy resistance.

However, in moving towards the vital bridge at the outskirts of the town, Maloney's force began to receive heavy fire. A number of men were hit and vicious house-to-house fighting ensued. By the time they had fought their way through the town, they found German troops had dug in on both sides of the bridge. Ostberg immediately attacked and succeeded in overrunning the German positions on the bridge closest to the town. Ostberg was actually on the bridge when he was shot and tumbled over it and into the waters below. Creek and another paratrooper got down to the riverbank and were able to pull the badly wounded colonel out of the water. Ostburg would live, but he was out of action for the duration of the fight at Chef-du-Pont. With the paratroopers on the bridge approaches exposed to a growing volume of German fire, their situation was precarious. It was made worse so by a radio message from General Gavin ordering Maloney to return to his position with as many men who could be spared to help bolster the defenses of La Fiere. After their victory at Cauquigny, German infantry and tanks were attempting to cross the causeway to La Fiere. Trapped on the narrow confines of the causeway, the tanks had little room to maneuver. This room was reduced still further by antitank mines that had been laid by the paratroopers. Bazooka teams and a 57-mm antitank gun destroyed one tank and then a second. German infantry tried to rush the end of the causeway, only to be beaten back by a storm of machine gun and rifle fire. Gavin reasoned that the developing fight for La Fiere meant that the force at Chef-du-Pont would have to be reduced to a minimum.

With Ostberg out of action, command was now assumed by Creek, who was the second highest ranking officer on the spot. Creek was left with just 34 men and German artillery rapidly reduced this to 20. Just as a company-sized enemy force was sighted, Creek's fortunes began to improve as a flight of C-47s on a resupply mission passed overhead. Containers carrying arms and ammunition began to float to earth. One container carrying 60-mm mortar ammunition landed directly on top of Creek's position. Fortunately, someone in Creek's squad had brought a mortar with them to Chef-du-Pont even though they had no ammunition for it. Mortar fire was rapidly brought to bear on the Germans advancing towards the bridge. As this was happening, a glider carrying a 57-mm antitank gun landed in the swamp near the bridge. The antitank gun was rapidly brought into action against the enemy artillery on the other side of the river that was firing to such devastating effect against

Creek's position. A direct hit was scored on the enemy gun, ceasing the artillery fire. Then a hundred paratroopers, reinforcements from La Fiere, appeared. The failure of the first attempt to cross the causeway had convinced the German forces at Cauquigny that they should spend the rest of the day regrouping. With the arrival of the force from La Fiere, the remaining German positions around the bridge at Chef-du-Pont were quickly stormed, and the vital link across the Merderet was at last fully in American hands. With La Fiere and Chef-du-Pont firmly secured by the Americans, the Germans had been robbed of the two principal means of advance across the marsh towards the invasion beaches. The 507th was fighting along both sides of the great marsh, and the actions of apparently disparate groups had conspired to deny vital territory to the enemy. Along the fringes of the marsh it was as though a great game of chess was being played. Like chess pieces, the disparate groups moved backward and forward in response to opportunity, enemy threat, and objective; but while they appeared separate, each group's actions impacted directly on every other piece on the board.

THE GRAIGNES GROUP

The one potential exception to this picture was a group of 507th men who had landed well to the south of their drop zones and the critical crossings at La Fiere and Chef-du-Pont. Nine C-47s from the 53rd Transport Command Squadron had managed to misdrop the entire Headquarters Company of the Third Battalion along with 55 equipment bundles containing machine guns, mortars, ammunition, rations, maps, demolitions equipment, and medical supplies. Sometime after 2:38 AM on June 6, Captain Leroy Brummitt, first man of his stick of paratroopers, found himself lost and alone. Searching vainly for the rest of his stick, he encountered mortar men and machine gunners from his unit, the Third Battalion of the 507th. They had managed to recover some of the bundles of heavy equipment that had landed in the marsh. Brummitt along with most of the rest of the Headquarters Company of the Third Battalion had fallen into the swamps and fields around the town of Graignes, six miles southwest of the critical route center of Carentan. At the base of the Cotentin Peninusula, Carentan occupied a key strategic position covering the coast road and sitting between Utah and Omaha beaches. Carentan, however, was not Brummitt's or the battalion's objective. With Graignes so far away from the regiment's objectives and the two landing beaches, Brummitt and his small force were miles from where they should have been dropped and even further away from the possibility of relief from forces driving inland from the beaches. Nevertheless Brummitt's force moved into Graignes and, expecting enemy opposition, they encountered none.

One of the other men lost and in the dark around Graignes in the early hours of June 6 was Sergeant Edward Barnes. Part of the communication team for the Third Battalion, Barnes had made the jump with a portable telephone switchboard attached to his legs. Barnes landed on firm ground beyond the swamp and released himself from the parachute and the switchboard. He immediately heard the sound of footsteps, which turned out to be an inquisitive cow determined to investigate the strange arrival in her field. Barnes later gave a revealing impression of what it was like to be a paratrooper on D-Day:

> A feeling of loneliness closed in on me, as I pictured the whole German Army was trying to locate and exterminate me. At first list of dawn, I took off again, where I thought our drop zone should have been. At about 5:00 a.m., I was challenged by a voice on the other side of the hedgerow. I gave the countersign and up popped another trooper. He was in the same spot as myself, hopelessly lost. We continued down the road and finally ran into some more troopers, also lost. By this time we had a mighty fighting force of six troopers. In the distance we could see the outline of a church steeple. So we decided to head for the church and maybe get some information as to our whereabouts and the whereabouts of any other troopers in the area. We continued cautiously on our way toward the church, expecting any minute to be fired on by the Germans, when we heard a challenge from the ditch up the road in front of us. We gave the countersign and were told to come forward slowly. When we got to within about fifteen yards from the spot where we heard the challenge, we could see they were troopers from the 82nd Airborne. We all went up to the church in the village, which turned out to be the village of Graignes, and reported in to the commanding officer in charge, Major [Charles D.] Johnson...It seems the major was as lost as the rest of us.[2]

It took some questioning of local villagers before Johnson, who had assumed command as senior officer with Brummitt as his second-in-command, could identify his position.

Daybreak revealed the precariousness and yet strength of their position. Situated on high land and surrounded on three sides by the waters of the great marsh, Graignes was at once defensible and a key observation point, especially the steeple of its 12th-century church, from which one could see for miles over the marsh and over several of the key approaches to Graignes. The village was also somewhat off the major routes connecting Carentan to the coast towns and to St. Lo in the South. As Brummitt's notebook, preserved in the National Archives, reveals, the morning of June 6 saw a steady stream of arrivals at Graignes:

> 0830 F[light] O[fficer] Morales & 1st Lt Ahmad & 2 E[nlisted] M[en] from glider which landed S[outh] W[est] of G[raignes] in swamp.[3]
> 0900 Capt Sophain, Capt Chapman, T Schiller in.
> 0950 Lt Hoffman & rest of stick plus Jenkinson, Hornbaker, Miller in.
> 1000 Major Johnson, H. Naughton, Cpl Reese in.[4]

During the course of the next 36 hours, the force at Graignes swelled to approximately 180 men. Most would be from the 507th, but men from other units would also find their way to Graignes. A patrol sent out late on June 6 would bring back 20 men from Company B, First Battalion, 501st Parachute Infantry Regiment. They too had been misdropped along with their commanding officer, Captain Loyal

Bogart. Bogart had jumped out of his C-47 along with the rest of his stick, even though he had been wounded in the legs by enemy flak. While the men from the 501st were valuable additions to the defenses of Graignes, Bogart was too badly injured to play a full combat role. Nevertheless, insisting on doing his duty, he set to work operating the telephone exchange, which served as the communications network for the defenses of Graignes. The defenses of Graignes were further reinforced by a party of Basque prisoners under the command of two French gendarmes, who wandered into the American positions. Most remarkably of all, they were joined by two men from the 29th Infantry Division, who had seemingly gotten off the beach and had advanced miles across enemy-held territory before arriving in Graignes. Their Browning automatic rifle made a valuable addition to the town's defenses. Incredibly, by the end of D-Day an American base, albeit cut off from and out of communication with other American units, had been set up in the rear areas of the German line.

In doing this, the men of the 507th received massive assistance from the local French populace. Finding so many Americans in their midst, the community of Graignes faced an agonizing choice. Alphonse Voydie, the acting mayor, with the support of Albert Leblastier, the Roman Catholic priest, decided to call for a meeting for the following day. Helping Americans cut off from their lines could easily invite the destruction of the town and reprisals by the German authorities. At that meeting, with the urging of Voydie, the people of Graignes gladly voted to take such risks and give the Americans all available help. To some extent, the decision was made on June 6. Several locals, including the Rigault family, had been giving their help spontaneously since the start of the landings. On June 6 locals ventured into the swamp to recover the precious equipment bundles with their blue parachutes, while others watched the swamps for signs of the enemy. Food was found and prepared for the paratroopers. Wounds were bound and guides were found to help American patrols through the swamp. Headquarters was set up on the hill at Graignes by the café and grocery shop owned by Madame Boursier. Ginette Decaumont, who was 15 in 1944, later recalled: "My father, my uncle, my brother... [went] out on the marsh many times to look for equipment which they [the paratroopers] had lost."[5] Ginnette, along with the other children of the commune, would receive American chocolate and chewing gum, which the paratroopers gladly shared with their hosts.

At first the paratroopers were suspicious of their hosts, especially as people walked from nearby villages such as St. Jean de Daye to see the strange arrivals. Some of them found themselves temporary prisoners of the 507th. However, the display of support for the Americans shown by the citizens of Graignes, and the excellent French of some of the parachutists such as Captain Sophain, the battalion medical officer swiftly ended the mistrust. By the end of June 6 a quite remarkable episode in the liberation of Normandy was taking place, as American parachutists and French civilians turned their town into an outpost of liberty in the heart of enemy territory. What the men of the 507th badly needed was a speedy linkup with the forces advancing off the beach. This would be neither swift nor easy.

OVERALL STRATEGIC SITUATION AT 2400 HOURS, JUNE 6, 1944

The situation faced by the men of the 507th was identical to that facing a number of Allied units at the end of June 6. Despite the slaughter on Omaha Beach, the landings had been a success. The German air force had made what amounted to little more than a token effort to oppose the invasion force. Similarly, the efforts of the German navy were largely ineffective. The danger from conventional submarines in the shallow English Channel was largely discounted, but the threat from fast E-boats was considered significant, especially in light of Exercise Tiger. Only German land forces had achieved any real success in opposing Allied ambitions.

On the eastern flank of the landings, the 3rd British Infantry Division had come ashore on Sword Beach between St. Aubin sur Mer and the mouth of the river Orne. In one of the leading landing craft, under heavy fire from the beach, Major C. K. King had read his men the famous call-to-arms speech before the battle of Agincourt in Shakespeare's *Henry V.* Lord Lovat's commandos, meanwhile, were led ashore by a lone bagpiper, and the British forced their way through the small port of Ouistreham and headed inland. Almost 29,000 men had landed on Sword Beach before the end of D-Day, and a linkup had been effected with the British paratroop forces covering the eastern flank of the landing. The advance had, however, not been as swift as anticipated. The city of Caen had not been captured as had been anticipated in the landing plan. Moreover, strong German forces lay between the Sword bridgehead and the nearest Allied forces, which had come ashore on Juno Beach. Over 21,000 men of the 3rd Canadian Division had come ashore on Juno on D-Day and had linked up with the men of the British 50th Infantry Division landing on Gold Beach. At Courseulles, the Canadians had been forced to fight their way through a town riddled with pillboxes, fortified houses, and enemy-held trenches. A further 25,000 men of the British 50th Infantry Division had come ashore on Gold Beach by the end of the first day of the Normandy campaign. Some of the leading units, like the First Battalion of the Hampshire Regiment, sustained heavy casualties as they waded through deep water, but they successfully created a bridgehead. Nine miles of enemy-held territory lay between the forces on Gold Beach and the easternmost section of Omaha Beach held by the U.S. 1st Infantry Division.

Despite the slaughter on Omaha Beach in the first few hours of the landing, by the end of June 6 over 34,000 men had come ashore. This force remained isolated from Utah Beach, on which 23,250 men had come ashore on D-Day. Between Omaha and Utah beaches lay almost 20 miles of enemy-held territory and the towns of Isigny sur Mer and Carentan. The latter was particularly important, for it controlled the routes to the interior along which enemy reinforcements were already en route. If the Germans could prevent the linkup between Omaha and Utah beaches, they had the opportunity to destroy the bridgehead at the latter. A unified bridgehead would be considerably harder to deal with. In the 20-mile gap between the two bridgeheads were small groups of friendly forces, including a small force of U.S. Rangers who had seized the Pointe du Hoc after much fighting on June 6. They would have to hold out until June 8 for relief. The gap also contained scattered groups of misdropped

American paratroopers at places like Graignes. At the end of June 6, Carentan had become perhaps the most valuable piece of real estate in Normandy. Combined Allied casualties breaking through the coastal crust on D-Day had been mercifully slight—10,300 men, some 6,000 of whom were American. What mattered now was to enlarge the bridgeheads into a single entity. That meant capturing Carentan, and those Americans cut off behind enemy lines in the 20-mile gap suddenly assumed major strategic importance.

A further imperative lay in bringing in as much men and material as quickly as possible and ensuring that they lay beyond the range of enemy artillery fire. Engineers were busy clearing the beaches of obstacles and opening up and reinforcing the roads which led off them. They were already busy building two artificial harbors at St. Laurent sur Mer and at Arromanches. The beaches, however, remained under enemy artillery fire. To relieve them from it would take several more days, as units such as the 22nd Infantry Regiment pushed further inland.

CHAPTER 11

The Drive Inland and the Crossing of the Merderet

On June 7 the 22nd Infantry Regiment resumed their task, with the Second Battalion advancing on Azeville and the First on Crisbecq. The Third Battalion advanced slowly up the beach, reducing enemy strongpoints. By late afternoon on June 7 both the First and Second battalions found themselves under heavy pressure. Under fire from German artillery, American counterbattery fire began to drop dangerously close to the regiment's lines. Wading through the inundated areas the First Battalion had lost all its .30-caliber machine guns and its mortars. The Second Battalion was badly in need of machine gun ammunition. So great was the pressure that between 1800 and 1815 the First Battalion retired 600 yards to reorganize and take up defensive positions for the night. The situation was highly dangerous as the First and Second battalions were separated from each other and from the 12th Infantry Regiment somewhere on their left. The dangers of enemy infiltration, or even full-scale counterattack to exploit the exposed flanks of the American units, were considerable. During the afternoon both the First and Second battalions had already faced German counterattacks, and it came as little surprise when, during the night, the First Battalion once again found itself under enemy assault. By dawn on July 8, the First and Second battalions had suffered total losses since landing of six killed, 72 wounded, and 59 missing. The strain was beginning to show as reports of tanks (in incredible numbers) were filtered through to the regimental command post, and every enemy artillery round was ascribed to the dreaded 88 mm.

At 0630 both the First and Second battalions resumed their advance on the enemy strongpoints at Azeville and Crisbecq. They met stiff resistance, and by mid-morning the advance was faltering. The writer of the regimental signal log recorded at 1040:

Edwards can't make contact with Co "F" – "F" Co is trying to take Azeville. "F" Co not doing so good. "E" Co has 35 prisoners but are meeting stiff residence [*sic*] from mortars. Ruggles is sending "E" Co a platoon of 4.2 to knock out motors [*sic*]. Snipers are still coming in 2nd Bn C.P. I could hear the snipers over the phone.[1]

Despite strenuous efforts by both battalions, the advance fell well short of both strongpoints. Part of the problem was that the heavy batteries at Azeville and Crisbecq could support each other with observed artillery fire. With the danger of enemy counterattack still high the Third Battalion was relieved of its duties and sent inland to act as regimental reserve. The First and Second battalions withdrew from enemy contact to dig in for the night. Company A, assaulting Crisbecq, was in such danger at the time that as the withdrawal began the commanding officer, Captain Tom Shields, who had been seriously wounded, ordered his men to leave him in order to effect their retreat. Shields then called in an artillery strike on his position as the Germans overran it. He sacrificed his life in order to protect his company. The regiment was bracing itself for a counterattack as a captured German soldier stated that the 248th Division was planning to attack regimental lines during the night. The return of the Third Battalion to the regiment had a marked effect on its morale. As was recorded in the Regimental signal log: "The 2nd Bn is back on line. They feel better now that they have the 3rd Bn in reserve".[2] Artillery and nebelwerfer rocket fire continued, but the attack by the 248th Division did not materialize. The strain was considerable, and rumors and stories circulated around the regiment. The writer of the regimental signal log, expecting the enemy counterattack at any moment, wrote shortly before midnight on June 8:

An American soldier who was captured by the Germans and escaped tells this story: He was captured with two of his buddies. A German NCO and others questioned them. They refused to give anything but their name, rank and serial number. One American was shot in the face as an example to the others. The next American got the same thing. Pvt Irvin would have been next. But just then our artillery opened up and the Nazis scattered out. Irvin took to the tall grass and escaped. He was followed for about a mile and shots kept hitting around him. He made it to the inundated area and met some paratroopers and joined up with them.... The recorder writes these notes from the story as told to him. More complete details were given to [the] executive officer.[3]

The men of the regiment spent the night of June 8–9 in uneasy expectation of a counterattack that did not come, and a dawn that would herald a return to the advance. Reports of booby traps, German aircraft disguising themselves as Allied, and landings by German paratroops continued to come in during the night.

Daybreak on June 9 saw a change in tactics to reduce the strongpoints. Instead of advancing on Azeville and Crisbecq, the full combat power of the regiment would be directed solely against Azeville. Crisbecq, in the words of the regimental history, was to be "contained and by-passed."[4] The Third Battalion would lead the assault with the support of a company from the 899th Tank Destroyer Battalion. The Second and First battalions would advance in a column of battalions behind them and would deal with the strongpoints north of Azeville after that strongpoint had been reduced. The assault, under the command of Brigadier General Henry A. Barber, was named Task Force Barber. Despite stubborn resistance, and the efforts of the Crisbecq battery, the concentration of combat power was sufficient to force the Azeville garrison to surrender. However, it was a closecall.

Company I led the assault, coming in sight of the first pillbox at 1200.[5] Supported by a tank, two assault sections worked their way through a minefield to eliminate three small pillboxes on the perimeter of the battery. Using a hedge as cover, they then worked their way toward the four casemates containing the heavy guns. Each casemate was protected by a machine gun on the roof. The supporting tank and the assault sections concentrated their fire on the nearest casemate. Bazooka and tank shells made little impact on the six-foot-thick walls of the casemate. Therefore, one assault section concentrated its efforts on the back door of the casemate. First, they discharged their flamethrower against the casemate without any visible effect. A 40-pound charge of TNT was then set off against the back door. Again there was no visible effect. A second charge was laid. When it exploded, it knocked unconscious the men who had laid it because they had not been able to retreat far enough. The door remained firmly closed.

The second assault section then came forward. Private Ralph Riley brought forward his flamethrower after a 75-yard crossing of an open field under fire. Unfortunately, the flamethrower wouldn't ignite. Riley pumped liquid fuel around the door before lighting a match and running. Riley made cover, although his canteen and gas mask were shot through in the process. Company I was now out of ideas and low on ammunition, but it was not out of luck. As Riley returned to the hedgerow behind which the rest of the assault sections were sheltering, the sound of exploding small-arms ammunition became audible. Riley's liquid fire had run under the casemate door and had set off some of the small-arms ammunition stored behind it. Fifteen minutes later, the casemate door opened and a German officer carrying a white flag appeared. With him was an American parachute officer, who had been captured by the Germans. The German officer explained that he was willing to surrender the battery if the Americans would cease fire. This was arranged, and I Company took the surrender of the Azeville battery. The men of the Third Battalion were somewhat shocked at the size of the Azeville garrison, which had grown steadily to over 160 men as the Americans pushed back the German units in front of them after June 6.

Perhaps the critical event in the reduction of Azeville was a single shot fired earlier by the Battleship USS *Nevada*. The guns of this veteran of Pearl Harbor were used to support the advance of the 22nd Infantry Regiment. Most of the shells went harmlessly over the casemates containing the German heavy guns. One, however, did not. It came straight through the aperture for the gun, shattering it and its shield. The gun's crew members were killed in an explosion of gun fragment and concrete. The shell punched through the reinforced concrete of two walls to exit through the rear of the casemate. Despite the destruction it wrought, the shell did not detonate. Indeed, it had to be dealt with by a bomb disposal team more than 50 years later.

In shattering one casemate, the *Nevada's* single round helped to convince the defenders of Azeville that it was time to surrender to I Company.

By the end of June 9, the regiment found itself on the outskirts of Ozeville and facing another strongpoint. It was also engaged by the heavily defended German position at the Chateau de Fontenay, which had once been the home of Voltaire. The Third Battalion would sustain heavy casualties attacking the Chateau before the Germans evacuated it on June 11. Ozeville and Crisbecq would fall the following day. Finally on June 14 the three battalions of the regiment would attack and seize the high ground west of Quineville. It would then take a well-earned rest in the line. Reorganization, reinforcement and reequipment were necessary to make up for the losses sustained by the regiment. Although the regiment would continue to play a leading role in the campaign in France and the drive towards Germany, its strange little episode in establishing the Normandy bridgehead had come to an end.

In a handful of days the regiment had been transformed. It was now a veteran unit, and its men had gone through many a personal evolution. David Rothbart was an NCO in the Service Company of the 22nd Infantry Regiment. He had stayed behind in England while the rest of the regiment had landed in France and fought its way across the Cotentin Peninsula. He caught up with the regiment on June 22 near Cherbourg. He was struck by the change that had come over the regiment and its men:

German gun position at Azeville showing combat damage. (Picture taken by author.)

Our casualties are very heavy. Some companies have already had 3 or 4 different first sergeants and company commanders. Names of rifle company personnel have changed
almost beyond recognition. In just one day we have become oriented; even we now
appear grimy and unshaven, though clean compared with those who landed over two
weeks ago and now carry German pistols, pocket knives, watches and other souvenirs
taken from German soldiers either dead or live prisoners. Some ride on captured motor-
cycles, have a ready stash of cognac or cider, and are considerably different than as we
knew them before.[6]

The 22nd Infantry Regiment had been prepared for a modern mechanized war of
maneuver. Thanks to the flooding, and the strength of German defenses, it had
found itself engaged in a kind of war that harked back to earlier times. Each strongpoint had to be demolished like some medieval castle. It was difficult, dangerous, and
unglamorous work. Yet it was needed to place Utah Beach well beyond the range of
German artillery fire. The determination and professional skills of the Germans who
manned the batteries at Azeville and Crisbecq were matched by the men who had to
take them. The concentration of regimental combat power on Azeville under Task
Force Barber, and the resulting success of the regiment in realizing its objectives,
illustrated the learning curve that American officers had to go through in the days
following D-Day. Strongpoints had to be reduced methodically and slowly at the
expense of the pace of the advance. Colonel Tribolet's reward for such methodical
progress was to be relieved of his command. At division and corps level, concern
had been mounting at the slow speed of the regiment's advance.

LA FIERE

While the 22nd Infantry Regiment was fighting its way through the German
strongpoints behind Utah Beach, the 507th was engaged in bitter fighting in the
swamps of the Merderet and Douvre rivers. The job of the paratroops was to facilitate the crossing of the Merderet River by the forces coming off Utah Beach. Much
of this was centered on La Fiere. After being beaten back on the afternoon of June
6, the forces of the German 91st Airlanding Division had regrouped around Cauquigny. Heavy artillery was brought up during the night to support at attack, which
began at 0800 on June 7. Again the French-built Renault and Hotchkiss tanks of the
91st Division took the lead. The lead tank advanced along the causeway until it
reached the tanks burnt out the previous day. It was then hit by a round from the
57-mm antitank gun on the banks above the marsh. A third knocked-out tank
blocked the road completely, with the result that the remaining three German tanks
could not move forward. The German infantry, however, used them as a cover to
support their rush along the causeway. With the Germans able to close to within gre-
nade range of the American positions, a furious exchange of fire took place. At close
range, attackers and defenders traded small-arms fire and grenades. Stationed on the
causeway, Company A of the 505th bore the brunt of the assault, with 507th and
508th men supporting them from the banks behind and above the manor. After

sustaining heavy losses, the Germans fell back. Shortly thereafter they asked for a truce to recover their wounded. This process took over two hours, at the end of which German artillery fire resumed.

By the evening of June 7, the 82nd Airborne Division faced an increasingly desperate task, even though the arrival that day of glider troops from the 325th Glider Infantry Regiment at La Fiere increased the chances of holding that position. Troops advancing from the beach had still failed to link up with the division. Relief was overdue, and at Chef-du-Pont and at La Fiere, German pressure remained considerable. Creek's force from the 507th was under orders to fall back to La Fiere if pushed out of Chef-du-Pont; and if La Fiere fell, the defenders who remained were to retreat to St. Mere Eglise. The 505th Parachute Infantry Regiment had captured this vital route center with relative ease on D-Day. German attempts to retake the town had been beaten back, and an army hospital established in the town treated the wounded who were brought into town. St. Mere Eglise was the base at which the 82nd Airborne Division would defend to the last. Forces were on their way to the town from the beachhead, but German resistance was proving unexpectedly resolute.

Dawn on June 8 saw a changed situation for the 507th and the other defenders of La Fiere. In the previous hours the leading elements of the VII Corps had finally reached St. Mere Eglise. On the causeway Company A, 505th Parachute Infantry Regiment, which had taken the brunt of the enemy attack from Cauquigny, was withdrawn from the line. Taking their place was a group of troopers from the 507th under the command of Captain Robert D. Rae. The night had also witnessed the failure of an attack intended to lift the siege of Timmes's Orchard. On June 7, the secret ford across the Merderet had been discovered by soldiers from Timmes's group. It was used to cross the swamp and contact General Gavin at La Fiere. At 2230 on June 7, Gavin had sent the First Battalion of the 325th Glider Infantry Regiment across the Merderet to relieve Timmes and to take Cauquigny and the other end of the causeway from La Fiere. Timmes's Orchard was duly relieved at around 0100, and the 325th continued its advance. However, given the strength of the German forces in the vicinity of Cauquigny, the rifle companies quickly found themselves in difficulties. They fell back independently to join the beleaguered defenders of Timmes's Orchard around daybreak on June 8. Gavin's attempt to free the causeway by stealth had failed. With the further advance of VII Corps blocked by the Merderet River, Gavin had little option but to prepare for a frontal attack across a causeway littered with dead men and vehicles from the preceding two days of combat.

The Third Battalion of the 325th Glider Infantry Regiment was selected to lead the attack. As the preliminary bombardment began on the morning of June 9, General Gavin relieved the commanding officer of the battalion, Lieutenant Colonel Charles A. Carrell, of his command. Carrell reported that he was sick and unable to undertake his duties in connection with launching the assault. The atmosphere was highly charged. Attacking across a narrow front against a well-equipped enemy would undoubtedly produce a considerable number of casualties. The failure of the First Battalion, 325th Glider Infantry Regiment, to take Cauquigny during the night left no one in any doubt as to the strength of the German forces on the other side of the Merderet River.

The relief of Carrell of his command sent a wave of uncertainty through an already tense battalion of men. Sensing that all was not well, Gavin spoke to Captain Robert Rae, whose company from the 507th had taken over principal responsibility for stopping a German threat across the causeway. Rae was ordered to move his force along the causeway towards Cauquigny if the advance of the 325th stalled. After two days of heavy combat, Rae knew only too well the difficulties that they would face in crossing the causeway. Many felt that Gavin had entrusted them with what amounted to a suicide mission. However, Rae's men were motivated by a higher force than simply obeying orders. Timmes and their fellow troopers from the 507th required relief urgently. It was their duty to their comrades to attempt a task that had failed others.[7] Rae eyed the preparations of the 325th with keen interest. Relations between paratroopers (who constituted a volunteer elite) and the glider men (who did not) were less than easy. They enjoyed vastly different status and rewards, with the "glider riders" enjoying the worst of both.

In the vanguard of the assault by the 325th would be Company G under the command of Captain John Sauls. At 1045 Sauls set off across the causeway with Lieutenant Donald Warran and Sergeant Wilfred Ericsson at his heels. The party covered the 500 yards from the manor at La Fiere to the end of the causeway in the face of heavy small-arms fire. Company G sustained casualties during the run, but as Sauls reached his goal he was amazed to see only another 30 men following him. A force of less than three squads had charged an enemy that had defeated an entire battalion the previous evening. The fight was as desperate as it was uneven.

The problem lay back at La Fiere. As Sauls set off for the attack, German machine gun fire had killed Private Johnson of G Company as he tried to cross a seven-foot gap in the manor's perimeter wall. That wall provided vital cover for the attacking glider men. The death of Johnson, and the seven-foot gap on which the Germans had registered their machine guns, brought home to the glider men the full horrors of the task at hand. The men behind Johnson hesitated, then froze, stalling the advance of the battalion stretched out behind them. By the time an officer arrived to force the remainder of G Company forward, Sauls and his party were heavily engaged. More importantly, the German forces whose heads had been kept down by the preparatory bombardments were now alert and prepared for the second stage of a stalled attack. As G Company, and then E Company, came across the causeway, they began to suffer heavy casualties. A Sherman tank attempted to support their advance, only to be disabled by an antitank mine on the causeway. It joined the tangle of wrecked machinery on the causeway, which, along with the dead and dying and enemy fire, caused the advance to bog down again. Sauls and his party at the end of the causeway did what they could to alleviate the pressure on the advance. Lieutenant Wasson was killed assaulting singlehandedly one of the machine guns that caused such damage to the men on the causeway. Rae and his company from the 507th provided covering fire from the opposite end of the causeway. While small elements of E Company and then F Company arrived to join Sauls's beleaguered force fighting in the hedgerows and fields around Cauquigny, the mass of G, E, and F companies remained pinned down on the causeway. The attack looked to have failed, never mind stalled, when Gavin indicated to Rae that his force from the 507th would have to restore the momentum.

The 90 men of Rae's company began their run across the causeway in two columns. Due to the congestion on the causeway, their dash stalled, and an artillery round caused four casualties among the leading group of men from Rae's command. To restore the momentum, Rae physically pulled some of his men to their feet while his runner, Private Keeler, organized a group of eight men to spearhead a renewed push through the mass of tangled men and machine. Pushing shell-shocked men aside, the eight-man spearhead succeeded in opening a passage along the causeway. Rae and the rest of his company proceeded along the causeway at top speed while medics used their renewed mobility to move casualties back towards La Fiere. In the wake of Rae's company came the rest of the Third Battalion, 325th Glider Infantry Regiment. Rae's arrival at Cauquigny rapidly began to turn the battle there. A stream of reinforcements followed him across the causeway. In close combat, the force of paratroopers and glider men drove the enemy back. The siege of Timmes's Orchard was soon lifted and his wounded evacuated back across the Merderet River. More significantly, on the strategic level, VII Corps became free to advance westward to cut off the Cotentin Peninsula and the vital port of Cherbourg from the rest of France.

CHAPTER 12

Cut-off Elements of the 507th

Beyond the fights at La Fiere, Cauquigny, Chef du Pont and Timmes's Orchard, many troopers of the 507th were conducting their war in small bands roaming the countryside. The countryside of the Bocage area of Normandy, with its small fields divided by thick hedgerows and substantial banks, was ideal for such operations. Fields of view were very limited and camouflage easy and effective. Small groups of 507th troopers were scattered across the west bank of the Merderet River. The Timmes group was the largest, and in isolated pockets such as at Graignes, paratroopers from all the regiments of the division were doing their best to play havoc with the Germans. Some of these groups, preferring hit-and-run tactics, spent their time roaming around the Norman countryside looking for targets of opportunity. One such group had ambushed and killed Major General William Falley, commanding officer of the 91st Airlanding Division as he raced to his headquarters at Picauville around dawn on June 6. Another group was led by the 507th's regimental commander, Colonel Millett. In the early hours of D-Day he had assembled a force of around 120 men and had set off to capture the regimental objective of the town of Amfreville. Like Timmes, the Millett group had come under heavy fire from the town. Rather than withdraw, as Timmes proceeded to do, Millett decided to hold his position. His force had grown steadily until it numbered some 250 men with 90 prisoners. On June 8, with ammunition beginning to run low and with little chance of capturing Amfreville, Millett decided to withdraw his forces towards the Merderet. Such a move would also support Gavin's attempt to rush the Cauquigny end of the La Fiere causeway. Exfiltrating such a substantial force was no easy task, and when two German machine guns opened fire, the advance of the column was halted. The column broke up under pressure of enemy action. Major David E. Thomas, a surgeon with the 508th Parachute Infantry Regiment, was part of the column. His after-action report later recalled: "The last approximately 40 members of the march column were brought under machine gun and sniper machine pistol fire.

The sniper was up in a tree. Half of this group tried to go forward and were well shot up with machine gun and mortar [fire]. The other half worked back to the original position. The tree sniper was located and shot."[1] However, the damage had been done and the column broken, although it took some time for everyone to realize it. Davies was one of the unlucky ones: "After waiting several hours we moved forward again and contacted the remaining people who had gone ahead. [We] hid in a hedge row and sent out a patrol and contacted [the] enemy within 200 yards. At this time the Infantry soldiers present took off without informing me, leaving me there with one Medical Detachment E[nlisted] M[an]" from the 507th. Further back down the column, Captain Paul Smith of F Company knew that something was wrong when the column had not moved for several minutes:

> We moved toward the head of the column but found that the front half of the column had moved off: a connecting file had fallen asleep. We were now located west of the Amfreville-Gourbesville highway. Suddenly I found myself in command of 150 men and 90 some prisoners with only a vague idea of where we were supposed to be going and of our mission when we got there. I did know, however, that Colonel Millett origi- nally was headed in the direction of the Merderet River which was located to our east, so I decided to keep in that direction.[2]

Along the way Smith's force encountered strong enemy forces and a group of men who had been with Davies in the front part of the column. They explained that Colonel Millett had been captured along with several other men from the head of the column. Together the men of Smith's column crossed the Merderet under heavy fire. Before they reached American lines near La Fiere, many of the prisoners had become casualties. On reaching American lines, Captain Smith advised Lieutenant Arthur Maloney, the regimental executive officer, of Millett's capture. Maloney was now acting regimental commander and Millett would spend the rest of the war in a prisoner-of-war camp until escaping in 1945.

Other members of Millett's column would make Allied lines over the course of the next few days. Major Davies was one. Finding himself alone except for the enlisted medic, Davies spent much of June 9–10 in the bottom of hedgerows trying to escape detection. In the darkness they walked through several groups of German soldiers without being challenged. Unfortunately, they were challenged by a sentry near Amfreville and captured. Stripped of all personal possessions in the command post of a German regiment, Davies treated the wounds of a fellow paratrooper who had been wounded by mortar fire. The colonel of the German regiment, realizing that Davies was a doctor, asked him if he would stay behind to treat the wounded. Davies remained there for three days, working alongside two German doctors as a steady stream of casualties came in. As he later related his story:

> I had been under informal guard up to this time, but in the commotion of digging silt trenches, etc., they forgot to put a guard on me. I busied myself moving from place to place so they wouldn't get used to seeing me in any one place, and then slipped away

and hid in a hedgerow. A Heavy Weapons Company came along on the other side and proceeded to dig in. When it was dark I travelled several hedge rows away form the personnel who had moved in on me. I opened up my escape kit to get my compass to direct myself to friendly troops. I found the compass was broken. I guided myself by the stars and travelled in an easterly direction until the moon came up, at which time it was too bright to travel. Then I holed up in a hedgerow. This hedgerow, incidentally, was about 100 yards in front of a German mortar battery and I spent the next day almost absorbing counter battery fire. With the coming of darkness I proceeded again, in a southeasterly direction when the Germans were not alert.[3]

Davis eventually walked into a 75-mm gun battery of the 90th Infantry Division. Other groups of cut-off paratroops would be less successful in their attempt to return to friendly lines.

THE FALL OF GRAIGNES

By the end of D-Day some 180 Americans, with the help of the local French populace, had established Graignes as an American base deep in the heart of the enemy's lines of communication. Command of the defenses of Graignes had passed from Captain Brummitt, who had led the initial entry into the town, to Major Johnson, executive officer of the Third Battalion. While other groups of the 507th battled desperately elsewhere in the swamps of the Cotentin Peninsula, the group at Graignes went unnoticed by the enemy. As Brummitt recorded in his report on the events at Graignes: "Defensive position was organized around Gragnes [sic]. Patrols were sent out to reconnoiter to the north in the vicinity of Carentan and to prepare the bridge over the Vire-Taute canal at Port des Planques for demolition if needs be. Approximately three or four days following D-Day patrolling was ordered nightly."[4] Brummitt's concise soldierly report does not convey the detail or danger involved in these patrols. However, his journal maintained throughout the days at Graignes does:

June 7
   Rumors of Americans at different places. Sighted a bit of activity across swamp to West...Tried salvaging equipment from glider. Could not get jeep.
   Capt. Brummitt led a 30 man patrol... to try to get some heavy weapons. Patrol was unsuccessful as far as mission concerned. We had one meal on this day.
   Patrol under H. Maxwell to Carentan got to meet an outfit retreating, horsedrawn believe BN [battalion] of Field Art[illery]. A skirmish followed resulting in the patrol scattering & coming in on their own. Sgt Hornbaker clipped on the wrist. From the manner in which the outfit was acting they were a bit battle weary.
   Lt. Maxwell's patrol all back in.
   Lt. Naughton with demolition guard went out.[5]

The "rumours of Americans at different places" were undoubtedly accurate. Captain Robert H. Phillips was in the process of gathering together a force of 17 to 18 men from B and C companies of the 501st Parachute Infantry Regiment in the vicinity of St. George de Bohon, on the western shore of the swamp opposite Graignes.[6] Aided by local French people, they would conduct ambushes against German forces for several days before retreating northwards towards Carentan..

Meanwhile, Major Johnson had resolved that even though they were miles from American lines, the forces at Graignes could play a valuable role in harassing the enemy rear and in conducting ambushes. This was despite the suggestions of Captain Brummitt, who on June 6 came up with a plan for a night march across the swamps to rejoin American lines around Carentan. Brummitt knew the vulnerability of their position and above all the need to attain battalion objectives. Major Johnson surmised that by holding Graignes, they could still play a valuable role in attacking enemy forces retreating from the beach and in threatening the enemy's lines of communication to the interior. The roads that connected Carentan to the interior would contain retreating enemy units broken by the American units coming off the beaches, as well as fresh units from the interior who would have to contain the Allied bridgeheads. Even though they came to differing conclusions, both Johnson and Brummitt were entirely logical in their appreciation of the situation. Both men were right in their favored choice of action for entirely different reasons. Brummitt's plan focused on the need to meet objectives. Johnson's was creative and recognized that, as with most military operations, the plan had gone out the window as soon as the first men began to land miles from their objectives. Graignes could become more than a thorn in the enemy's side, and if they could hold the land to the south of the great marsh until they were relieved, they would make the process of breaking out from the bridgeheads that much easier. Landing at Graignes was an accident, but in Johnson's eyes, it could be turned into a major opportunity.

Offensive patrolling was the order of the day, and after Maxwell's patrol had encountered the retreating German Field Artillery Battalion, efforts were made to relocate the enemy. On June 8 they were located with a field kitchen close to the neighboring village of Montmartin en Graignes. Alphonse Voydie, the acting mayor of Graignes in June 1944, remembers what happened next:

> The American commander, Johnson, sent seven of his men to wipe them out, for there could be no question of taking so many men prisoner. I said to Captain Sophain that it was very bold to send seven men to wipe out 200. He replied, "M. Le Maire, you must realise that one of my men is worth 60 German gunners." But they arrived too late, the Germans had disappeared.[7]

As the number of Germans retreating from the beaches continued to increase, inevitably there would be increasing contact between the defenders of Graignes and the enemy. The town would not be allowed to threaten the German lines of communication in the way that Johnson had hoped. From June 8 onwards, German activity around Graignes increased markedly.

On the morning of Sunday, June 11, the defensive perimeter around Graignes was quiet. Many of the townspeople went to church for ten o'clock Mass, joined by some of the American paratroopers. Partway through the service, two of the women of the town burst into the church to announce the arrival of a substantial German force. Raymond Lereculey, who was 12 at the time, remembered:

> Mme Bazir came into Church shouting, "My children, look out, the Boches are coming." The paratroops ordered us to stay in the Church while they themselves went out to fight. People prayed or chatted. As for me, I had a religious studies examination the following Tuesday, so I revised all day. We stayed there until the middle of the afternoon, until a Canadian who spoke French gave us permission to leave following the hedgerows and above all say nothing about the Americans if we encountered any Germans.[8]

Outside the church, a pitched battle raged as German troops advanced from the south. One member of the 507th would note at the time: "They seem to be throwing everything at us but the kitchen sink. One man 501st hit—also one of ours."[9] Inside the church the 64-year-old priest, Father Leblastier, read from *The Appearances of Fatima* to try to maintain the morale of the congregation.[10] His choice of texts was particularly appropriate. In 1917 the Virgin Mary had appeared to three children at the village of Fatima in Portugal. The children had proceeded to relay the message she brought. War, said the Virgin Mary, was a punishment for sin. War, famine, and persecution of the church were God's way of punishing the world. As well as a message, *The Appearances at Fatima* contained a prophecy of a world engulfed by war unless it returned to faith. *The Appearances* was officially endorsed by the Catholic Church in the 1930s. With a battle raging around Graignes, the prophecy seemed to have come to pass for the inhabitants of this one small commune. Father Leblastier was helped in ministering to his congregation by one of his old pupils Father Lebarbenchon, 32 years his junior. A member of the Franciscan order, Lebarbenchon had been sent to Graignes to recuperate from tuberculosis.[11] At five o'clock there was a lull in the battle, and at 1900 the Americans ordered Raymond Lereculey and the other members of the congregation to slip away, a sign that the defenses of Graignes were about to fall. Already a breach in the perimeter had been prevented only by the prompt movement of forces within the village.

The defenders of Graignes did not know it, but they had been engaged by the 17th SS Panzer Grenadier Division Gotz von Berlichingen. Moving northward from St. Lo, the division was ordered into the line at the base of the Cotentin Peninsula to reinforce the 6th German Parachute Regiment holding Carentan and to contain the Omaha Beach bridgehead. Taking the back roads from St. Lo to Carentan, which offered greater security from Allied fighter bombers, one of the advance guards of the division had been ambushed by the defenders of Graignes on June 10 by the roadside Calvary on the route to St. Jean De Daye.[12] The motorbike and sidecar and lorry carrying the German patrol were shot up by Lieutenant Murn and troopers from the 501st, with four probable enemy casualties.[13] The motorbike and sidecar were captured along with documents indicating that the small force was the advance guard of an armored division.

On the morning of June 11, the paratroops were about to bury the dead from the previous day's engagement when the enemy was sighted and warning given to the people inside the church. Reconnaissance elements from the 17th SS Panzer Grenadier Division were exploring the back roads to and from Carentan. In so doing they had already tangled with the mixed force under Captain Phillips in the vicinity of St. George de Bohon. Two German motorcyclists fired their schmeisser machine pistols at the paratroopers, who outmaneuvered the motorcyclists and brought them down. Phillips went to inspect one of the Germans who lay on the road and whom he had brought down with his carbine. The man was still alive but mortally wounded. One trooper shouted that "he was going to blow his head off."[14] As Phillips issued the necessary corrective order, a truck carrying German soldiers came down the road towards them, and the paratroops quickly set an improvised ambush. As Captain Phillips later recalled: "We caught them from a cross-fire from both sides of the road and they emptied fast. The Germans who weren't killed in the trucks were running down the road madly. One of our men jumped on the lead truck, using the machine gun mounted over the cab, opened fire on the krauts."[15] Phillips and his men rapidly left the area and headed away from the swamp. As Sergeant Sessions from C Company later explained: "We didn't stick around very long to count the casualties. We knew once we got back at the Germans they would be looking for us." [16]

At Graignes, German soldiers also made an appearance. First of all a schwimwagen jeep was ambushed, with three of its occupants killed and one wounded. Shortly thereafter, 12 truckloads of infantry were sighted coming across the marsh from Tribehou, beyond which is St. George de Bohon. This reinforced company deployed in the fields around Le Mesnil Angot, a small village immediately to the south of Graignes. Using the landscape to the best effect, the Germans attempted to keep out of sight of the paratroopers as they patrolled around the locality. By 1430 in the afternoon, a full-scale firefight was in progress as the Germans tried to probe the American defenses. The Germans used mortars to try to pound the Americans into submission. After a lull in the late afternoon, which allowed the people trapped in the church the opportunity to try to return home, the Germans renewed their attack, having used the lull in the fighting to reinforce their forces. Most tellingly of all, the Germans brought up and positioned artillery at Thieuville. With a direct line of sight over much of Graignes, the artillery played a major role in breaking down the defenses. The church steeple, with its vital observation point, was one of the first targets to be reduced by the German artillery. The fighting became increasingly frenzied as the Germans pressed home their attacks. Well-sited machine guns took a heavy toll on the advancing Panzer Grenadiers. As Sergeant Frank Costa would later recall, at times the American defenders would duck down in their foxholes, allow the enemy to get beyond them, and then shoot them down from the rear. The defenders stuck doggedly to their tasks. Lieutenant Reed tried to get Lieutenant Farnham and another soldier to abandon their observation post in the church tower before the enemy could put their artillery into action. Farnham and the soldier refused to abandon their post. Together they died when the first round of artillery hit the tower. Elsewhere, Major Johnson was at his command post with Lieutenant Lowell Maxwell, who had become ill after the landing, when it was destroyed by another shell. American mortar teams rained their bombs down on the enemy to try to stem the onslaught. Slowly but surely the Americans were forced back, especially as fighting continued into the night. The cohesiveness of the defense began to weaken as enemy soldiers infiltrated the defenses. Around 0300 on June 12, the village was finally overrun. The surviving defenders of Graignes, at least those able to walk, began to withdraw in small parties either into the marsh or along the hedgerows that would carry them north toward neighboring small villages. The evacuation could not be properly coordinated, with unfortunate consequences. Private John Hinchliff later recorded his experiences in the desperate moments as the Germans overran the town:

> I grabbed my machine gun and instructed my assistant gunner to pick up the machine gun ammo and we retreated to the bottom of the hill. I knew we had suffered severe losses when I saw that my assistant and myself were the only two troopers in the vicinity. On reaching the bottom of the hill, we realized, that in his haste, my assistant had left the ammo back at our original position. I asked him to cover me while I ran back to get it. I left my carbine and personal belongings, as well as the machine gun with him to avoid any encumbrance.... [Reaching our former position Hinchliff came under fire] I quickly grabbed the ammo and ran a "zig-zag" down the hill with bullets flying all around me.[17]

Hinchliff arrived at the point where he had left his assistant, only to find that he had already gone. Picking up his abandoned carbine, he fired off several shots to give himself the opportunity to retreat into the swamp in the direction that he thought his assistant would have taken. Hinchliff eventually teamed up with his assistant and made his way through to Allied lines with a larger party under the command of Captain Brummitt. Hinchliff , despite his narrow escape, was one of the lucky ones. At daybreak some members of the 507th would find themselves in isolated foxholes at the edge of a town full of Germans.

At the fall of Graignes the Panzer Grenadiers captured the aid station that had been set up in the church. Some 19 soldiers were in the station. Captain Sophain and probably all the members of the medical detachment were busy ministering to the needs of wounded men. Those who could move were taken outside the church, where they were divided into two groups. It is probable that three men who could not be moved were simply murdered in the church. The division of those able to walk into two groups is interesting, and it seems likely that the men were divided according to their perceived intelligence value. The smaller group, some five men, were marched away from the church and into a nearby field where they were shot and bayoneted and pushed into a pond. The larger group was marched off in the direction of the neighboring hamlet of Le Mesnil Angot. Le Mesnil was probably the command post for the German attack on Graignes. Lying relatively close to Graignes, it is out of direct line of sight from the town and its church steeple. With several large farms at the edge of the hamlet, Le Mesnil Angot offered an excellent location from which to mount an attack on Graignes. It seems likely that at Le Mesnil the surviving American paratroopers were interrogated. They were then made to dig a large pit. Once completed, the Americans were executed and their bodies thrown into the pit.

Similar vengeance was meted out to the citizens of Graignes. Father Leblastier and Father Lebarbanchon were murdered at the rectory along with the two housekeepers. Elsewhere, the Germans ordered local people to leave the village. Those who argued were simply shot on the spot. The violence extended beyond Graignes to surrounding villages. At Tribehou, Joseph Anne was shot in his garden for arguing over the order to evacuate.[18]

Americans were scattered all over the area around Graignes. Frank Juliano of the 501st Parachute Infantry Regiment was one of the men who found himself in an isolated position: "I was on an outpost by myself. . . . by night fall falling back to the center of. . . town. . . but by pure luck I escaped through the swamp. . . some of us were fighting on our own. . . not knowing it.[19] Sergeant Frank Costa and two privates, in a foxhole by the marsh, were bypassed both by the Germans and their own retreating comrades. Not long after daybreak, Costa saw Germans digging in around the village. Surmising that the village had fallen and they were alone, Costa sent Private Page to get to a position where he could have a view into the village.[20] Page reported that hundreds of German troops were in the village. They agreed to wait until nightfall before abandoning their hideout, but when night came, the group again debated what they should do. Probably influenced by the sounds of battle during the day from the direction of Montmartin-en-Graignes, where elements of the 17th Panzer Grenadier Division were engaging Allied troops advancing off the beaches, Costa and the other men in the foxhole weighed their options. Should they hold tight and wait for the advance to reach them? Should they slip away into the marsh? Or should they try to find a friendly farmer to hide them? The debate was inconclusive, with the result that at daybreak on June 13 the three men were still in their foxhole and out of food and water. Thirst and hunger compelled the men to abandon their position later that day. Trying to keep in the bottom of the tall hedgerows and moving quietly, they called at a nearby farm. In addition to cider and pancakes, they were given directions to Carentan, and they set off in that direction. They again kept off the roads and away from the hedgerows. At one point they heard someone approaching and took up defensive positions. Through a gap in the hedge came a 15-year-old boy. Jean Rigault, a cousin of the Rigault family at Port St. Pierre, which had offered plentiful assistance to the Americans on June 6 and thereafter, offered to guide them to safety. While keeping their guard up, Costa and the other men allowed Jean Rigault to guide them to the Rigault farm at Port St. Pierre where 10 other troopers from the 507th were already in hiding in a hayloft. Costa and his group were not the only arrivals that day and soon 21 troopers were in the hayloft, creating enormous problems over how to feed them and keep them under cover. With the prospect of death for the Rigault family if the SS discovered they were hiding Americans they went to enormous lengths and considerable ingenuity to keep the visitors in the hayloft a secret. The Rigault family demonstrated that its members were as clever as they were brave. At one point Madame Rigault averted a firefight on the farm as 30 German soldiers retreating from Carentan unexpectedly turned up. Madame Rigault gave them directions to St. Jean de Daye and St. Lo and sent them on their way. After the promised Allied breakthrough failed to materialize on June 13–14, with Germans ever present in the vicinity, and feeding a real problem, the Rigault family decided to evacuate their visitors to Allied lines at Carentan by night. Joseph Folliot, a family friend of the Rigaults, used a large barge to ferry the 21 troopers to safety across the marsh. It was incredibly tense as the barge slowly crossed the watery expanses of the marsh. Too much noise could excite the interest of German observers and their machine gun teams. Flares routinely lit up the sky around the barge, and small-arms fire could be heard in the distance. Reaching the far side of the marsh, Folliot pointed the men in the direction of Allied lines, advising them that in a hundred yards they would be in American lines. The men in the barge wanted to do something to show their appreciation of Folliot's heroism. Collecting together all their invasion currency, they pressed Folliot to take it. He was reluctant to do so but eventually accepted. The troopers were quickly inside American lines but it would be 3;00 AM before Folliot made it back to Port St. Pierre.

The experiences of Sergeant Costa and his party in being left behind in Graignes and having to exfiltrate enemy lines were shared by many other troopers. Costa survived, and so the story of the "Rigault 21" has made the historical record. The stories of other members of the 507th who survived the fall of the town can be glimpsed only through oral accounts given by some of the townspeople with whom they came into contact. What happened to them after those contacts, whether they did indeed make it all the way back to Allied lines, cannot be discerned. In the immediate aftermath of the battle, one trooper continued to hide in the church belfry until given temporary shelter by Madame Meunier, the schoolteacher. She led him to the Port de Planques and pointed him in the direction of Allied lines. Another hid in a capacious bread oven at one of the local farms. Yet another turned up at the house of the Decaumont family. Gaston Decaumont remembered: "Eight hours after the battle, I saw one of them arrive. He came just after a party of Germans; and he'd had a narrow escape. He had a shave, and someone gave him something to eat. He stayed for almost a week. When he had to leave he saluted us. I don't know what happened to him after that."[21] American soldiers, some wounded, continued to hide in the immediate battle area for several days. On June 13 Marcel Roger, resident of the neighboring village of Montmartin-in-Graignes, was murdered by SS Grenadiers. He had aided a wounded American officer. What happened to that officer is not recorded.[22] Men reached Allied lines on their own or in small groups. In addition to two main groups, one of which Sergeant Costa was a part, some survivors stayed on their own or in pairs. Frank Juliano of the 501st Parachute Infantry Regiment teamed up with another member of his regiment in the marsh. Aided repeatedly by French civilians, they eventually made contact with American soldiers from the 90th Infantry Division.

The main group of survivors reached Allied lines south of Carentan on June 13. With the death of Major Johnson, Captain Brummitt had found himself in command of the force at Graignes. He had issued orders to exfiltrate their positions and head into the marsh. Brummitt, grabbing a .30-caliber Browning machine gun whose crew had been killed, left the town with a group of about 20 men.[23] Other officers led similar sized parties out of the town and into the marsh. These groups coalesced into a party of some 75 men under Brummitt's command. Returning to his original plan, which Major Johnson had dismissed, Brummitt led them in a night march towards Carentan. Two of the Spaniards who had joined the defense of Graignes and a Frenchman acted as scouts. They also foraged for food from local farms using the French francs issued to officers as part of their escape equipment. Vitally, the scouts secured the use of two boats, which could be used to cross the deep water areas of the swamp. Navigation in the swamp was extremely difficult, and Brummitt found that he had to take the point in order to be certain of their movements. With the Germans looking for them and retreating from the advancing forces coming off the beaches, the journey was also highly dangerous. Brummitt's men were overjoyed to reach the lines of the 2d Armored Division on June 13. Brummitt immediately reported to the headquarters of the 101st Airborne Division in Carentan and gave an account of what had happened at Graignes. He also gave details of those personnel believed to have been captured by the enemy. It would take some time for the horror of Graignes to become known. The town would be liberated on July 18, and four days later an American priest and a French priest from St-Jean-de-Daye celebrated Mass in the courtyard of the vicarage in the name of the murdered townsfolk and their American visitors.

The defense of Graignes played a significant, but largely forgotten, part in securing the Allied beachhead. It had restricted the enemy's freedom of maneuver in the days after June 6. Most importantly, Graignes prevented the speedy advance of the Gotz von Berlichingen Division at a time when the fate of Carentan hung in the balance. Estimates of the number of casualties inflicted on the enemy by the defenders of Graignes varied from 500 to 1,000. During lulls in the fighting, German troops were seen to load their casualties into lorries for removal from the field of battle. However, the estimates were almost certainly exaggerated. On June 15 the division reported that their total losses since June 1 amounted to 79 men killed, 61 missing, and 316 wounded.[24] Many of these were sustained as a result of enemy air attack on the drive to the coast and in the counterattack against Carentan, which was launched after the fall of Graignes. The divisional war diary's report that the action at Graignes amounted to mopping-up operations gives some indication of German perceptions of what was undoubtedly a fierce and prolonged battle.

The murder of surrendered paratroops at Graignes appears like a terrible and unusual event. The deliberate killing of unarmed and wounded men is shocking and atypical of the fighting in Western Europe during World War II, at least as far as the conceptions of the American and European publics are concerned. Three massacres in Western Europe during 1944–45 have left an impression on the public consciousness: the murder of Canadian prisoners of war by the SS Hitler Jugend Division in Normandy; the destruction of the French town of Oradour-sur-Glane and the murder of its civilian inhabitants by the SS Das Reich Division; and the murder of American POWs at Malmedy during the Battle of the Bulge in December 1944. In the public mind, the fighting in Western Europe after D-Day was in some way more civilized than that in the Pacific, or on the Eastern front during World War II. However, in reality, and whether or not one accepts that in some Allied units orders not to take prisoners had been given, a close appraisal of the fighting in Normandy reveals incident after incident of the cold-blooded murder of surrendered men. Prisoners of war were executed by both sides on numerous occasions. Often this was not done in a fit of rage or blood lust. Rather, an impediment to the continuation of an advance, a potential threat, or a drain on rations and manpower resources was eliminated with a single bullet. The realities of the fighting have been lost in the decades since 1944, but it takes little effort to unearth the story. The 115th Infantry Regiment landed alongside the 116th on D-Day. The regimental history of the 115th, written in the late 1940s, pulled few punches: "Fighting during the first few hours was rough with few of the rules of warfare observed. German snipers seemed to like the targets offered by the Red Cross armbands of the medics, while few prisoners taken by our troops reached the collecting cages."[25] The killing of POWs by Allied troops and their German counterparts was routine.

Robert Bowen of the 401st Glider Infantry Regiment, 101st Airborne Division, landed on Utah Beach on D-Day. Beyond the inundated area, he encountered several disturbing sights: "We passed a party of nine dead Germans lying in a roadside ditch. All had been shot through the back of the head, their foreheads blown out. The sight turned my stomach. It had been cold-blooded, completely unnecessary. Lieutenant Aspinwall turned to me saying, 'They sure look good to me.'"[26] A little later, near fields strewn with dead paratroopers, he encountered more than a dozen dead German bicycle troops. Again he noted that some had been shot through the back of the head. On Juno Beach, one young British seamen who had come ashore on a tank landing craft made an unwelcome discovery as he tried to secure for himself a souvenir. Following some distance behind some Canadian troops escorting six German prisoners into the sand dunes, he came across their bodies. Reaching down to take a helmet, he realized that they had all had their throats cut.[27] Murder and mayhem were evident everywhere in June 1944.

Genevieve Duboscq, the 12-year-old daughter of a level-crossing keeper who lived by the Merderet River, watched in horror what happened to a group of American paratroops captured by the Germans shortly after D-Day:

> They had gone some three or four hundred yards when two German soldiers grabbed one of the prisoners and pulled him from the American ranks. They forced him to undress at gunpoint, then tied a rope around his ankles and threw the other end of the rope over the branch of a nearby tree, and hoisted him up so that he was hanging head-down a couple of feet above the ground. I remembered what my parents had told me: in wartime, they'd said, prisoners and wounded soldiers were relatively well treated by their captors. So what was going on here? Suddenly one of the Germans pulled out a knife and started slashing at the man who was dangling from the tree. He twisted and turned at the end of the rope in an effort to protect himself, but in vain. The German went about his business almost methodically, as though he had all the time in the world.[28]

The 12-year-old girl looked away in tears. When she looked again, she saw the Germans disposing of their remaining captives.

The Supreme Headquarters of the Allied Expeditionary Force in Europe became aware at the end of June that notices were going up in Brittany saying that "parachutists and those giving them shelter would be considered Francs-Tireurs and shot."[29] The origin of these notices probably lay not with the SS but with the 266th Infantry Division. Based at St. Malo, the 266th was a low-establishment division consisting of men unfit for service in a regular division. A battlegroup from the 266th was by this stage fighting in the line in Normandy in the vicinity of Graignes. Its potential involvement in a policy of executing Allied paratroopers indicated in the clearest terms that the laws of war were being violated by units of the German army ranging from the elite to the most humble. On the Allied side, violation of the laws of war was similarly widespread.

CHAPTER 13

Aftermath and Conclusions

Randolph Ginman of Company D, 116th Infantry Regiment, who would be promoted to staff sergeant following June 6, noted: "We had left England with a beefed-up Company of 229 men. On the first night when we reached the hedgerows and took a head count we numbered less than 100. Out of a total of 9 officers we had lost 8....Almost 50% of our Non-Coms and Privates were either killed or knocked out of action."[1] A similar picture of a diminished military force greeted Lieutenant Colonel David G. MacIntosh III on June 8 as he took over command of the 111th Field Artillery Battalion, the artillery element of the regimental combat team of the 116th Infantry Regiment. On D-Day the battalion had lost an astonishing array of equipment, including 13 DUKWs, seven trucks, a piper cub spotter aircraft, and 11 howitzers. It also lost seven officers, including the commanding officer, and 41 enlisted men.[2] MacIntosh found the men of his new command in the foxholes and trenches around the Vierville draw: "Since all the howitzers and most of the essential equipment had been lost at sea on D-Day we were not a very effective fighting force. The men were clothed in a motley fashion with whatever the Navy had been able to spare them or what they had picked up on the beach during the past two days. We had accumulated almost every type of small arms including German burp guns—and machine pistols."[3]

Many of the families and friends of the men involved in the fighting on June 6 would spend several weeks anxiously waiting for information. Some had more reason than others to be nervous:

At her home on Long Island, Mrs. Theodore Roosevelt had slept fitfully. About 3am she awoke and could not get back to sleep. Automatically she turned on the radio—just in time to catch the official D-Day announcement. She knew that it was characteristic of her husband to be somewhere in the thick of the fighting. She did not know that she was probably the only woman in the nation to have a husband on Utah Beach and a

129

son—twenty-five-year-old Captain Quentin Roosevelt of the 1st Division—on Omaha Beach.[4]

Harold Baumgarten was born on March 2, 1925, in New York City. In June 1943 he was drafted into the U.S. Army and, after undergoing basic training at Camp Croft in South Carolina, he was sent to England to join the 116th Infantry Regiment. Attached to A Company, on May 20 he was transferred to B Company to make up their numbers after a training accident. He swiftly made friends with some of the boys in B Company, including PFC Clarius Riggs, Sergeant Barnes, and Lieutenant Donaldson. Perhaps the closest of his new friends was PFC Robert Dittmar of Fairfield, Connecticut. Landing in front of the Vierville draw on June 6, he watched as Barnes and Donaldson died in front of him. Dittmar was shot as they hit the beach:

I saw...[him] hold his chest and yell, "I'm hit, I'm hit!" I hit the ground and watched him as he continued to go forward ten more yards and then trip over a tank obstacle. As he fell, his body made a complete turn and he lay sprawled on the damp sand with his head facing the Germans, his face looking skyward. He seemed to be suffering from shock and was yelling, "Mother, Mom..." As he kept rolling around on the sand.[5]

Baumgarten would carry the images of Dittmar's death with him for the rest of his life. He was not the only one affected by the death of Robert Dittmar.

Days after June 6, a telegram would arrive at 42 Merton Street in Fairfield to inform Lothar and Mildred Dittmar that their only son had been killed in the service of his country. The local newspaper would carry notice of his death, and prayers would be said in the local community. In August 1944 the newsletter of Trinity Parish Church reported:

It is with great sorrow that we pass along the very sad news that Pvt. Robert C. Dittmar had been killed in action...Bob was a strapping young lad of 19, the only child of Mr and Mrs Lothar F. Dittmar, and he laid down his life in the cause of freedom in the first rush to the shores of France in the never-to-be-forgotten invasion of "D-Day". We sincerely hope that the enigmatic "D" in "D-Day" stands for "Deliverance" (for all time), for in no other way can we hope to justify his sacrifice.[6]

Dittmar's death touched a town in so many different ways.

At the outset of the war, the local Rotary Club in Fairfield had thrown its weight behind the war effort. Each month they produced a little newsletter of Fairfield news that was sent out to the city's service personnel from training camps in the United States to the jungles of New Guinea, the fighter bases in England, and the ports of Italy. In June the Rotary Club received a copy of its May newsletter marked "return to sender," as the addressee had been killed in action. Unopened, the letter was dutifully filed. In time it would be joined by the June newsletter, which had been sent to Robert Dittmar before his death had become public knowledge. That, too, would be filed away unopened, and would remain so for the next half a century. By the end of the war the Rotary Club would have over 30 such letters sent to Fairfield men, returned to sender with "killed in action" or "missing in action" marked on each envelope.[7] Dittmar's death was one of so many tragedies, so many sorrows for Fairfield.

During the course of the Normandy campaign, the 116th Infantry Regiment sustained 375 killed or missing in action. Three hundred and seventy-five families would have to endure the same experience as Mr. and Mrs. Dittmar. The blow would fall most heavily on the town of Bedford, Virginia. Twenty-two of the dead, who had served mostly with A Company, came from there. By early July many families had begun to suspect the worst. Their loved one had not written to them while other families had received a letter back from the front. Occasionally such letters would refer to the death of other Bedford men, leaving their readers with the decision of whether to relay the news to the deceased family. Some families feared the worst when their most recent letters addressed to their men folk were returned, although no official explanation was offered. It would be over a month after D-Day before most families received official confirmation of their fears.

On July 17, 1944, in Bedford, Elizabeth Teass, a teletype operator for Western Union, arrived at the drug store, where her office sat behind the cosmetic counter. At 0830 she turned on the teletype connecting her to the Western Union office at Roanoke:

"Good morning. Go Ahead Roanoke. We have casualties." Teass's heart sank as she read the first line of copy: "The Secretary of War desires me to express his deep regret." Teass had seen these words before. By July 1944, telegrams announcing the death of a local boy arrived on average once a week. She waited for the message to end, expecting the machine to fall silent. But it did not. Line after line of copy clicked out of the printer. Within a few minutes, as Teass watched in a "trance-like state," it was clear that something terrible had happened to Company A. "I just sat and watched them and wondered how many more it was going to be."[8]

Teass had to call on the town undertaker, doctor, local sheriff, and the boss of a local taxi company to deliver the telegrams to family after family. Some were to addresses in town, others to farms in the country. By midday a community was in shock as news spread like wildfire across town and through the workplaces. Some wondered at the kind of disaster that had overtaken the regiment in which so many local men had served. Had their troopship been sunk? Had the Nazis used a new secret weapon? Slowly the answers would come back as men returned or wrote home. Some locals would later question aspects of the landings—for instance, should Eisenhower have waited for better weather in which to launch the invasion? Slowly, however, like so many other battles in American history from Bunker Hill to Gettysburg, the landings on Omaha Beach would become a national calvary, a mythic sacrifice as one generation bequeathed to the next American values of liberty, patriotism, freedom of speech, and religion. The landings on Omaha Beach would become an integral part of the national story that one did not seek to question. Basic questions such as "what went wrong" were relegated to a secondary position behind the need to talk about bravery, sacrifice, and the reaffirmation of American values. In consequence, the landings on Utah Beach would pale in the public memory. While the landings on Omaha Beach would be talked about and represented in a dozen different ways from film to memoir to history to computer game, the sacrifice at Utah Beach would be overshadowed almost to the point of invisibility.

FORGOTTEN BATTLES

In May 1945, at the end of the war, Flight Officer Irwin Morales of the 74th Troop Carrier Squadron took a jeep and returned to the town of Graignes, where he and Lieutenant Thomas Ahmad had landed their glider on June 6. They had joined the defenders of Graignes. Morales had last seen Ahmad on the left flank of the defenses of Graignes near the church. With the fall of Graignes, Morales was able to make it back to American lines, but his friend did not return. While Morales received the Croix de Guerre with Palm from the French government, Ahmad was simply posted as missing in action. With the end of the war, Morales returned to Graignes to see if he could find out what had happened to his friend. Local

Utah Beach today. (Picture taken by author.)

townspeople explained to Morales what had happened. He eventually found his friend's grave at a temporary military cemetery on the St. Lo–Carentan road. Many others also wondered what fate had befallen their comrades at Graignes.

In the aftermath of 1945 there were few war crimes investigations into the mass of potential cases scattered across Normandy, France, and elsewhere in Western Europe. As became obvious from the Nuremburg trials, any war crimes trial had the capacity to allow the accused to turn the spotlight on the behavior of their accusers. At Nuremburg, Admiral Doenitz turned the tables on the prosecution, who alleged that he had ordered the murder of shipwrecked survivors, by inviting British and American naval officers to reveal that their respective navies had, on occasion, been involved in exactly the same crimes against German and Japanese sailors. The massacre at Graignes was not an isolated event. Rather it was part of a wider pattern of unlawful killing in Normandy that has largely been almost lost to history. The murder of Canadian prisoners of war by the Hitler Jugend SS Division on and after June 7 was the only high-profile case to be prosecuted.

In the circumstances of the cold war, many wanted to forget the excesses of the old war. West Germany was suddenly a valuable friend against the communist enemy. There seemed to be little point in antagonizing German opinion with war crimes trials if they could be avoided. Even in the most high-profile public cases justice would singularly not be done. In 1945 SS Major-General Kurt Meyer was tried and convicted of involvement in the murder of Canadian prisoners of war at the Abbaye d'Ardenne. Eleven men had been executed and buried by the Hitler Jugend Division under Meyer's command on June 7. The division would go on to murder at least 156 Canadian prisoners at various locations over the forthcoming days. War crimes investigators held that Meyer was present at some of the executions and was an inspiration to his troops in their murderous behavior towards prisoners. An Allied court duly convicted him and he was sentenced to death. In 1946 the death sentence was commuted to life imprisonment. The sentence was commuted again in 1954, and he was a free man by the end of that year. Many felt that justice had not been done.

The Meyer case was part of a pattern of failure to see that justice was done in war crimes cases in Europe. Only the most public cases would be pursued, and punishments were to be minimal. The murder of a large number of American prisoners of war, including an infamous massacre near Malmedy, by Kampfgruppe Peiper during the Ardennes offensive in December 1944 attracted international press attention. After the war, over 70 members of the Kampfgruppe would be charged with the murder of 538 to 749 unarmed American prisoners and 90 Belgian civilians during the offensive. Death sentences were passed on 42 of the accused. Thanks to the efforts of the defending officer, Lieutenant Colonel Willis M. Everett, who produced evidence that confessions and other incriminating testimony had been forced out of the defendents, those sentences were commuted to life imprisonment. Evidence that Obersturmbannfuehrer Jochen Peiper's men had been tortured, including beatings, mock executions, and deprivation of food, caused such alarm as to result in the interest of the U.S. Senate. Senator Joseph McCarthy attacked the army for its "Gestapo" tactics. Eventually all of Peiper's men would be released after relatively short periods of imprisonment. He would be the last to be released after serving 11 years of his sentence.[9]

In a further example of the near-total failure of the justice system, there was similarly little punishment for the men who, after the Ardennes offensive, had run a concentration camp for Jewish GI prisoners of war. Sixty or so GIs were mistreated to the point of death, or were murdered at the camp. Two Germans were sentenced to death for their crimes. Both would have their sentences commuted and would be freed by the mid-1950s. The families of the murdered GIs were not consulted. Similarly those GIs who had suffered in the camp were not informed of the reductions in sentence. The silence indicated that the U.S. military authorities at least felt a certain shame and embarrassment, even if they had forsaken the principles of justice and comradeship.

Attempts by the French government to secure justice for crimes committed on its soil during the war ended in similar failure. The postwar trial of the men of the Das Reich Division for the murder of 642 civilians at Oradour-sur-Glane on June 10, 1944, turned into a national farce. The accused were tried in Bordeaux in early 1953. Several of the accused were from the French province of Alsace, which had been incorporated in Germany in 1871, but which was returned to France at the end of World War I. The 14 Alsatian defendants claimed that they had been forced to join the SS. A death sentence was passed on one German and one Alsatian, with prison terms of up to eight years handed out to the rest. The sentences drew protests across France. In Limoges 50,000 people marched in protest at the leniency of the sentences. In Alsace the Bishop of Strasbourg led protests against the harshness of the sentences. With the country threatening to divide down the middle, an amnesty law was rushed through the French parliament absolving the Alsatian defendants of their punishments and responsibilities. For postwar French governments there would be little political mileage in dragging up the wartime period. Trials would only expose and exacerbate the divisions in a society that had split between resisters, collaborators, and the great mass of the population, which had been neither.

The dead of Oradour-sur-Glane would not get justice. The dead of Graignes and a dozen other places in Normandy would not even get their day in court. In view of the outcomes of some of the other atrocity cases in Western Europe, it was probably just as well. The probable travesty of an outcome would have mocked the bravery of those who sacrificed so much. Given the instruction/suggestion about prisoners to some of the parachute infantry regiments in their briefing before D-Day, any case would have involved a certain element of double standards. The plain fact remains that even today there are almost certainly veterans of the 17th SS Panzer Grenadier Regiment living in retirement in Germany who could shed significant light on the events at Graignes in June 1944.

After the war a Franco-American memorial to the dead was established at Graignes. Utilizing what remained of the church, the memorial was dedicated in a ceremony attended by the American ambassador. On the 60th anniversary of

D-Day in 2004, a plaque listing the names of the dead was added to the memorial. In the years between 1947 and 2004, the action at Graignes was almost completely forgotten. The men of the 507th and 501st parachute infantry regiments at Graignes had fallen too far away from any of the major centers of action on D-Day to merit consideration in the official histories written after the war. The 507th itself, which transferred to the 17th Airborne Division after D-Day, was itself largely overlooked by historians until the 1990s. The town of Graignes quietly rebuilt its houses and established a new church in the 1950s. It was not until over 50 years after D-Day that the story of the 507th began to be reclaimed by French and American historians.

At the same time that an addition was being made to the memorial at Graignes, public attention turned to another massacre of American paratroops from the 507th. On D-Day a group of men from the regiment were misdropped near the town of Hemevez to the north of St. Mere Eglise. Seven of them were quickly taken prisoner and dispatched with a shot to the back of the head. At least one was subsequently stabbed with a bayonet to make sure that he was dead. The seven corpses were discovered by a local farmer in a hedge bottom. With other people from the village, he recovered and buried the bodies in the local churchyard. Their presence was later reported to the advancing American troops from the 90th Infantry Division, who liberated the village on June 17. The exhumation of the dead American paratroops was carefully filmed. The exhumation team and camera crew went to considerable lengths to ensure that their film could be used to substantiate charges of murder. However, as in the case of Graignes, no charge was brought, and the incident had been largely forgotten until 2004, when a memorial was placed in the local churchyard. One veteran member of the 507th commented at the memorial ceremony: "Could you believe that...The amazing thing is, none of us even knew about this!"[10]

A large part of the reason for this was the heavy casualties sustained by the Airborne Division in Normandy. Graignes and a dozen other incidents were swallowed in a wave of bleak statistics. Of the 11,700 men who had jumped with the 82nd Airborne Division on D-Day, 5,436 (46.18 percent) became casualties. Of these 1,142 (9.7 percent) were killed in action and 2,373 (20.16 percent) wounded in action. A further 1,081 had to be evacuated through sickness or injury, mainly sustained during the drop. Postcombat analysis suggested that at least 36 men were drowned in the initial drop, and 63 men were abandoned to the enemy as a result of injuries sustained in jumping. Losses among battalion commanders were extremely heavy. Of the twelve battalion commanders that went into action with the 82nd Airborne Division in June 1944 only one was able to fight through to the end of campaign. Of the rest, two were killed, five wounded, three injured and one relieved of his command.[11] Unsurprisingly, casualties among the ranks of the 507th Parachute Infantry Regiment had been heavy. Some 303 officers and men had been killed in action, some 354 had been wounded, and 178 were classed as missing in action.[12] By comparison, later fighting in the Ardennes and in the campaign to cross the Rhine and bring about Germany's defeat would cost the regiment fewer fatalities than its first combat jump over Normandy. Members of the 507th made a depressingly large contribution to the overall losses of the 82nd Airborne, and men of those classed as missing in action in 1944 would later be adjusted to have been fatalities. For most families of the missing men from the 507th, the liberation of the German prisoner-of-war camps in 1945 would not produce a happy ending. Instead it would be left to the army to make inquiries and, in 1946–47, to quietly change the status of MIA men to that of KIA.

Two years later, in the presence of the American ambassador to Paris, the rebuilt tower of the church in Graignes was dedicated as a memorial to the dead. The main walls of the church were reduced to their lower courses of stone to enable the visitor to imagine what the church was like when it held its last Sunday Mass in June 1944. The worn entry step still bears testimony to the coming and going of worshippers since the twelfth century. Beneath the tower is the last resting place of the bones of Father Leblastier and Father Lebarbenchon. The bodies of both were burned by the Germans after their murder, but some remains were later recovered by returning citizens.

It would take another decade for the memorial to list the names. One local news-paper recorded its thoughts on the erection of a marble plaque honoring the dead: "It will not be possible, alas, to inscribe on the great marble plaque fixed to the wall of the church's apse, where the names of 32 civilian victims and 12 dead Americans are brought together, the names of the dead paratroopers, because they are unknown: nor those who were drowned, nor those who were shot at Mesnil-Angot."[13] Thirty years later another plaque would be unveilved thanks to the help of the American veterans of Graignes.[14] Colonel Frank Naughton, who as a lieutenant in 1944 had been responsible for blowing the bridge at Port des Planques, was guest of honor at the unveiling ceremony. He and other veterans had done much to ensure that the story of the 507th at Graignes and elsewhere in Normandy was not entirely forgotten. In 1986, as a result of Colonel Naughton's efforts along with those of a fellow Graignes veteran, Earcle Reed, 11 citizens of Graignes were recognized for their bravery by the U.S. military. Marthe and Odette Rigault would be among those honored.

The new plaque in 1989 would list 66 names: 34 Americans and 32 inhabitants of the local commune. The passage of thirty years had placed another 20 American names belonging to the fallen of the 507th and 501st Parachute Infantry Regiments on the memorial. Undoubtedly more than 34 Americans lost their lives at Graignes. With something like 20 Americans massacred at Graignes and Le Mesnil Angot the loss of only 14 American lives in the intense fighting around Graignes seems remark-ably low. Perhaps the passage of another 30 years will be sufficient to place another handful of names on a new plaque at Graignes. Comparison of the jump rosters for the 507th against the casualty lists for the regiment suggests the names of a num-ber of men who may have met their fates in and around Graignes.[15] Everywhere across Normandy, the pain and suffering of the regiments and men which breached

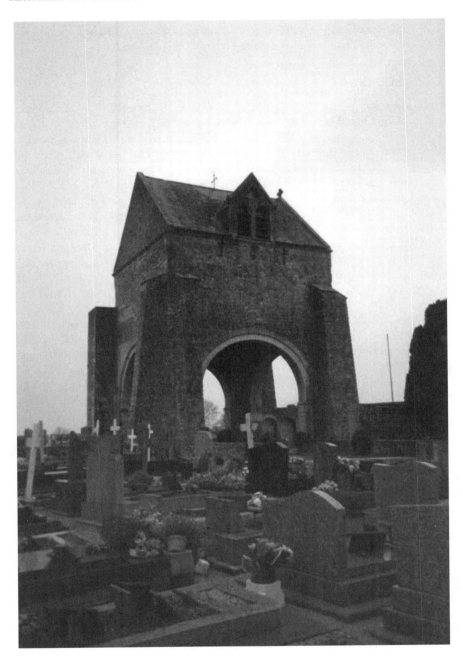

Graignes old church. (Picture taken by author.)

Hitler's Fortress Europe are inscribed on memorials from the Airborne memorial at La Fiere to a string of memorials along Omaha and Utah beaches.

CONCLUSION

History, Hollywood, and public memory play funny tricks on the historical record. Cornelius Ryan's *The Longest Day,* Steven Spielberg's *Saving Private Ryan,* and a hundred or more works by professional historians have obscured as much as they have revealed. The films are especially problematic. As Trevor McCrisken and Andrew Pepper have commented: "As a whole, although they contain some challenging images, they tend to reinforce the perception of World War II as the Good War, or indeed as the Best War Ever in American history."[16] Small wonder that America's wars since 1945 have failed to reach the publicly-set benchmarks of the moral certainties and crushing victory of the European war, which ended with the link up of American and Russian troops on the Elbe River in 1945. Over time the complexities of America's involvement in World War II have been obscured. The story that has emerged is a simple tale of good versus evil, on which rests America's self-perception of her own foreign policy. America's role in the world is to defend freedom and democracy. The sacrifice on Omaha Beach was part of this and a validation of America's lack of self-interest in her foreign policy. If popular depictions of the D-Day landings have helped to obscure some of the more self-interested currents in American foreign policy, they have also done much to obscure the historical realities of those landings. In the public consciousness, the story of Omaha Beach is the story of the American army on D-Day. The story of the American parachute landings is summed up by Ambrose/Spielberg's *Band of Brothers* and Cornelius Ryan's image of Private John Steele of the 82nd Airborne hanging from the church steeple in St. Mere Eglise. The struggles of the 507th Parachute Infantry Regiment at La Fiere and Graignes lie below the public consciousness in the land of the lost. The 4th Infantry Division's landings on Utah Beach were undoubtedly easier than those of the 1st and 29th infantry divisions on Omaha Beach. The success at Utah Beach appears in the public consciousness as little more than a footnote to the slaughter on Omaha. However, as the experiences of the 22nd Infantry Regiment show, the situation on Utah Beach, and the struggle to secure it, was difficult, demanding, and dangerous work. Lieutenant George Wilson, who landed on Utah Beach in late June as a replacement officer for the 4th Infantry Division, made the point most effectively in his memoirs. Talking about comparisons between the landings on the beaches and the tendency to belittle the difficulties faced on Utah Beach, he commented: "Of course, those who were wounded and died there would never agree that it had been an easy battle."[17]

For many of the men of the 116th Infantry Regiment, their campaign in Normandy, and their lives, were over in a matter of seconds on the morning of June 6. The regiment would continue to play a role in fighting the war to a successful conclusion through the Normandy campaign and beyond, but the survivors of that day formed a close-knit brotherhood of sacrifice and experience. After D-Day the

29th Infantry Division, along with the 35th Infantry Division, advanced on St. Lo, which the Germans fought hard to retain. As one member of the 35th Infantry Division later commented: "St. Lo was the worst because we were green. The Germans had more planes, men and material in there than they ever had later on."[18] It took American forces five weeks to reach the town, and just before the final assault Major Thomas Howie of the Third Battalion cheerily told his men: "I'll see you in St. Lo." Howie was killed shortly thereafter, and General Gerhardt, officer commanding the 29th Infantry Division, ordered his men to carry Howie's body into the town square. The regiment would continue to battle its way all the way to Germany. On January 6, 1946, the regiment back in the United States would be declared inactive. D-Day had been the regiment's finest and worst hour.

The men of the 22nd Infantry Regiment went through similar experiences after D-Day. There would be days of steady advance under artillery and mortar fire, facing determined enemy infantry in well-prepared positions. Men would die and be replaced, and then the replacements would become casualties. The strain was almost unrelenting. Although the casualty figures would only partly reflect it, the cost on the nerves of the men subjected to it would be considerable. This would be the war that the majority of GIs would know from June 1944 to May 1945. It was an inglorious war that did not hit the headlines, did not impact the public consciousness, and did not have historians eager to write about it. However, for a generation of young Americans on the battlefields of Europe, it would be their daily lives and their personal histories.

The paratroopers of the 507th, who would transfer to the 17th Airborne Division after D-Day, would return to Tollerton in July. Losses would be made good and the regiment would await the next combat deployment. That would come in December as the 507th was thrown into the fighting in the Ardennes. In March 1945 the regiment made a combat jump into Germany as part of Operation Varsity. From that point on they would fight as infantry until the end of the war in Europe.

The German army looked on with amazement at the ability of the American regiments to take heavy punishment. The regiments constituted a fighting force designed for one end—the conquest of the enemy. In Normandy in 1944, that enemy daily witnessed the effectiveness of the American army and the units that comprised it. The regimental system proved remarkably resilient. Regiments could be decimated, rebuilt, and destroyed again and again. Greenhorn regiments fresh from the United States would fight like tigers in the Ardennes and the Battle for Germany. Regiments like the 507th could be shifted from one division to another and retain their integrity and character. This was much to the consternation of the enemy. As one German officer confessed:

> I cannot understand these Americans. Each night we know that we have cut them to pieces, inflicted heavy casualties, mowed down their transport. We know, in some cases, we have almost decimated entire battalions. But—in the morning, we are suddenly faced with fresh battalions, with complete replacements of men, machines, food, tools, and weapons. This happens day after day.[19]

Some GIs were undoubtedly eager for combat. Many were eager to see Britain and the rest of Europe, and to see dead Nazis. The realities of combat forced many to reappraise their lives. After the war, that process of reappraisal stopped in many cases as men struggled to come to terms with their experiences while building new lives in booming postwar America. By the 1960s, spurred perhaps by a new war in Asia, and the passage of time from the events of the mid-1940s, former GIs began to come together to meet long-lost friends, revisit past lives and to do a little more reappraisal. This would be done particularly through regimental associations. Men who had left the army in 1945 found themselves drawn back to their old units. In time, spurred by anniversaries such as in 1984, many would revisit the old battlefields and the graves of absent friends. They would do so alongside their old regimental comrades and would find themselves and their exploits feted by presidents and prime ministers. It was no matter that some of the places, regiments, and events had been lost from public history, or eclipsed by more bloody, decisive, or tragic events. In old age, former farm boys from Iowa and factory workers from Cleveland would know that in June 1944, in sand dune and hedgerow, they had changed the course of history.

116th Infantry Regiment Losses in Action, June 6–7, 1944

(Courtesy of the National Archives, Washington DC)

Assault on Omaha Beach and Adjacent Towns (St. Laurent Sur Mer, Vierville Sur Mer), June 6–7, 1944

Numbers highlighted in bold indicate where on the original document the regimental typist has duplicated the same number twice.

(a) Killed:

Maj. John W. Sours, 0337213
Capt. Walter O. Schilling, 0330838
Capt. Sherman V. Burroughts, 0330025
Capt. Taylor N. Fellers, 0381409
Capt. Robert B. Ware, 0387982
Capt. Ettore V. Zappacosta, 0399291
1st Lt. Benjamin R. Kearfoot, 0407671
1st Lt. Alfred S. Anderson, 01291076
2nd Lt. Alton B. Ashley, 01286225
1st Lt. Merle T. Cummings, 012990722
1st Lt. Harold C. Donaldson, 01292150
1st Lt. William (NMI) Gardner, 0024051
1st Lt. Vincent P. Labowicz, Jr., 01290091
2nd Lt. Rudolph (NMI) Skrek, 01320661
1st Lt. Clyde R. Tidrick, 01316243
1st Lt. Robert B. Williamson, 0425827

2nd Lt. John R. Hussey, 0439206
2nd Lt. John B. Clemments, 01318282
1st Lt. Thomas R. Dallas, 01290723
2nd Lt. Herman G. Hilscher, 01292175
2nd Lt. James J. Limber, 01292019
2nd Lt. Stanley H. Schwartz, 01298447
1st Lt. Emil (NMI) Winkler, 01316257
S.Sgt. Leslie Abbot, 20363621
PFC Robert T. Ainsworth, 33431055
Tec. 4 Herbert R. Aldred, 20363137
PFC Henry F. Augin, 31057737
S.Sgt. Meade H. Baker, 33043409
PFC James A. Bakewell, 33417631
Pvt. William D. Barnett, 33706102
PFC Edward L. Bechtel, 36148034
Pvt. Raymond C. Bell, 38520198
PFC Joseph M. Bercholz, 33152986
Tec. 5 Robert H. Bergmann, 32335562
PFC Clarence W. Bloxom, Jr., 3313660
PFC Carl E. Bowen, 32047659
PFC Moritz H. Brall, 32300019
Sgt. Thomas E. Bratten, 35688309
PFC Walter S. Brinton, 3267437
Cpl. Walter E. Broscious, 3315274
PFC Claude H. Brownell, 38518332
PFC Donald E. Burke, 33133676
Pvt. Charles T. Byrnes, 32974846
PFC Clarence H. Campbell, 33046870
S.Sgt. Rufus B. Carr, 33047772
PFC Raymond D. Carver, 20365466
PFC Frank J. Cheek, 38487392
PFC William R. Chipps, 35757478
PFC John R. Clifton, 20363635
S.Sgt. John R. Cox, 20365451
Pvt. William G. Crawley, 34737626
PFC Victor L. Culberson, 34145362
Pvt. Charles C. DeVeaney, 33278822
PFC Thompson G. Dicks, 14115893
Pvt. Frank J. Ditoma, 32857053
Pvt. Alexander F. Dominquez, 39018036
Pvt. Carman P. Drolles 33481835
Pvt. Ellis S. Abney, 34635336
PFC Louis J. Alberigo, 31067716
S.Sgt. Samuel R. Anderson Jr., 20366028
PFC Richard G. Ayers, 33047604
S.Sgt. John G. Barnes, 33043543
Pvt. Andrew D Bean, 33316910

PFC Charles G. Beckwith, 32837592
PFC Frederick L. Bennett, 31013927
PFC Edward B. Berghoff, 33043413
Sgt. John T. Blacknall, 33042558
PFC Albert A. Boucher 31067618
PFC William T. Boyd, 33046968
Pvt. Richard C. Brandtojnes, 33694935
Pvt. Claude V. Bray, 36757075
PFC James L. Brooks, 20363846
Sgt. Staunton M. Brown, 33043501
Pvt. Roger G. Burlotte, 31322746
PFC John M. Burkhart, 33526478
Pvt. Celford C. Bampbell, 35266046
Sgt. Frank E. Carnrike, 33152809
PFC Wallace R. Carter, 20363699
Pvt. Frutoso R. Chavez, 38215609
PFC Benjamin (NMI) Chesney, 33153006
Pvt. William B. Clark, 34736752
PFC William J. Cowan, 31064212
Pvt. Wilber S. Crane, 39218639
Pvt. Mauricio G. Cuellar, 38553193
Pvt. Leonard F. Dearing, 33519267
Pvt. John (NMI) Beneditti, 38352237
Pvt. August W. Diedesch, 36756619
Pvt. Robert L. Dittmar, 31336619
T.Sgt. Frank P. Draper, Jr., **20363679**
PFC William A. Drumheller, **20363679**
Pvt. Herman Dunham, Jr., 3575717
PFC John C. Dylik, 32369900
PFC Charles F. Edgar, 32300332
PFC James L. Elam, 33047984
Pvt. Roger J Ellison, 32015659
T.Sgt. Elvin T. Estee, 30264752
PFC Willard W. Fader, 31067416
Sgt. Joseph A. Felix, 33077226
Pvt. Frank J. Ferraro, 42000775
Pvt. John H. Ficken Jr., 34737436
Pvt. Frank I. Fissette, 31265482
PFC Charles (NMI) Fritz, Jr., 35170911
PFC Charles (NMI) Ford, 32320197
PFC Orcar J. Gasewind, 32301896
PFC Edward L. Gillingham, 35166934
Pvt. James D. Godwin, 34811808
Pvt. Harry C. Gunter, 33046850
PFC Oliver J. Hammond, 35166770
PFC George A. Hawn, 33070225
Pvt. Bedford T. Hoback, 20363617

Pvt. Bernard W. Homerding, 36713446
PFC Zigmunc (NMI) Horodecki, 32301878
Pvt. Kenneth C. Howie, 37566136
Pvt. Carl H. Huddleston, 35712777
PFC William E. Hughes, 33152628
Sgt. Russell N. Ingram, 20364221
PFC Claudie (NMI) Jennings, 33533707
T.Sgt. Leaslie L. Jewett, 31042010
S.Sgt. Hogan M. Johnston, 33043600
PFC George W. Keinz, 37550196
Pvt. Russell T. Kernoll, Jr., 33414473
Pvt. Robert (NMI) Kilduff, 11131463
Tec. 5 John T. Kincer, 20366063
Pvt. Willie E. King, 34634761
PFC Ernest L. Kiser, 33046917
PFC Francis E. Koshinski, 33152945
PFC John E. Kozak, 33039624
PFC Anthony (NMI) Krwfsky, 32177002
PFC Henry B. Krzcick, 36516110
PFC Conrad V. Kufta, 32925165
Pvt. Lester K. Laing, 33540888
PFC Henry J. Lang, 16095650
PFC Prudencio A. Lavin, 31253091
PFC Basil (NMI) Lee, 36585384
S.Sgt. Stuart L. Leonard, 6879532
Pvt. George R. Losey, 32939645
PFC Jack (NMI) Lowe, 33381062
PFC Eugene (NMI) Macaluso, 33419213
PFC Willard C. Dyer, 33000279
PFC George F. Eckardt, 32300406
PFC Henry M. Eiseman, 33512971
PFC Melvin O. Ellinger, 33047815
PFC James E. Embry, 35717509
Pvt. Paul E. Evans, 33046938
Pvt. Whitney J. Faulk, 3871754
Pvt. Gino (NMI) Ferrari, 32808292
Sgt. William E.D. Ferrell, 33053548
PFC Hershel L. Finke, 37443548
PFC Forrest (NMI) Fitchett, 33133534
Pvt. Thomas H. Fridley, 33047952
PFC Robert L. Garbett, Jr., 33043163
Pvt. Stanley P. Gembala, 32839587
S.Sgt. Fred W. Goad, 33046937
Pvt. Junior (NMI) Graves, 35588106
Sgt. Harry P. Hamilton, 33043429
PFC John O. Harris, 33042139
Pvt. James A. Hayes, Jr., 32971798

S.Sgt. John (NMI) Holmes, 16016683
Tec.5 Frederick W. Hopping, 32301157
Pvt. Earl (NMI) Howe, 38263432
Pvt. Ralph H. Hubbard, 33048029
Pvt. John N. Hughes, 33479093
Pvt. Wesley J. Husted, Jr., 33761825
Cpl. William R. Jarrett, 33153137
T.Sgt. Ralph E. Jennings, 20363866
Sgt. George D. Johnson, 20364222
Pvt. Nicholas S. Kafkales, 33690296
Sgt. Paul M. Kennedy, 33033494
PFC Rosco E. Kidd, 35668437
PFC Edgar H. Kimball, **39856696**
Pvt. Leo E. King, Jr., **39856696**
S.Sgt. Bernard E. Kirkendall, 33153053
PFC Alva J. Knight, 33720048
PFC Walter T. Kostrzewski, 37324422
Pvt. Robert L. Krahenbuhl, 37531718
Pvt. Jordan R. Krummes, 39693810
Sgt. William (NMI) Kucera, 33513968
S.Sgt. William C. Laffin, 33153197
PFC Ingram E. Lambert, 42001422
Pvt. Charley B. Langston, 39698365
Pvt. Thomas S. Leahey, 35066175
Pvt. Raymond J. LeBeau, 31347366
Pvt. Clifton G. Lee, 20363651
PFC Bernard H. Lipscomb, 35391464
PFC Orlow H. Lovejoy, 32585850
PFC Harry (NMI) Lurie, 36364342
Sgt. Kayo T. Malmberg, 36188746
PFC Vincent J. Mandino, 32574507
Pvt. Ralph L. Markowitz, 13058316
Pvt. James W. Martin, 34777566
Pvt. Warren M. Maul, 32591742
PFC Thomas E. McArtor, 33043355
PFC Wilson H. McDairmid, 14116665
Pvt. Donald E. McGrath, 33459554
Sgt. Orville (NMI) McNew, 35468127
Pvt. Frank B. Miller, 33439664
Sgt. Clarence (NMI) Moore, 33046849
S.Sgt. Ted F. Moubray, 20364146
PFC Cleo B. Munday, 33133515
Sgt. Julius A. Nessing, 31064023
PFC Frank (NMI) Muzzo, 33088356
Pvt. Thomas S. Offutt, 6285527
Pvt. John J. O'Neil, 32820825
Pvt. Clifford C. Overman, 38472153

Pvt. Robert E. Palmer, 32974318
Sgt. James W. Paulick, Jr., 33153324
Sgt. Henry B. Pearson, 33043338
PFC William G. Perdue, 33529530
Pvt. Wallace F. Pinkham, 31252636
PFC Everett K. Polley, 35651450
PFC Jack G. Powers, 20363657
Pfd George (NMI) Pricopoulos, 11017737
PFC Joe W. Pullen, 34537334
Pvt. Miguel Ramon, 35558287
Pvt. Robert C. Reece, 32839742
PFC Robert B. Reyes, 39696580
PFC Clairus L. Riggs, 33568943
S.Sgt. Clarence E. Roberson, 20363890
PFC Weldon A. Rosazza, 20363659
Pvt. Lee T. Rychleski, 33058293
Pvt. Stewart D. Saffelle, 33641987
S.Sgt. John B. Schenk, 30263661
PFC Daniel B. Schmidt, 37458514
PFC Cono R. Severino, 32691513
PFC Harold C. Short, 33047997
PFC Robert J. Simmonds, 36522461
Cpl. Jack R. Simms, 20364207
PFC Sherman J. Skeens, 33047979
PFC Mike (NMI) Slivka, 32300049
PFC Alvin D. Smith, 33153211
PFC Lloyd H. Smith, 32769392
PFC Bryon L. Stanton, 33152923
PFC William A. Stedman, 20363898
Pvt. Robert Stover, 33000886
PFC Elmer Swift, 33047859
Pvt. Andrew F. Marczyk, 32300234
PFC Thomas J. Marks, 33476796
Pvt. Robert A. Martin Jr., 33496737
Pvt. George (NMI) Mayer, 32898328
Pvt. William J. McCarthy, 32977540
Pvt. John J. McGarty, 31385933
Pvt. Benjamin F. McKenney, 17056995
Pvt. John L. Messer, 31256332
Pvt. Joseph D. Mobile, 32594997
Pvt. Clyde (NMI) Moore, 33047958
Pvt. James A. Mullen 31067398
Sgt. Paul O. Neff, 33047558
Pvt. Dallas A. Nickel, 35618155
M.Sgt. James H. Obenshein, 20364197
Tec.5 Eugene E. Oikari, 14119775
PFC Jacob (NMI) Osofsdy, 31067685

Tec.5 Richard M. Palmer 33012828
Pvt. Samuel C. Palmer, 35803938
PFC Ascy F. Peacock, 34109899
Pvt. Clarence E. Peck, 33047995
Pvt. Joe F. Peters Jr., 38392337
Pvt. Metro (NMI) Pluts, 33152968
Sgt. David G. Powers, 33047806
PFC Noel O. Price, 33043038
Tec.5 Alex H. Prigden, 34176535
PFC John H. Radzierjewski, 36577715
Sgt. Carl W. Raymond, 33195210
Pvt. James R. Reed, 38514997
PFC John F. Reynolds 20363700
PFC Garnet L. Rinker Jr., 33133611
PFC Pearl M. Robertson, 20364693
PFC Alex (NMI) Rosenthal, 36415403
PFC Frank (NMI) Sadusky, 31274604
PFC Bartolameo (NMI) Satti, 31037082
Pvt. Harry (NMI) Schiraldi, 32706686
PFC William E. Schools, 33132231
PFC Forrest C. Shope, 33153200
Pvt. Edward J. Siemiion, 36827929
PFC George H. Simmons, 33007718
Pvt. Johnnie Singleton, 35803725
Pvt. Robert J. Slate, 32934895
S.Sgt. James B. Smallwood, 33047888
Pvt. Harvey P. Smith, 20363432
Tec.5 Robert P. Smith, 12047501
PFC George A. Stearns, 33152445
T.Sgt. Ray O. Stevens, 20363619
PFC Dominic (NMI) Surre, 31099356
PFC Clare E. Sypal, 37542496
S.Sgt. Earl P. Talley, 20365645
PFC George (NMI) Thomson, 11080009
Cpl. Andrew J. Toback, 33153142
PFC James F. Unger, 35725635
Pvt. Joseph Veenstra Jr., 36643253
Pvt. Milton V. Wagner, 32818636
Pvt. Richard A. Waite, 33680487
PFC Anthony M. Walter, 32669703
PFC William W. Weaver, 33046946
PFC Francis W. Wheeler, 36628213
M.Sgt. John L. Wilkes, 20633629
Cpl. James W. Williams, 33152458
PFC Thomas H. Williams, 33047498
Pvt. Charlie H. Wilson, 20364525
Sgt. Roy O. Wilson, 33047456

PFC John E. Wise, 33266626
PFC Anthony J. Wlodarek, 35539457
S.Sgt. Daniel P. Womack, 20363908
Cpl. Atlas E. Wright, 33043419
S.Sgt. James L. Wright, 20364229
Sgt. Grant C. Yopp, 20363698
Pvt. Willie E. Young, 34737057
PFC Frank A. Zawicki, 31065555
PFC George (NMI) Kerber, 32911410
Pvt. Vincent J. Mastroilli, 32893949
PFC John H. Self, 37536247
PFC Thomas W. Stevens, 33043015
Pvt. John E. Thommessen, 36807360
Sgt. Tyrus H. Tisdale, 33043130
Pvt. Daniel L. Torowski, 35065990
S.Sgt. Edward A. Vargo, 33043150
PFC Edward S. Verdugo, 39687657
PFC Joseph P. Waichulonis, 36731198
Pvt. Nevin N. Walk, 33153128
S.Sgt. Noel P. Washburn, 20365044
PFC Harold J. Weber, 31284968
S.Sgt. Gordon H. White, Jr., 20363664
Pvt. George E. Williams, Jr., 331551486
S.Sgt. Maurice M. Williams, 33043445
Pvt. Charles R. Wilson, 33672555
PFC Jerome E. Wilson, 36058456
Pvt. Albert D. Wingate, 33047383
Pvt. Henry G. Witt, 32817411
T.Sgt. John S. Wohlford, 20365269
S.Sgt. Arthur Woods, 12019903
S.Sgt. Elmere P. Wright, 20363693
S.Sgt. James A. Wright, 20363839
PFC Mahlon R. Yeates, 20364531
PFC Daniel W. Young, 33043424
PFC John P. Zabludowski, 36280830
Pvt. Guillermo (NMI) Bedard, 31278018
PFC Giasomo (NMI) Martorana, 31067644
Pvt. Joseph (NMI) Periandri, 33828838
Sgt. Wesley D. Sisson, 330000251
PFC Samuel A. Whipkey, 33152858

(b) Wounded: June 6, 1944

1st Lt. William B. Williams, 0379493
1st Lt. John W. Ballenger, 0436329
1st Lt. Robert T. Hackett, 0447139
2nd Lt. Ralph E. Frisby, 01325210
1st Lt. Carl W. Dickhoff, 0407482
2nd Lt. Theron S. Ward Jr., 0483739
CWO Thomas E. McKnight, W–2109148
2nd Lt. Ira C. Nelson 0202965
2nd Lt. Frederick J. Hopkins, 01312081
Capt. William F. Burke, 0415621
1st Lt. George (NMI) Lenchner, 01290093
2nd Lt. Forrest K. Ferguson Jr., 01322014
2nd Lt. Leon A. Pingenot, 01298920
2nd Lt. Wilbur F. Marsh, 01290100
2nd Lt. Paul O. Mortweet, 01316187
Capt. Laurence A. Madill, 024216
PFC Patrick (NMI) De Cicco, 32769399
Pvt. Walter A. Edney, 33105773
PFC Louis (NMI) Green, 32538540
Pvt. Murrell T. Haymes, 35731860
Pvt. Edmund R. Kirkwood, 3767118
Pvt. James C. Lingo, 37519602
PFC Harry M. Martz, 33153028
Sgt. Theodore E. Hamm, 33153040
Tec.3 Marion C. Gray, 15071621
Pvt. Charlie R. Gardner, 34774954
PFC Leon (NMI) Friedman, 32329211
PFC Ottoway O. Fore, 33043219
PFC Warren C. Fitzgerald, 32700294
S.Sgt. Wesley M. Estes, 20364689
Pvt. Angelo E. DeMattia, 32974307
Sgt. James J. Cunningham, 33046908
PFC Benny B. Crowe, 20364471
PFC Joseph E. Corr, 323227304
Pvt. William G. McCausey, 32132783
Tec.5 Gerald H. Morrow, 33231582
PFC Glen L. Nelson, 373823530
PFC John H. Calfee, 33133484
Pvt. Leo J. Bildeau, 31253085
Pvt. Louis A. Biacchi, 33606581
PFC Robert J. Austen, 35595852
S.Sgt. William S. Allen, 7009952
PFC Harold (NMI) Adler, 32808242
Tec. 5 Walter J. Ornowski, 32304756
Tec. 5 Bernard L. Layne, 20366012
PFC Gary W. Laughon, 20363154

PFC Dominick J. Colavito, 32638950
Pvt. Fred A. Caviness, 33047792
Pvt. Joseph E. Kwiatkowski, 33152988
PFC John W. Kruper, 33152450
Cpl. Thomas J. Joyner, 33043067
Pvt. Donald R. Huckstedt, 36674168
Pvt. John D. Hinton, 34736908
Pvt. Atney (NMI) Deshotels, 384806515
Pvt. John T. Goglia, 32927664
Pvt. Floyd (NMI) Hatcher, 20364485
PFC Freddy (NMI) Kaufmann, 32738203
Pvt. Victor (NMI) Lapinsky, 36647056
S.Sgt. Robert E. Marsico, 20363677
Pvt. Allan (NMI) Harwich, 10500880
PFC Raymond W. Hackler, 33047749
Sgt. Robert L. Goode, 20363680
PFC George J. Gallagher, Jr., 32301815
Tec. 5 George W. Fox, 33046863
Pvt. Charles T. Fletcher, 34736942
Pvt. Barney C. Everett, 35326949
PFC John D. Dorzi, 31067686
PFC Samuel A. DeMaria, 32799369
PFC Earl F. Cundiff, 20363400
Pvt. Francis J. Couch, 32856045
Pvt. Edwin F. Cooner, 34658847
S.Sgt. Joseph (NMI) McHocko, 33073729
Pvt. Leonard A. Nead, 35069240
Pvt. Thomas P. Carey, 13081506
Pvt. Clarence H. Blessard, 20363399
PFC John W. Biggers, 33047590
Tec.5 John A. Azzaretti, 12157106
S.Sgt. William C. Allen, 20365242
Pvt. John W. Akers, 23585963
Pvt. Virgil E. Bennett, 36835227
PFC Charles K. Linton, 35570308
Tec. 5 Hatley N. Lawson, 33042627
Pvt. William R. Collins, 35558564
PFC James T. Lambert, 33046995
Pvt. Charles L. Caruso, 32756111
Pvt. Victor J. Kujat, 33606949
Tec. 5 Robert J. Koos, 13109055
PFC Leroy R. Hutchins, 20364492
Pvt. Wilson Hodge, 34658953
PFC Harold C. Zelss, 36290902
Pvt. James E. Hill 35231544
Sgt. Loxley L. Wooldridge, 20363910
PFC Jack D. Wheeler, 33047770

PFC James W. Watson, 20363627
Pvt. Kenneth H. Willard, 31339981
S.Sgt. Melvin L. Waggoner, 20363166
Pvt. Michael (NMI) Utiss, 32262566
Pvt. Irwin H. Unger, 12221304
PFC Ervin G. Tweed, 14142882
PFC Richard J. Thompson, 32304077
PFC William F. Stone, 32706084
PFC Robert J. Scott, 32180510
Pvt. Walter D. Sink, 20364257
Pvt. George (NMI) Pisar, 32776793
Pvt. Bernard G. Brush, 36853089
PFC Forest L. Rosamond, 34613295
PFC Willis W. Thaxton, 20364699
PFC Donald J. Szymczak, 36578100
Pvt. James E. Payette, 36675742
Pvt. Clarence (NMI) Svoboda, 35518818
PFC Frank (NMI) Strizak, 35172990
PFC Joseph (NMI) Milwit, 33133662
S.Sgt. George E. Stone, 20365021
PFC Francis M. Malinowski, 36586206
PFC Earl H. South, 35062716
Pvt. Georhe A. Somers, 33475645
PFC Walter F. Kizer, 20364451
PFC Herbert (NMI) Kaufman, 15382485
Pvt. Cecil F. Hodges, 33533650
PFC Ralph B. Gardner, 33075107
Pvt. Thurman (NMI) Green, 33047671
Pvt. Albert (NMI) Falzini, 35521025
PFC Donald N. Severtson, 37542436
Sgt. William N. Dula, 33046453
Pvt. Roland H. Coates, 39469519
Sgt. Joseph B. Churchill, 32267825
PFC Alfred H. Carlton, 36440588
PFC Robert H. Schiele, 34276914
Pvt. Alex (NMI) Bereski, 32300479
Pvt. Marlin B. Ryan, 33511925
PFC Samuel A. Rothernberg, 12204935
PFC Lawrence L. Brannan, 15338531
Pvt. John M. Heindorf, 12214345
PFC William R. Wise, 33272553
T.Sgt. Oakley Q. Wilson, 33046873
PFC Walter W. Wagner, 20365610
Pvt. Martin I. Williams, 34123276
S.Sgt. John (NMI) Van Der Meulen, 36150360
T.Sgt. Charles B. Turner, 20365854
PFC Frank (NMI) Tyskiewicaz, 32821215

Sgt. Francis L. Snyder, 33043011
S.Sgt. Thomas B. Turner, 20365836
PFC John R. Truman, 33041915
PFC Morris (NMI) Shelton, 35467795
Sgt. Albert H. Thrift, 33041865
Pvt. Raymond F. Prince, 36852729
PFC Larry J. Roach, 33133223
Pvt. Doyle B. Thomas, 34635334
Pvt. Leslie D. Teegardin, 36865752
PFC Edward L. O'Toole, 32269416
PFC Joseph L. Pellegrini, 32706057
PFC Sam J. Neighbors, 37236221
PFC Derrill G. Mellon, 37283438
Sgt. Allen P. Moberly, 35468273
PFC Keith W. Stever, 33009965
PFC James D. Manipolo, 32389197
PFC James T. Songster, Jr., 12135545
PFC Joseph B. Kelliher, 33133677
Pvt. Wilbert L. Smith, 37673723
Pvt. Everett L. Keister Jr., 35917516
S.Sgt. James C. Herndon Jr., 20364447
S.Sgt. Melvin H. Granger Jr., 20364673
Sgt. John W. Hall, 33047794
S.Sgt. John W. Fischer, 20364817
Pvt. Maurice W. Collins, 32639919
Pvt. Allen T. Collier, 20364443
PFC Henry F. Seal, Jr., 20365208
PFC John (NMI) Gerone, 32300303
PFC Cosmo G. Scorzelli, 32331472
PFC John R. Byers, 33561285
PFC Garland B. Ashworth, 20364459
PFC William L. Rucker, 34437468
Pvt. Clarence J. Blair 31114701
T.Sgt. Everette C. Cardwell, 20365027
PFC James J. Rhodes, Jr., 33459893
PFC Francis M. Payne, 33000367
S.Sgt. Elmer E. Lunsford, 33043289
Pvt. William J. Mask, 33727224
S.Sgt. Douglas A. Orndorff, 20365289
Pvt. Felix J. Perez, 32819506
Pvt. Ernest Z. Peacock, 34890658
Pvt. Ardell W. Payne, 34787827
PFC Glenwood E. Overstreet, 20363624
Pvt. Robert L. Osgood, 35805961
Pvt. Francis E. O'Brien, 33641822
Pvt. Lonnie P. Nowell, 330422201
T.Sgt. Peter L. Mulligan, Jr., 32300359

PFC Angelo M. Morales, 32330865
Cpl. Charles S. Meade, 32330198
Pvt. Abraham Passman, 32972372
Pvt. Carl T. Mauser, 35068003
Pvt. Herman (NMI) Martin, 14035716
Tec.3 Paul S. Malachowski, 11044634
Sgt. Ernest L. Wilborn, 20364700
PFC James R. Yeatts, 20364884
Pvt. Ozell Weeks, 34809832
PFC William A. Umberger, 20364259
S.Sgt. Joseph P. Trona, 33153326
Tec. 4 Elbert J. Sult, 20366079
Pvt. Mack L. Smity, 34008259
Pvt. Oscar J. Powell, 398861373
Pvt. Gilbert E. Pittenger, 32769588
PFC Woodrow W. Payne, 33000524
Pvt. Harold (NMI) Baumgarten, 32975300
PFC Royce O. Branscom, 37186078
PFC Roy V. Church, 20364470
PFC Charles L. Collins, 39150349
Pvt. Mile J. Radwan, 36717995
PFC Donald A. Pyle, 33152863
PFC Raymond J. Prior, 31067723
PFC Herman H. Midgett, 33042436
Pvt. Reeder H. Pettus, 34339455
S.Sgt. Graham (NMI) Pearce, 33043068
Pvt. John D. Yowell, 20365713
PFC Raymond E. Painter, 20365687
PFC James K. Page, 33531688
Pvt. Eugene V. Ostoj, 37560934
Tec. 4 John S. Orlando, 32340513
PFC Cecil G. Nuckols, 33042452
PFC Garrett S. Neff, 33047692
Pvt. Leonard F. Koluch, 37463237
PFC Douglas M. Martin, 33535547
Cpl. Oliver (NMI) Ness, 37177894
Pvt. Thomas R. McCammon, 33512562
PFC William H. Mauro, 33431092
T.Sgt. Thomas D. Tinnin, Jr., 20364403
Pvt. Edmund M. Magilam, 32666540
Pvt. Joseph M. Lynch, 33737182
PFC Sidney (NMI) Wolkoff, 32655209
PFC Edward J. Watts, 33042522
Pvt. Ernest E. Towbridge, 31363644
S.Sgt. Dewey O. Tredwaym 20364404
PFC James B. Snyder, 33459913
T.Sgt. Isaac W. Rainey, 20364835

Pvt. Lloyd A. Pond, 31198136
S.Sgt. Henry J. Peters, 20365085
Pvt. Eugene A. Paczesny, 36827869
PFC Gerald M. Bohn, 20363139
PFC Lawrence M. Cassell, 330447743
PFC Ronald O. Clark, 20364710
Pvt. Louis A. Culla, 31246858
Cpl. Earl L. Davis, 33046935

(c) Missing: June 6, 1944

PFC Leo C. Balon, 32839931
PFC Charles C. Camacho, 12086269
PFC William F. Dillon, 20363418
PFC Nick N. Gillespie, 20363645
S.Sgt. Raymond S. Hoback, 20363618
PFC William J. Maffe, 33673098
PFC Charles G. McSkimming, 33455666
S.Sgt. Fulton E. New, 20364677
PFC James (NMI) Ohler, 33152866
S.Sgt. Earl L. Parker, 20363625
Pvt. N.R. Spillman Jr., 37152253
PFC Fairfield (NMI) Butler, 33108519
S.Sgt. James K. Desper, 20365639
Pvt. Glenn M. Dow, 37482332
Pvt. Heinz J. Grunig, 32875055
Pvt. Carl S. Johnson, 36630396
Pvt. Hobart Maness Jr., 34439516
PFC Charles R. Milliron, 20364248
PFC Charles W. O'Dee, 32375475
PFC James M. Padley, 32751616
PFC Jack (NMI) Smith, 33047670
Sgt. Ivor D. Thornton, 33047375

(d) Taken Prisoner: June 6, 1944

WOJG Frank W. Holland, W–2120296
Tec. 4 Edward J. Cashner, 33153157
PFC Sam J. Vicari, 38284702
Pvt. Nickolas (NMI) Barnosky, 42000042

507th Parachute Infantry Regiment Losses in Action, June 6–July 14, 1944

(Courtesy of the National Archives, Washington DC)

(a) Officers Killed in Action:

1st Lt.	Bloethe, Leonard W.	June 16, 1944
1st Lt.	Carson, Joseph A.	June 23, 1944
2nd Lt.	Clark, Max D.	June 7, 1944
1st Lt.	Crooks, Claude V. Jr.	June 23, 1944
2nd Lt.	Donlan, Robert D.	June 7, 1944
2nd Lt.	Dunham, Edward A.	June 7, 1944
1st Lt.	Eyerly, Jack B.	June 15, 1944
1st Lt.	Farnham, Elmer F.	June 11, 1944
Capt.	Frank, Stanford M.	June 12, 1944
1st Lt.	Freeman, James W. Jr.	June 10, 1944
2nd Lt.	Gorl, Frederick C.	June 6, 1944
Capt.	Keller, John J.	June 16, 1944
1st Lt.	Levy, Louis	July 5, 1944
1st Lt.	Maxwell, Lowell C.	June 11, 1944
1st Lt.	McClure, James C.	June 7, 1944
2nd Lt.	McGonigle, Gerald C.	June 7, 1944
1st Lt.	Moran, Frank R.	June 15, 1944
2nd Lt.	Paterson, Donald E.	June 9, 1944

1st Lt.	Rinehart, Charles A.	July 7, 1944
2nd Lt.	Shelly, Richard D.	June 15, 1944
1st Lt.	Stanhope, Phillip R.	June 16, 1944
Capt.	Tolle, Clareance A.	June 17, 1944
2nd Lt.	Wagoner, Elliott W.	June 6, 1944
2nd Lt.	Zielke, Edward B.	June 10, 1944
Capt.	Allyn, Gordon S. Jr.	June 15, 1944
2nd Lt.	Aubel, William C.	July 5, 1944
1st Lt.	Todd, Kay	June 12, 1944

(b) Officers Wounded in Action:

1st Lt.	Ardziejewski, Stanley L. J.	June 15, 1944
2nd Lt.	Ballard, John K.	June 15, 1944
Capt.	Bennett, William	June 6, 1944
Capt.	Bennett, Thomas R. Jr.	June 15, 1944
1st Lt.	Boyer, Robert H. Jr.	July 4, 1944
2nd Lt.	Burnett, James A.	June 14, 1944
2nd Lt.	Calabro, Philip J.	June 14, 1944
1st Lt.	Cofer, Horace J.	June 29, 1944
1st Lt.	Cole, Marior K.	June 28, 1944
Capt.	Cotham, William Z.	June 10, 1944
1st Lt.	Cowan, Otis K. Jr.	June 15, 1944
2nd Lt.	Darling, John G.	June 14, 1944
Major	Davis, John T.	June 28, 1944
1st Lt.	Dillon, Gerard M.	June 14, 1944
1st Lt.	Dixon, Roland B.	June 27, 1944
2nd Lt.	Ericson, Elmer F.	July 4, 1944
Capt.	Esposito, Louis C.	June 8, 1944
Major	Fagan, Joseph P.	June 6, 1944
2nd Lt.	Harmon, Robert L.	June 14, 1944
2nd Lt.	Hayden, Ralph M.	June 25, 1944
1st Lt.	Hayes, John J. Jr.	June 8, 1944
2nd Lt.	Haynes, Earl C.	June 5, 1944
1st Lt.	Hessberger, George W. Jr.	June 15, 1944
1st Lt.	Hopkins, Robert S.	June 17, 1944
1st Lt.	Jamison, Henry S.	June 6, 1944
1st Lt.	Johnson, Evans H.	July 5, 1944
1st Lt.	Joseph, John T.	July 5, 1944
2nd Lt.	Keenan, Edward S.	June 7, 1944
2nd Lt.	Killion, Robert J.	June 7, 1944
1st Lt.	Kline, Jules J.	June 7, 1944
2nd Lt.	Kormylo, Joseph	July 5, 1944
Lt. Col.	Kuhn, William C.	June 6, 1944
2nd Lt.	Larsen, Gerald E.	July 7, 1944
1st Lt.	Law, Robert W. Jr.	June 29, 1944
1st Lt.	Lillge, Carl W.	June 12, 1944

Lt. Col.	Maloney, Arthur A.	July 7, 1944
1st Lt.	Marr, John W.	July 4, 1944
1st Lt.	Martin, Jack S.	June 19, 1944
1st Lt.	Mayers, Isadore	June 7, 1944
2nd Lt.	McCarty, Willis P.	June 6, 1944
Capt.	McCoiv, Chester V.	June 7, 1944
1st Lt.	McGill, Ralph S.	June 6, 1944
1st Lt.	McNamara, William F.	June 7, 1944
Capt.	Miller, Saul	June 8, 1944
Capt.	Nunn, James R.	June 12, 1944
1st Lt.	O'Brian, George R. Jr.	June 7, 1944
2nd Lt.	O'Rourk, Donald C.	June 8, 1944
Lt. Col.	Ostberg, Edwin J.	June 7, 1944
Major	Pearson, Benjamin F. Jr.	July 7, 1944
Capt.	Pine, Irving	June 17, 1944
Capt.	Rosenbloom, Allen D.	June 6, 1944
1st Lt.	Stephens, Albert L. Jr.	June 14, 1944
Capt.	Stephens, Howard A.	June 6, 1944
Capt.	Taylor, Allen W.	June 19, 1944

(c) Officers Missing in Action:

2nd Lt.	Alderton, Albert G.	June 6, 1944
1st Lt.	Browne, William J.	June 6, 1944
2nd Lt.	Cecil, Albert M. Jr.	June 6, 1944
2nd Lt.	Clarke, James F.	June 13, 1944
2nd Lt.	Comstock, William G.	June 6, 1944
2nd Lt.	Danziger, Benjamin	June 18, 1944
1st Lt.	Devlin, William J. Jr.	June 6, 1944
1st Lt.	Farnham, Elmer F.	June 11, 1944
1st Lt.	Heisler, Walter C.	June 6, 1944
1st Lt.	Henderson, Robert A III	June 6, 1944
1st Lt.	Hoffmann, Elmer F.	June 6, 1944
1st Lt.	Hopkins, John V.	June 6, 1944
1st Lt.	Houle, Arthur J. Jr.	June 6, 1944
2nd Lt.	LeClair, Lloyd L.	June 6, 1944
Capt.	Pfeffler, John F.	June 6, 1944
2nd Lt.	Rooney, Edward E.	June 6, 1944
2nd Lt.	Shutt, Robert W.	June 6, 1944
Major	Smith, Gordon K.	June 6, 1944
1st Lt.	Smith, Richard E.	June 6, 1944
Capt.	Sophian, Abraham Jr.	June 11, 1944
1st Lt.	Stevens, John M. Jr.	June 7, 1944
2nd Lt.	Winton, Clifford A.	June 7, 1944

(d) Officers Taken Prisoner:

1st Lt.	Graul, Donald O.	June 6, 1944
Capt.	Hennon, Robert M.	June 6, 1944
Major	Johnston, Charles D.	June 11, 1944
Colonel	Millett, George B. Jr.	June 6, 1944
1st Lt.	Monson, Nelson P.	June 11, 1944
2nd Lt.	Wade, James M.	June 6, 1944
1st Lt.	Whiting, Roger	June 11, 1944

(e) Enlisted Men Taken Prisoner:

Baldwin, Robert L.	June 6, 1944
Brightbill, William L.	June 6, 1944
Cahill, Vincent F.	June 6, 1944
Conley, Steve H.	June 6, 1944
De La Cruz, Salvadore A.	June 6, 1944
DeRosa, Harlow J.	June 6, 1944
Carrigus, Robert O.	June 6, 1944
Hahn, Edward C.	June 6, 1944
Horvath, Holman Jr.	June 8, 1944
Kelly, Bernard E.	June 6, 1944
Koenig, Frank W.	June 6, 1944
Leptuck, Anthony S.	June 6, 1944
Lindberg, Oliver	June 6, 1944
Manning, Shelton	June 8, 1944
Peschl, Fred E.	June 6, 1944
Petrullo, John	June 6, 1944
Phillips, Robert M.	June 8, 1944
Prince, Joe R.	June 5, 1944
Puckett, William C.	June 7, 1944
Slothouber, Derk	June 6, 1944
Szarzi, Joseph A.	June 6, 1944
Tessier, Geane	June 6, 1944
Trimm, Paul	June 6, 1944
Trivett, Willard R.	June 6, 1944
Vavro, Joseph J.	June 7, 1944
Watkins, Granvel J.	June 6, 1944
Watling, Harry R.	June 7, 1944
Wilbert, William J.	June 6, 1944
Williams, Val R.	June 6, 1944
Wellen, Donald M.	June 6, 1944

(f) Officers Died of Wounds:

1st Lt.	Keenan, Walter F.	June 17, 1944
1st Lt.	Koehler, Elmo F.	June 17, 1944
1st Lt.	Wagner, Edward H.	June 28, 1944

(g) Enlisted Men Died of Wounds:

Bigham, Felix S.	July 26, 1944
Boots, George E.	June 5, 1944
Chabot, Ludger J. Jr.	June 15, 1944
Clark, Alton D.	June 11, 1944
Colbroth, Robert E.	June 12, 1944
Coppersmith, Donald C.	July 5, 1944
Fink, Charles E. Jr.	June 18, 1944
Goldstein, Jordan L .	June 18, 1944
Hebbe, Frederick J.	June 30, 1944
Holcombe, Roger F.	July 5, 1944
Hurthle, Preston C.	June 16, 1944
Jenkins, George E.	June 16, 1944
Kennedy, Ray C.	June 8, 1944
McClure, Ira L.	June 20, 1944
Ragsdale, Willard L.	June 16, 1944
Savage, Wilburn	July 11, 1944
Shearer, Kenneth L.	July 9, 1944
Siler, Merton	June 8, 1944
Stewart, William W.	July 5, 1944
Toomey, John J.	June 23, 1944
Tullidge, George B.	June 7, 1944
Wiley, Jerry E.	June 15, 1944

(h) Enlisted Men Killed in Action:

Ahlgrim, Robert W.	July 4, 1944
Albert, Wayne H.	June 14, 1944
Amyx, Oval G.	July 2, 1944
Anderson, Nolan R.	June 12, 1944
Anders, Henry A.	June 24, 1944
Antanaitis, Bernard C.	June 12, 1944
Barnes, Billy J.	June 13, 1944
Barnes, Harold V.	June 5, 1944
Barton, Donald M.	July 5, 1944
Bauer, George E.	June 13, 1944
Belden, William N.	June 15, 1944
Bello, Reynolds J.	June 13, 1944
Benoit, Robert L.	June 17, 1944
Benton, Robert O.	June 18, 1944
Bergendahl, John R.	June 6, 1944
Bliss, Allison T.	June 6, 1944
Borowski, Egenuirz	June 7, 1944
Bradley, Herbert L.	July 4, 1944
Brown, Lawrence H. Jr.	June 16, 1944
Camarena, Manuel M.	June 6, 1944
Campbell, James E.	June 18, 1944
Carmichael, Hershel	June 7, 1944
Carroll, William F.	June 7, 1944
Chico, Fidel	July 4, 1944
Cleary, Donald P.	June 16, 1944
Costes, Charles H.	June 6, 1944
Coffer, Charles C.	June 23, 1944
Collins, Arthur L. Jr.	June 6, 1944
Collins, Glenn R.	June 14, 1944
Condran, John W.	June 24, 1944
Conley, Anthony J.	June 7, 1944
Colombana, Geno	July 3, 1944
Corley, Nathan D.	June 6, 1944
Crone, Chester R.	June 6, 1944
Curtin, Edward J.	June 8, 1944
Curtis, Louis H.	July 7, 1944
Daugela, Bruno A.	June 19, 1944
De Mestri, Thomas J.	June 11, 1944
Denton, Carl E.	June 15, 1944
Dignon, Francis J.	July 8, 1944
Dillard, Russell B.	June 24, 1944
Dixon, Kenneth E.	June 23, 1944
Dubreuil, Louis A.	June 25, 1944
Eichelberg, Otto	July 3, 1944
Elizarraraz, Fidel A.	June 18, 1944
Elliott, Chester R.	June 6, 1944

Ellis, Clarence F.	July 3, 1944
Emmet, William P.	July 3, 1944
Ernsberger, Howard J.	June 7, 1944
Farver, Arwillis E.	June 6, 1944
Feninez, Michael	June 22, 1944
Ferguson, Charles Jr.	June 7, 1944
Fernandes, John A.	June 20, 1944
Fero, Joseph P.	June 28, 1944
Fessler, John H.	June 10, 1944
Filbey, James H.	July 4, 1944
Fiore, Vincinzo V.	June 10, 1944
Fischer, Robert W.	June 6, 1944
Fowler, James H.	June 7, 1944
Foster, Cleo C.	June 22, 1944
Fought, Edgar R.	July 11, 1944
Fradet, James L.	June 21, 1944
Francis, Louis Jr.	June 15, 1944
Leonard, Douglas R.	June 11, 1944
Lewis, Wilford I.	July 5, 1944
Lipham, Bryant H.	June 16, 1944
Lisenby, Walter W. Jr.	June 5, 1944
Lloyd, Grady W.	July 17, 1944
Long, Houston H.	June 22, 1944
Lucas, Willard J.	July 24, 1944
Lusk, Eugene	June 14, 1944
Lusk, Frank L.	June 18, 1944
Maltby, Thomas E.	July 8, 1944
Mansfield, Clarence	June 16, 1944
Martin, Ira	July 4, 1944
Martinez, Arnold J.	June 6, 1944
McClaim, Hubert	June 8, 1944
McCord, William Jr.	June 12, 1944
McCormick, Francis J.	June 13, 1944
McCormick, James M.	June 10, 1944
McElhaney, Delmar C.	June 6, 1944
McEntire, Cyril B.	June 10, 1944
McIntosh, Christopher C.	June 8, 1944
McKee, William R.	June 10, 1944
McKinney, James R.	June 15, 1944
Mezarick, Frank	June 11, 1944
Micknowski, John A.	June 23, 1944
Miller, Robert R.	July 23, 1944
Mitchell, Albert J.	June 19, 1944
Mote, Gail B.	June 11, 1944
Moumousis, Nicholas F.	June 24, 1944
Munroe, William A. Jr.	June 6, 1944
Murray, Harry W.	July 7, 1944

Myers, Melvin	June 14, 1944
Niles, Robert S.	June 6, 1944
Nocera, Russell S.	June 6, 1944
North, Billy	June 30, 1944
O'Donnell, Michael R.	June 8, 1944
Olinik, John	June 16, 1944
Palmer, William F. Jr.	June 7, 1944
Parker, Chester J.	June 13, 1944
Patterson, Paul E.	June 14, 1944
Penland, Henry M.	June 23, 1944
Perley, Joseph W.	June 11, 1944
Pettus, George P.	June 9, 1944
Phillips, Ivan R.	June 16, 1944
Pinnix, William F.	June 7, 1944
Popivchak, George	June 24, 1944
Postin, Frank E.	June 28, 1944
Preece, William S.	June 7, 1944
Prescott, Albert R.	June 14, 1944
Quimby, Howard I.	June 12, 1944
Rapp, Wayne E.	June 22, 1944
Rector, Ralph D.	June 12, 1944
Reynolds, Oren D. Jr.	July 23, 1944
Robertson, Paul E.	June 13, 1944
Rockwell, Robert R.	July 24, 1944
Rodgers, Thomas L.	June 15, 1944
Rosales, Calistron	June 22, 1944
Russell, Lazare E.	June 7, 1944
Sandman, Walter G.	June 6, 1944
Sansky, Joseph J.	June 15, 1944
Schulken, Arthur	June 24, 1944
Scott, John E.	June 9, 1944
Shake, Bernard E.	June 22, 1944
Shapiro, Jerome	July 5, 1944
Showers, William H.	June 24, 1944
Silseth, Orville M.	June 14, 1944
Simpson, Vester E.	July 22, 1944
Speer, Ralph A.	June 13, 1944
Sral, Walter T.	June 23, 1944
Stachowiak, Joseph A.	July 24, 1944
Stetz, Stanley F.	July 7, 1944
Stevens, Glenn A.	June 6, 1944
Stippich, Walter P.	June 6, 1944
Stratton, Joel	July 1, 1944
Stroud, Lewis E.	June 6, 1944
Stuart, Jim T.	July 7, 1944
Sullivan, Lawrence W.	June 24, 1944
Sutherland, Lynuel D.	July 6, 1944

Tapscott, Roger F.	June 15, 1944
Taylor, Billy J.	June 23, 1944
Taylor, Walter B.	June 18, 1944
Thomas, Clarence	June 16, 1944
Thomas, Raymond W.	June 23, 1944
Thore, Paul B.	July 7, 1944
Tillett, George E.	September 8, 1944
Tillman, Daniel B.	June 24, 1944
Todd, William A.	June 7, 1944
Toye, Lewis S.	June 12, 1944
Treloar, Warren	June 14, 1944
Trojchak, Michael	June 6, 1944
Underwood, Ernest L.	June 26, 1944
Urban, Peter C.	June 8, 1944
Van Cure, Edward	July 5, 1944
Vaughn, Tom R.	June 7, 1944
Vecchiarelli, Dominick	June 23, 1944
Waldorf, Louis C.	June 12, 1944
Waller, Stephen E. Jr.	June 8, 1944
Ward, Richard W.	June 6, 1944
Warwick, John W.	June 10, 1944
Watson, Robert G.	June 6, 1944
Watts, Hunter D.	June 15, 1944
Werner, Robert E.	June 24, 1944
Whiteford, Fred D.	June 30, 1944
Wilcox, Eugene D.	June 30, 1944
Wolf, William R.	July 4, 1944
Wood, Frank J.	June 28, 1944
Woodall, Clarence R.	July 13, 1944
Wright, Willard K.	July 13, 1944
Yarrington, Carl H.	June 6, 1944
Zahorsky, Theodore J.	June 6, 1944
Zielinski, Walter	July 13, 1944
Zielke, Edward D.	June 10, 1944

(i) Enlisted Men Wounded in Action:

Acosta, Selestino A.	June 8, 1944
Aller, Loren E.	June 14, 1944
Alvarez, Ricardo R.	June 27, 1944
Angello, Samuel	June 14, 1944
Aros, Arthur R.	June 14, 1944
Austin, Oscar E. Jr.	June 8, 1944
Ballon, Albert J.	June 7, 1944
Barker, James L.	June 15, 1944
Barlow, James W.	June 7, 1944
Barnum, Alfred H.	July 5, 1944
Barrett, John E.	June 11, 1944
Bartley, Edwin C.	July 7, 1944
Barton, John H.	July 7, 1944
Beasom, Donald R.	June 6, 1944
Beatty, James G.	July 9, 1944
Beatty, William R.	July 5, 1944
Becker, Lawrence F.	June 12, 1944
Beier, Alfred M.	June 15, 1944
Benjamin, Elliott	June 6, 1944
Bentz, Robert L.	June 27, 1944
Berry, Joseph P.	June 7, 1944
Bizub, Anton F.	June 23, 1944
Blair, Thomas B.	June 7, 1944
Blalock, Newell D.	June 14, 1944
Blalock, Claude R.	June 14, 1944
Blood, Paul P.	July 5, 1944
Bodolsky, John A.	June 24, 1944
Bokrosh, Andrew Jr.	June 7, 1944
Bolick, Earl A.	July 7, 1944
Bonnell, Reinhold W.	June 14, 1944
Booth, Orville J.	July 7, 1944
Booth, Wayne J.	June 7, 1944
Bostick, Merideth	June 9, 1944
Bosworth, Donald E.	June 8, 1944
Bowell, William D.	June 15, 1944
Boyd, Russell	June 15, 1944
Brianzo, Thomas E.	June 12, 1944
Brophy, Vincent	July 7, 1944
Brosnan, Joseph S.	June 16, 1944
Bruce, Lewis R.	June 15, 1944
Brundige, Oscar E.	June 17, 1944
Brzezowski, John J.	June 6, 1944
Buholtz, Franklin Jr.	June 7, 1944
Burch, Kenneth E.	June 19, 1944
Burchardt, Harry	June 13, 1944
Burk, Edward C.	June 12, 1944

Burman, Robert E.	June 14, 1944
Burns, Fred L.	June 8, 1944
Burns, Harry M.	June 27, 1944
Camblin, David L.	June 15, 1944
Cantar, Ronald O.	June 15, 1944
Cantu, Trinidad P.	June 9, 1944
Carlson, Donald M.	June 7, 1944
Carr, George F.	June 17, 1944
Carter, Melvin D.	June 13, 1944
Carter, Norman V.	June 13, 1944
Casazza, Ralph L.	July 7, 1944
Casey, Oscar D.	June 14, 1944
Caton, Arthur Jr.	June 11, 1944
Ceraso, John A.	June 7, 1944
Chaney, William T.	June 14, 1944
Charatte, Roland G.	June 9, 1944
Charles, Herman	July 6, 1944
Chriswell, Linsly G.	June 14, 1944
Clark, Elmer H.	July 3, 1944
Cleveland, Charles W.	June 12, 1944
Cole, Paul B.	June 15, 1944
Coleman, Joe H.	June 22, 1944
Collins, Paul L.	June 19, 1944
Collins, Clarence W.	June 9, 1944
Collins, Herman V.	June 15, 1944
Cook, Raymond E.	June 7, 1944
Cooper, Carl E.	June 9, 1944
Cooper, Ross L.	July 4, 1944
Costa, Frank S.	July 6, 1944
Cothren, Raymond W.	June 14, 1944
Cottrell, Robert M.	June 19, 1944
Courneotes, Chris	June 14, 1944
Couveau, Bernard L.	June 19, 1944
Cox, Arthur W.	June 6, 1944
Coyle, Luther F.	June 8, 1944
Crouder, Edward T.	July 5, 1944
Curran, James G. Jr.	June 15, 1944
Czyzewicz, Charles D.	July 4, 1944
Daly, Patrick J.	June 27, 1944
D'Andrea, Thomas F.	June 6, 1944
Davis, Arthur M.	July 7, 1944
Davis, Clifford L.	July 4, 1944
Davis, John W. Jr.	June 12, 1944
Day, Jerome G.	June 10, 1944
Denham, Thomas O.	June 7, 1944
Denson, Henry M.	June 18, 1944
DeKrenzo, Antonio	June 21, 1944

DeVore, Reuel J.	June 15, 1944
Dewvall, John H.	June 15, 1944
Dickerson, Gilbert V.	June 27, 1944
Dickerson, Howard M.	July 5, 1944
Dillon, Jimmie	June 13, 1944
Dodd, Halsey H. Jr.	June 14, 1944
Dubree, Odel L.	June 13, 1944
Duff, Rolland J.	June 21, 1944
Edel, Bernard J.	June 9, 1944
Edwards, James P.	June 9, 1944
Elliott, Eugene B.	June 15, 1944
Ellsworth, Kenneth J.	June 8, 1944
Elshire, Gerald M.	June 27, 1944
Ely, Bernard D.	June 27, 1944
Embree, Ray M.	July 5, 1944
Emerick, Clyde W.	June 14, 1944
England, Eugene E.	June 13, 1944
Epifanio, Clyde H.	June 7, 1944
Ergler, Stanley E.	June 8, 1944
Erickson, Austen G.	June 16, 1944
Escobar, Gaspar A.	June 7, 1944
Estep, Floyd E.	July 3, 1944
Evans, Lloyd R.	June 8, 1944
Farmer, Frank D.	June 14, 1944
Feasley, Howard T. Jr.	June 6, 1944
Feldman, James B. Jr.	June 16, 1944
Festa, Nicholas	June 7, 1944
Fetzer, Carl A.	June 14, 1944
Fiscina, Gilbert	June 11, 1944
Flauto, Ralph E.	June 19, 1944
Fleming, John F.	June 8, 1944
Flynn, Edward B.	June 6, 1944
Flynn, Edward Jr.	June 18, 1944
Foor, John L.	June 19, 1944
Foster, Sinclair B.	June 13, 1944
Fox, Edward F.	June 15, 1944
Franchi, Armando H.	June 8, 1944
Frank, Charles	June 14, 1944
Franks, Floyd R.	June 14, 1944
Fredericks, Howard	June 14, 1944
Freedman, Martin	June 6, 1944
Fritts, Bose B. Jr.	June 27, 1944
Funes, Joseph R.	June 23, 1944
Gallery, Joseph P.	June 14, 1944
Gannon, Wayne G.	June 15, 1944
Garner, Thomas S.	June 18, 1944
Garrison, Howard E.	June 14, 1944

Gately, William	July 7, 1944
Gaydon, Alexander B.	June 14, 1944
Gaydos, George	June 15, 1944
George, Thurman L.	July 4, 1944
Giacoletti, Dominic P.	June 8, 1944
Gibbs, Lloyd B.	June 14, 1944
Gibeck, Andrew H.	June 6, 1944
Gilbert, Emmitt P.	June 27, 1944
Gillian, Henry L.	June 9, 1944
Glass, Harvey J.	June 18, 1944
Gonzales, Alvelardo M.	June 6, 1944
Googe, Freeman L.	June 13, 1944
Gorney, Anthony G.	July 8, 1944
Goss, William E.	June 18, 1944
Gosztyla, Joseph V.	July 4, 1944
Gray, Manis E.	June 19, 1944
Groomes, Carl	June 12, 1944
Groff, Richard F.	June 14, 1944
Gross, Sydney T.	June 13, 1944
Hadella, Charles A.	June 8, 1944
Hale, Charles R.	June 15, 1944
Hall, Louis C. Jr.	June 7, 1944
Hall, Luther M.	June 13, 1944
Hall, Richard H.	June 8, 1944
Hamner, George H.	June 12, 1944
Hanley, Michael W.	June 7, 1944
Hansen, Chalmer D.	June 13, 1944
Hanssen, Elof A.	June 14, 1944
Hardin, James M.	July 4, 1944
Harris, Thurmond	June 19, 1944
Harvey, Carroll J.	June 12, 1944
Hausch, Sidney	June 15, 1944
Hayford, Francis R.	July 5, 1944
Herlevich, Louis R.	June 27, 1944
Herwitz, Sidney J.	June 9, 1944
Hickey, George M.	June 28, 1944
Hicks, Donald B.	June 8, 1944
Hiles, Harry B.	July 2, 1944
Hinson, Loyd	July 4, 1944
Hitchcock, George R.	June 19, 1944
Hoback, Richard W.	June 7, 1944
Hodges, Thad L.	June 8, 1944
Hogan, Mylo F.	June 15, 1944
Hohn, Cleo L.	June 12, 1944
Holava, Frank J.	July 7, 1944
Holman, Aarne A.	July 4, 1944
Homnick, Peter P.	June 27, 1944

Hornhayk, Joseph G.	July 4, 1944
Horvath, Stephen P.	June 14, 1944
Howard, Edward M.	July 7, 1944
Howard, Robert P.	June 15, 1944
Hromco, John G.	June 18, 1944
Hubbard, George B.	June 15, 1944
Hughart, Clarence S.	June 27, 1944
Hughes, George W.	June 8, 1944
Hughes, Glenn E.	June 11, 1944
Humphrey, James E.	June 8, 1944
Humphrey, Charles W. Jr.	June 19, 1944
Huncovsky, Donald E.	June 14, 1944
Hurda, Raymond L.	June 14, 1944
Hurst, Joseph C.	June 9, 1944
Hutto, Paul L.	June 8, 1944
Ialongo, Ernest V.	June 6, 1944
Ikwald, Adolph	June 7, 1944
Jackson, Wallace R.	June 8, 1944
Jarosik, John	June 7, 1944
Jenkins, Regel G. Jr.	June 7, 1944
Johns, Luther W.	June 10, 1944
Johnston, James W.	June 9, 1944
Johnes, Carl D.	July 5, 1944
Jones, Lloyd M.	June 15, 1944
Jones, Thomas	June 13, 1944
Justice, Harry	July 4, 1944
Kamphey, Howard	June 7, 1944
Kaska, Arthur A.	June 17, 1944
Kaufmann, James W.	June 6, 1944
Keating, Robert L.	July 1, 1944
Kent, William R.	July 8, 1944
Kesler, Francis E.	June 15, 1944
Kirby, Joseph	June 7, 1944
Kish, Julius M.	June 9, 1944
Kline, George F.	June 7, 1944
Kniess, Eugene L.	June 14, 1944
Knight, Bryson E.	June 7, 1944
Kohute, Edward G.	June 27, 1944
Koladish, Stephen A.	June 6, 1944
Kolok, Joseph F.	June 15, 1944
Koncaba, Charles A.	July 4, 1944
Koneczny, Bernard W.	June 14, 1944
Kostarowski, John H.	June 27, 1944
Kowalczyk, Joseph	June 7, 1944
Kosuch, Steve M.	June 13, 1944
Kraemer, Stephen T.	June 8, 1944
Kramer, Stephen J.	June 10, 1944

Kramer, William A.	June 8, 1944
Kraushar, Harold S.	June 25, 1944
Krugg, Robert A.	June 13, 1944
Kruk, Joseph A.	July 5, 1944
Kuchta, Mike A.	June 15, 1944
Kuhnert, Raymond L.	June 14, 1944
Kuntz, Paul R.	July 7, 1944
Lacy, Edward J.	July 3, 1944
LaFleur, Robert D.	June 9, 1944
Lang, Joseph D.	June 13, 1944
LaPine, Glen H.	July 7, 1944
Larsen, Robert	June 7, 1944
Larson, Norman C.	June 15, 1944
Lavazza, John G.	June 14, 1944
Lawler, Daniel J.	July 5, 1944
Lawrence, Calvin J.	June 13, 1944
Lawson, Ellis	June 14, 1944
Lawton, Harold M.	June 8, 1944
Lee, James C.	June 18, 1944
Lee, Palmer M.	July 7, 1944
Leiter, Nestor	June 8, 1944
Level, Newell W. Jr.	June 27, 1944
Lewis, Harvey D. Jr.	June 27, 1944
Lidaka, Peter	June 19, 1944
Ligon, Robert B.	June 8, 1944
Lindsey, Morris E.	June 8, 1944
Lindsey, William H.	July 5, 1944
Lipham, Fred H.	June 15, 1944
Lock, Luther D. Jr.	June 7, 1944
Lopez, Guadalupe Jr.	June 30, 1944
Lowe, James M. Jr.	June 18, 1944
Lozich, Anthony T.	June 16, 1944
Lynn, Romeo C.	June 9, 1944
Lyons, James	June 16, 1944
MacDonald, Richard E.	June 14, 1944
MacGregor, Ian D.	July 5, 1944
Manderscheidt, Francis W.	June 8, 1944
Mantz, Frank E.	June 12, 1944
Martens, Cecil G.	June 15, 1944
Martinez, Ricardo	June 9, 1944
Massey, Fillmore D.	June 7, 1944
Mathews, Thomas E.	June 27, 1944
Mattingly, James L.	June 14, 1944
Max, Edward J.	June 14, 1944
Mayo, Clyde E.	June 21, 1944
McCarroll, Robert E.	June 8, 1944
McCarthy, Thomas J.	June 10, 1944

McCurry, Samuel Jr.	June 19, 1944
McElroy, Thomas T.	June 28, 1944
McGlothran, Clarence	June 27, 1944
McHaney, Alfred E.	July 5, 1944
McMahan, James W.	June 19, 1944
Mennella, Anthony	June 15, 1944
Mercer, Norman D. Jr.	June 15, 1944
Merideth, Joe H. Jr.	June 7, 1944
Meritt, James F.	June 13, 1944
Metz, Raymond J.	June 9, 1944
Mihalcik, Edward A.	June 19, 1944
Miller, Bruce E.	June 8, 1944
Miller, Harold F.	June 17, 1944
Miller, Harry E.	June 11, 1944
Miller, Robert G.	June 19, 1944
Moeller, Roy V.	June 14, 1944
Monson, Carl A.	July 5, 1944
Moore, Charles F.	June 17, 1944
Morgan, Clyde V.	June 6, 1944
Morris, Thompson J.	June 7, 1944
Morrison, William M.	June 14, 1944
Morse, Charles A. Jr.	June 6, 1944
Moscozo, Arnold	June 13, 1944
Motes, James M.	June 9, 1944
Moucheron, James R.	July 7, 1944
Moyer, Milton C.	June 18, 1944
Muffo, Augustine V.	June 22, 1944
Mullen, Andrew J.	June 8, 1944
Mumey, Robert M.	June 15, 1944
Mundon, Thomas E.	June 13, 1944
Munyer, George R.	June 8, 1944
Murphy, Redmond J.	June 22, 1944
Musur, Aloysius J.	June 9, 1944
Nagel, Gordon F.	June 9, 1944
Nageldinger, Roy A.	June 21, 1944
Nardo, Vincent	June 7, 1944
Natale, Nick	June 15, 1944
Neel, Hottle C.	June 15, 1944
Nelson, Carl J.	June 12, 1944
Nelson, Russell E.	July 3, 1944
Newgard, Walford R.	June 19, 1944
Nicholson, Joseph	June 7, 1944
Nicholson, Ronald B.	July 3, 1944
Nicoll, Leslie H.	June 7, 1944
Neider, Clifford P.	June 8, 1944
Nies, Bernard L.	June 14, 1944
Nielsen, Milton F.	June 18, 1944

Norris, Roy E.	June 7, 1944
Norskog, Kenneth J.	June 16, 1944
Oakes, George F.	June 15, 1944
Oldham, Vernon P.	June 14, 1944
Olesh, Walter B.	July 5, 1944
Oliver, Richard A.	July 4, 1944
Orndorff, Robert A.	June 6, 1944
O'Rourk, James W.	June 6, 1944
Osinski, Frank	June 6, 1944
Ostrowski, Lee A.	June 14, 1944
Oughterson, William T.	June 9, 1944
Palmese, Joseph	June 14, 1944
Palo, Tyko A.	July 5, 1944
Panzera, Louis G.	June 10, 1944
Parham, James L.	July 7, 1944
Parker, Frederick G. Jr.	June 12, 1944
Parletto, Mario A.	June 11, 1944
Pasikowski, Charles M.	June 7, 1944
Pauxtis, Sylvester J.	July 5, 1944
Pavkov, John I.	June 6, 1944
Pavlicek, James E.	June 9, 1944
Pawlik, Joseph E.	June 7, 1944
Peck, Robert H.	July 5, 1944
Peckham, Charles C.	July 14, 1944
Peebles, Eugene H.	June 7, 1944
Peluso, Angelo R.	June 7, 1944
Pendlebery, John W.	June 22, 1944
Peringian, Charles A.	8 July 1944
Pertusi, Antonio P.	June 28, 1944
Peterson, Harry A.	June 7, 1944
Peterson, Marshall J.	July 4, 1944
Phillips, Leslie V.	June 18, 1944
Pilant, Melvin A.	July 7, 1944
Pipolo, Sandy E.	June 14, 1944
Pippin, Raymond B.	July 4, 1944
Pirtle, George W.	June 7, 1944
Plesco, Nick C.	June 19, 1944
Pluta, Walter C.	June 15, 1944
Poindexter, Thomas J.	July 7, 1944
Pok, Wayne E.	June 8, 1944
Porter, George W.	June 14, 1944
Potter, Roy V.	June 8, 1944
Potts, Lenton L. Jr.	June 14, 1944
Powell, Jerry I.	June 23, 1944
Powers, Archie R.	June 13, 1944
Powers, Thomas I. Jr.	June 8, 1944
Pritchard, Audra	June 10, 1944

Pritchard, William H.	June 9, 1944
Przewozniak, Chester S.	July 7, 1944
Pucel, Steve A.	June 14, 1944
Race, John H.	June 25, 1944
Rader, Ceilan H.	June 15, 1944
Rafalko, Henry	June 8, 1944
Ramey, Aaron D.	June 16, 1944
Ramsay, William E. Jr.	June 28, 1944
Ransom, Matias C.	June 18, 1944
Rassi, Robert L.	June 12, 1944
Ratliff, George H.	June 19, 1944
Reardon, Roy V.	June 12, 1944
Redmon, Sewell	June 14, 1944
Reed, Mitchell C.	June 20, 1944
Reider, Carson L.	June 6, 1944
Reilly, Francis P.	July 6, 1944
Reilly, James	July 7, 1944
Reis, Erneset F.	June 14, 1944
Reynolds, Perry F.	June 14, 1944
Richesson, Harry E.	July 3, 1944
Riding, James R.	June 27, 1944
Rigatti, Julian	June 13, 1944
Reilly, Stanford G.	June 7, 1944
Rivers, Clifton W.	July 4, 1944
Roberts, Mitchell C.	June 27, 1944
Robertson, Cecil V.	June 15, 1944
Rodgers, Jerome A.	June 6, 1944
Roman, Jose L.	June 8, 1944
Rombold, William M.	June 14, 1944
Romeo, Carmen M.	July 4, 1944
Rooks, Noah F.	June 7, 1944
Ross, Clarence E.	June 8, 1944
Roussey, Robert F.	June 14, 1944
Rowan, Francis S.	June 15, 1944
Russo, Vincent J.	June 9, 1944
Rust, Arthur B.	June 16, 1944
Ryan, Earl P.	June 15, 1944
Ryan, James	June 14, 1944
Salter, Henry R.	June 27, 1944
Samutt, Frank Jr.	June 11, 1944
Sampson, Gerald R.	June 15, 1944
Santini, Donald P.	June 27, 1944
Sapp, William C. Jr.	June 7, 1944
Sauer, Gail	June 9, 1944
Sawley, George A.	June 6, 1944
Sawyer, Farwell F.	July 4, 1944
Schaefer, Charles W.	June 10, 1944

Schaub, Adolph J. Jr.	June 14, 1944
Scheuerman, Frederick J.	June 19, 1944
Schletz, Raymond C.	July 5, 1944
Schwab, Rafael C.	July 7, 1944
Schwartz, Edward J.	June 19, 1944
Self, Ernest C.	June 14, 1944
Sellers, Mack J.	July 4, 1944
Senior, Robert	June 13, 1944
Seymour, Samuel V.	June 27, 1944
Shaver, James S.	June 6, 1944
Shelton, James B.	July 5, 1944
Shepperd, George A.	June 12, 1944
Sheridan, Joseph E.	June 15, 1944
Shipp, Raymond L.	June 14, 1944
Shippee, Giles R.	June 22, 1944
Shipton, Bernard G.	June 8, 1944
Shigers, Edward L.	June 17, 1944
Sica, Alexander V.	June 14, 1944
Siekierski, William J.	June 14, 1944
Sienko, Joseph	June 22, 1944
Simon, John L.	June 8, 1944
Skarie, Herbert M.	June 9, 1944
Skorupski, Edmund J.	June 17, 1944
Struck, William M.	June 5, 1944
Slosson, George F. III	June 9, 1944
Slough, John R. Jr.	June 11, 1944
Smith, John C.	June 15, 1944
Smith, Roger C.	June 9, 1944
Smith, William H.	June 14, 1944
Snyder, Albert H.	June 9, 1944
Snyder, Richard W.	June 7, 1944
Sowdro, Thomas A.	June 8, 1944
Songstad, Melvin J.	June 7, 1944
Sonka, Frank J.	June 6, 1944
Sorge, Arthur L.	June 13, 1944
Sparks, Clement	June 8, 1944
Spatz, Walter E.	June 6, 1944
Spaulding, Sherman L.	July 2, 1944
Speer, Kenneth	June 6, 1944
Spinetti, John R.	June 15, 1944
Spitler, Everett H.	June 13, 1944
Stahler, William J.	June 15, 1944
Stanley, Paul	July 8, 1944
Stanziale, John A.	June 30, 1944
Steele, Herbert	July 5, 1944
Steuart, George E.	June 8, 1944
Strauss, Harry H.	June 7, 1944

Stumpf, George P.	June 19, 1944
Sudderth, James F.	June 8, 1944
Swank, Owen V.	June 19, 1944
Swanson, Everette C.	June 6, 1944
Sylvester, Eugene R. Jr.	July 4, 1944
Tampleon, Eddie A.	June 13, 1944
Tanner, Adrian B.	June 15, 1944
Taylor, Boonie R.	June 14, 1944
Taylor, Paul C.	July 5, 1944
TenNapple, John	June 12, 1944
Tenerelli, Robert D.	June 19, 1944
Terpening, Floyd	June 30, 1944
Thacker, James A. Jr.	June 21, 1944
Thomas, Boyd E.	July 6, 1944
Thomas, Callen J.	July 2, 1944
Thompson, Earl W.	June 13, 1944
Thompson, Ulrich Z.	July 4, 1944
Tirella, Joseph J.	July 15, 1944
Tolbert, Francis J.	July 9, 1944
Toneguzzo, Dante P.	June 11, 1944
Torrez, Celestino	June 17, 1944
Tougher, Martin J.	June 14, 1944
Traca, Santo P.	June 7, 1944
Tubbs, Joel R.	June 7, 1944
Tullio, Bartholomew M.	June 9, 1944
Tutt, Arthur	June 15, 1944
VanVolkenburg, John J.	July 7, 1944
Vigil, Ramon B.	June 10, 1944
Viher, George A.	June 11, 1944
Villaloves, Atanacio	July 3, 1944
Vinski, John A.	June 6, 1944
Vlcek, Joseph C.	July 7, 1944
Vovak, Chester	June 14, 1944
Wadford, Thomas J.	June 15, 1944
Wall, Richard H.	June 10, 1944
Walters, Russell A.	July 3, 1944
Ward, Charles W.	July 5, 1944
Warren, Carl W.	June 14, 1944
Wasson, Claude H.	June 12, 1944
Wattles, Frank Jr.	June 15, 1944
Weathers, Peter J.	July 4, 1944
Weinman, Harry	June 13, 1944
Weissman, Peter	June 14, 1944
Wenglar, Albert J.	June 16, 1944
Whalley, Bertram J.	June 16, 1944
Wheeler, Kenneth R.	June 15, 1944
Whipple, Joseph Q.	June 9, 1944

White, E. C.	June 7, 1944
White, Howard P.	June 14, 1944
Whittlesey, John B.	June 19, 1944
Whitworth, Hugh C.	June 9, 1944
Wibright, Henry E.	June 7, 1944
Wieck, Willard W.	July 4, 1944
Wilgis, Edwin M.	June 14, 1944
Wilkinson, Robert K.	June 12, 1944
Williams, James F.	June 8, 1944
Wilson, Harold W.	June 8, 1944
Wilson, Herbert V.	June 14, 1944
Wilson, Homer L.	June 15, 1944
Wilson, Reino	June 7, 1944
Wilson, Robert D.	June 10, 1944
Wiltrout, Howard L.	June 15, 1944
Winfield, William M.	June 6, 1944
Wingate, George W.	June 8, 1944
Winnie, William M.	June 8, 1944
Wisecup, Robert E.	June 21, 1944
Wiser, Arthur C.	June 13, 1944
Wolfgram, William A.	June 9, 1944
Wollsyn, Walter	June 12, 1944
Wondell, Fred G. Jr.	June 6, 1944
Wood, Earnest C.	July 5, 1944
Wood, Richard J.	July 4, 1944
Woodard, John R.	June 27, 1944
Woods, Cecil G.	June 21, 1944
Woratschek, John N.	June 12, 1944
Worswick, Robert A.	June 10, 1944
Wright, Charles L.	June 14, 1944
Writer, Milton M.	July 7, 1944
Wydra, Anthony L.	July 7, 1944
Yates, Cecil R.	June 15, 1944
Yearwood, Evan L.	June 15, 1944
Yee, Leon V.	June 6, 1944
Yoake, George	June 14, 1944
Yoho, Thomas T.	July 4, 1944
Yuricek, Ferdinand	July 26, 1944
Zuccher, James	June 23, 1944

(j) Enlisted Men Missing in Action:

Adams, Frederick D.	June 6, 1944
Aguilera, Lester	June 6, 1944
Allen, Marvin H.	June 11, 1944
Angrick, Norman D.	June 6, 1944
Arnold, Joel C.	June 6, 1944
Atkinson, Jesse F.	June 6, 1944
Ayllon, Peter C.	June 10, 1944
Baliel, Anton	June 10, 1944
Ball, Glenn	June 6, 1944
Ballard, Ray V.	June 6, 1944
Baragon, George S.	June 6, 1944
Barnes, Franklin C. Jr.	June 6, 1944
Bauers, Lyle W.	June 6, 1944
Beacham, George M.	June 16, 1944
Beall, Norman W.	June 6, 1944
Baudine, Robert J.	June 6, 1944
Beardon, Robert L.	June 7, 1944
Blakeman, Robert E.	June 7, 1944
Bond, Walter	June 6, 1944
Boswell, Harvey L.	June 7, 1944
Botts, Herbert R.	June 6, 1944
Bowers, Charles E.	June 6, 1944
Britton, Robert W.	June 6, 1944
Broussard, Benton J.	June 11, 1944
Brown, Billie M.	June 7, 1944
Brown, John D.	June 6, 1944
Buehler, Clarence F.	June 7, 1944
Butler, Lawrence L.	June 7, 1944
Byers, Robert E.	June 8, 1944
Campbell, Shade	June 6, 1944
Carper, James F.	June 6, 1944
Carraway, Raymond P.	June 18, 1944
Casas, Jesus	June 11, 1944
Cavallin, Oscar N.	June 6, 1944
Cessna, Norman A.	June 6, 1944
Clark, Harold E.	June 18, 1944
Clark, Harvey W.	June 17, 1944
Coffin, Alfred J. Jr.	June 6, 1944
Columbus, Edward E.	June 6, 1944
Condich, John J.	June 7, 1944
Conger, Herbert	June 6, 1944
Cook, Edgar G.	June 6, 1944
Crandall, Forrest W.	June 6, 1944
Cuff, Frank E.	June 6, 1944
Cummings, Don W.	June 6, 1944
Dahlia, Joseph A.	June 6, 1944

Davidson, James L.	June 6, 1944
Dearing, Charles W.	June 6, 1944
DeMidio, Dominick T.	June 6, 1944
DeRise, Sidney	June 6, 1944
Dikinson, John R.	June 6, 1944
Donnelley, Robert F.	June 6, 1944
Donohue, Thomas J.	June 7, 1944
Dover, Harry J.	June 6, 1944
Druner, George M. Jr.	June 6, 1944
Dudley, Jack	June 6, 1944
Dumke, Leonard C.	June 6, 1944
Dupuy, James L.	June 6, 1944
Edmundson, Grant	June 6, 1944
Ehas, Carl J.	June 6, 1944
Evanick, Michael	June 6, 1944
Fay, Leland E.	June 6, 1944
Fessler, Robert P.	June 6, 1944
Fitzpatrick, Harold H.	June 6, 1944
Flood, Edward L.	June 6, 1944
Forte, George M.	June 7, 1944
Fox, Walter	June 9, 1944
Gaddis, Ray R.	June 7, 1944
Gaj, Leonard S.	June 6, 1944
Gauch, Joseph H.	June 6, 1944
George, Robert L.	June 6, 1944
Gifford, Thurman D.	June 6, 1944
Gillispie, Robert J.	June 6, 1944
Gladney, Alfred J.	June 7, 1944
Golomb, James F.	June 7, 1944
Gomez, Carl E.	June 6, 1944
Graham, Peter A.	June 6, 1944
Gray, William L.	June 6, 1944
Green, Thomas B.	June 6, 1944
Grgurich, Joseph	June 6, 1944
Griffin, Marshall F.	June 6, 1944
Groom, Jim V.	June 6, 1944
Guy, Henry	June 7, 1944
Halbert, Earl	June 6, 1944
Haley, John M.	June 6, 1944
Hanson, Donald C.	June 6, 1944
Hanson, Henry M.	June 6, 1944
Hard, J.Z.	June 6, 1944
Harris, Charles J.	June 6, 1944
Hassell, Herbert D.J.	June 6, 1944
Hatton, Marion Jr.	June 6, 1944
Hays, Norman A.	June 6, 1944
Heffner, Louis J.	June 7, 1944

Hen, Edward G.	June 7, 1944
Hereford, George B.	June 8, 1944
Hindman, Cecil W.	June 6, 1944
Hiner, Ralph B.	June 6, 1944
Hlavacek, Leonard J.	June 6, 1944
Hollman, John E.	June 6, 1944
Hollowell, Van B.	June 6, 1944
Hornbaker, Nelson F. Jr.	June 11, 1944
Howarth, Walter G. Jr.	June 6, 1944
Hughes, Preston R.	June 6, 1944
Humphries, Shuford M.	June 11, 1944
Hurley, Francis E.	June 6, 1944
Hurley, Robert T.	June 6, 1944
Hyatt, Roy W.	June 6, 1944
Imman, Clyde E.	June 6, 1944
Isbell, Edward M.	June 6, 1944
James, James P.	June 6, 1944
Johnston, Clyde D.	June 6, 1944
Jones, Oland	June 6, 1944
Jones, Warren H.	June 6, 1944
Jordan, Hubert H.	June 15, 1944
Karafotis, Frank G.	June 6, 1944
Kassner, Charles	June 6, 1944
Keith, Wilson W.	June 7, 1944
Kelley, Fred C.	June 7, 1944
Kelley, Raymond J.	June 8, 1944
Kelly, Robert E.	June 7, 1944
Kernel, Emil C. Jr.	June 6, 1944
Kestler, John R.	June 6, 1944
Keyes, Claude B.	June 6, 1944
King, Warren G.	June 6, 1944
Kirk, Frank S.	June 6, 1944
Kirkbridge, Erret R.	June 6, 1944
Knight, Bryson E.	June 7, 1944
Koblischshke, Frank	June 6, 1944
Korch, Theodore A.	June 7, 1944
Kotzian, Edward J.	June 6, 1944
Larkin, James E.	June 6, 1944
Lawrence, John.	June 6, 1944
Lefchik, Charles J.	June 7, 1944
Leonardo, Walter J.	June 6, 1944
Lesseter, Idris E.	June 7, 1944
Letson, Carl R.	June 6, 1944
Lelandowski, John	June 6, 1944
Lewis, Archie F.	June 6, 1944
Lewis, James	June 18, 1944
Lewis, Paul L.	June 6, 1944

Lilienthal, Robert C.	June 6, 1944
Loughnana, John W.	June 6, 1944
Lucero, Francisco A.	June 6, 1944
Mack, Joseph D.	June 6, 1944
Maher, William L.	June 7, 1944
Malinchak, Andrew	June 6, 1944
Marco, Thomas G.	June 7, 1944
Martinez, Alfonso	June 6, 1944
Mazurkewitz, Alfred	June 6, 1944
McCarty, Victor H.	June 6, 1944
McGhee, George W.	June 6, 1944
McKeel, Thomas E. Jr.	June 6, 1944
McKeever, William P.	June 6, 1944
McKenzie, Clarence L.	June 6, 1944
McMahon, Robert J.	June 7, 1944
Merschen, Kenneth E.	June 6, 1944
Miller, George T.	June 8, 1944
Miller, Herbert L.	June 7, 1944
Miller, Lawrence V.	June 6, 1944
Miller, William K.	June 6, 1944
Mitchell, Orla W.	June 6, 1944
Mockridge, Marshall D.	June 6, 1944
Montgomery, John Y.	June 7, 1944
Moore, Ralph E.	June 6, 1944
Mulhall, John D.	June 6, 1944
Myers, Morenza	June 6, 1944
Myers, Raymond	June 6, 1944
Neff, Charles R.	June 7, 1944
Nelson, Carl A.	June 6, 1944
Nelson, George A.	June 6, 1944
Nesticky, Edward J.	June 6, 1944
Neumann, Jerome P.	June 7, 1944
Nichols, Johnnie R.	June 6, 1944
Noll, Theodore	June 7, 1944
Owings, John W.	June 7, 1944
Parker, Delmar A. Jr.	June 6, 1944
Pavkov, John I.	June 6, 1944
Pessland, Theodore P.	June 6, 1944
Pelczar, Stanley J.	June 6, 1944
Pellegrino, Joseph P.	June 6, 1944
Pendergrast, Horace J.	June 6, 1944
Perea, Charlie J.	June 6, 1944
Pfeifer, Louis A.	June 6, 1944
Pickup, Christopher V. Jr.	June 6, 1944
Pillis, Edward J.	June 6, 1944
Plis, Joseph E.	June 6, 1944
Plummer, Kenneth B.	June 6, 1944

Ponder, John L.	June 6, 1944
Premo, Harold J.	June 6, 1944
Ptacek, Albert	June 7, 1944
Pullen, Howard T.	June 6, 1944
Pytel, Stanley J.	June 11, 1944
Raven, Donald C.	June 6, 1944
Reeves, Lacey H.	June 6, 1944
Reese, Richard E.	June 11, 1944
Reeve, Walter E.	June 6, 1944
Rice, Willie B.	June 7, 1944
Riolo, Samuel C.	June 7, 1944
Robbins, William L.	June 6, 1944
Romas, Joseph	June 6, 1944
Ross, Oliver H.	June 6, 1944
Rudgmann, Lawrence L.	June 6, 1944
Rusch, Leroy C.	June 7, 1944
Rushing, Jesse J.	June 6, 1944
Rutkauskas, Vincent J.	June 6, 1944
Schack, William F.	June 6, 1944
Schwervell, Russell J.	June 6, 1944
Scornavacca, Thomas	June 6, 1944
Seay, Alfred S.	June 6, 1944
Seiler, Rodgers E.	June 6, 1944
Severston, Donald L.	June 6, 1944
Shaffer, Paul G.	June 6, 1944
Shaw, Warren	June 6, 1944
Simpson, Roscoe E.	June 6, 1944
Sindelar, Francis S.	June 6, 1944
Skinner, Melvin C.	June 6, 1944
Slough, Dale W.	June 6, 1944
Smith, Frank	June 6, 1944
Smith, Richard G.	June 6, 1944
Smolik, Joseph	June 6, 1944
Smudin, George	June 6, 1944
Snell, Rudolph F.	June 6, 1944
Soares, John	June 9, 1944
Sokol, Sylvester	June 6, 1944
Spandauer, Joseph D.	June 6, 1944
Spurlock, Joseph M.	June 6, 1944
Sroufe, Richard E.	June 8, 1944
Staats, Edward G.	June 6, 1944
Stevens, Miles W.	June 7, 1944
Stillman, Edwin L.	June 6, 1944
Stout, Charles G.	June 6, 1944
Strickland, Charles H.	June 6, 1944
Sullivan, Charles W.	June 6, 1944
Swaney, Lee H.	June 5, 1944

Taylor, Robert R.	June 6, 1944
Terryberry, Blair M.	June 6, 1944
Thomas, Arthur F.	June 7, 1944
Thomas, Callen J.	June 6, 1944
Tomason, Van B.	June 6, 1944
Thordson, Clifford V.	June 5, 1944
Todaro, Peter S.	June 6, 1944
Tomko, Victor E.	June 6, 1944
Toth, George J.	June 6, 1944
Travers, Thomas J.	June 11, 1944
Trimm, Welton	June 6, 1944
Truett, Weldon F.	June 6, 1944
Turner, Horace R.	June 6, 1944
VanDerwerken, John H.	June 7, 1944
VanSickle, Jack B.	June 6, 1944
Vaughn, Thomas V.	June 6, 1944
Wagner, John C.	June 6, 1944
Waldman, Norman W.	June 7, 1944
Wallace, Raymond C. Jr.	June 6, 1944
Ward, Melford L.	June 6, 1944
Warnick, Archie L.	June 6, 1944
Way, James M.	June 6, 1944
Webb, Homer A.	June 6, 1944
Weber, Samuel R.	June 6, 1944
Welch, Orie T.	June 6, 1944
White, Gerald E.	June 6, 1944
White, James C.	June 6, 1944
White, William C.	June 8, 1944
Whiteford, Fred D.	June 6, 1944
Williams, Ted R.	June 6, 1944
Wilson, Everette C.	June 7, 1944
Winn, Robert C.	June 6, 1944
Wolfinger, H.J. III	June 18, 1944
Wood, Gerald	June 6, 1944
Wood, Harold M.	June 6, 1944
Worme, Clifford C.	June 6, 1944
Yoshida, George	June 6, 1944
Youker, William C.	June 6, 1944
Zimmerman, Lester H.	June 6, 1944

116th Infantry Regiment Decorations for Bravery— Omaha Beach

(Courtesy of the National Archives, Washington DC)

Brigadier General CHARLES D. W. CANHAM, 016496; demonstrated extraordinary heroism in reorganizing and leading his troops under intense fire; Distinguished Service Cross, GO 29, HW, First United States Army, June 29, 1944.

Lt. Colonel SIDNEY V. BINGHAM, Jr., 023267; demonstrated extraordinary heroism in personally leading attack on enemy machine gun nest. Located gun and organized flank and rear attacks which knocked out enemy position, thus permitting unit to advance. Distinguished Service Cross, GO 29, HW, First United States Army, June 29, 1944.

Captain JOHN J. COTTER, 0429492; landing early in initial assault on coast of France, administered medical aid to the wounded under heavy army fire. Distinguished Service Cross, GO 29, HQ, First United States Army, June 29, 1944.

Captain ARCHIBALD SPROUL, 0406823; at a time when his battalion was pinned down on beach because of intense enemy fire, exposed himself to this fire, encouraged his men and fearlessly led them across the fire-swept beach. Distinguished Service Cross, GO 29, HQ, First United States Army, June 29, 1944.

Captain FORREST ZANTOW, 0474270; landing early in initial assault on coast of France, attended wounded on the beach under heavy enemy fire, and undauntedly moved about the beach caring for the wounded. Distinguished Service Cross, GO 29, HQ, First United States Army, June 29, 1944.

1st Lt. EDWARD N. GEARING, 0495585; landed with his platoon in face of heavy enemy fire in initial assault on coast of France. With his men pinned down and the enemy fire causing numerous casualties and considerable disorganization, exposed himself to fire, reorganized his platoon and led a successful assault on enemy positions. Distinguished Service Cross, GO 29, HQ, First United States Army, June 29, 1944.

1st Lt. ROBERT C. HARGROVE, 01296853; his men pinned down in initial assault on coast of France, exposed himself to intense enemy fire, reorganized his platoon and led successful assault on enemy positions. Distinguished Service Cross, GO 29, HQ, First United States Army, June 29, 1944.

1st Lt. VERNE V. MORSE, 01292044; with his entire platoon pinned down by heavy enemy fire in initial assault on coast of France, exposed himself to deadly fire to reorganize platoon and lead successful assault on enemy positions. Distinguished Service Cross, GO 29, HQ, First United States Army, June 29, 1944.

1st Lt. LEO D. VAN DE VOORT, 0885530; exposing himself to intense enemy fire which had pinned down his platoon on a narrow beachhead, reorganized platoon and led successful assault on enemy positions. Distinguished Service Cross, GO 29, HQ, First United States Army, June 29, 1944.

2nd Lt. LEONARD A. ANKER, 0529110; aided by an enlisted man, assaulted enemy machine gun position, killing 16 and capturing five of the enemy. Distinguished Service Cross, GO 29, HQ, First United States Army, June 29, 1944.

2nd Lt. FOREST K. FERGUSON, 01322014; observing that the initial assault units were pinned down by intense enemy fire and further advance blocked by an extensive barbed wire obstacle, undauntingly moved forward with a Bangalore torpedo and blew a gap in barbed wire. Wounded while leading troops through this gap. Distinguished Service Cross, GO 29, HQ, First United States Army, June 29, 1944.

1st Sgt. WILLIAM H. PRESSLEY, 33147994; located enemy strongpoint and artillery OP while his small unit was cut off from the main body by intense enemy fire. Exposed himself and located a Naval Shore Fire Control Party and led it to a position where it could fire on enemy positions. Remained in an exposed position while Naval group was directing its fire. Distinguished Service Cross, GO 29, HQ, First United States Army, June 29, 1944.

Tech. Sgt. CARL D. PROFFITT, 20365448; when his company landed in initial assault on coast of France, beach was covered with withering enemy fire. On a number of occasions, fearlessly exposed hiself to encourage his men to move across the beach. Distinguished Service Cross, GO 29, HQ, First United States Army, June 29, 1944.

Tech. Sgt. OZIAS C. RITTER, 20365297; led machine gun section ashore in initial assault on coast of France, set his guns in position and placed fire on enemy positions. Exposing himself time and again, he also entered a sector of observed mortar fire to carry out the wounded. Distinguished Service Cross, GO 29, HQ, First United States Army, June 29, 1944.

Tech. Sgt. JOHN A. ROACH, 20363889; wounded when he came in with initial assault on coast of France and noting his platoon leader was a casualty, reorganized the platoon and, in the face of intense enemy fire, led it in a push which overran the enemy positions. Distinguished Service Cross, GO 29, HQ, First United States Army, June 29, 1944.

Tech. Sgt. HOWARD W. ROGERS, 33047696; separated from his own unit soon after landing with the first wave of troops in initial assault on coast of France, he found himself in a group of soldiers also separated from their units. Upon discovering an enemy pillbox from which intense fire was emanating, led this group on an assault of the pillbox and destroyed same. Distinguished Service cross, GO 29, HQ, First United States Army, June 29, 1944.

S.Sgt. RALPH S. COFFMAN, 20365662; upon landing on coast of France with first assault troops, noted troops were pinned down by intense enemy fire. Fearlessly gathered a group of soldiers and led an assault on several enemy machine gun positions, destroying same. Distinguished Service Cross, GO 29, HQ, First United States Army, June 29, 1944.

S.Sgt. LYMAN K. PATTERSON, 33042869; fearlessly exposed himself to intense enemy fire and led his men in an assault that overran enemy positions protected by mines and barbed wire. Distinguished Service Cross, GO 29, HQ, First United States Army, June 29, 1944.

Sgt. DOUGLAS (NMI) ORNDORFF, 20365289; noting that deadly enemy fire had pinned down two battalions, led his platoon in the assault of responsible enemy positions. This move inspired the other troops, and they aided in carrying the enemy positions. Distinguished Service Cross, GO 29, HQ, First United States Army, June 29, 1944.

T/4 ELMER G. SHINDLE, 33494073; after the craft in which he came ashore in initial assault on coast of France had received a direct shell hit and had sunk, T/4 Shindle, as he swam ashore, aided others. He also made many trips across the beach under heavy fire to rescue wounded and drowning soldiers, taking them to best available cover and treating them. Distinguished Service cross, GO 29, HQ, First United States Army, June 29, 1944.

PFC WILLIAM C. RIBBS, 34499006; when the landing craft on which Riggs was coming ashore was struck by enemy shell fire, it began to sink in the rough sea. Despite the intense enemy fire, Riggs plunged into the sea and swam 500 yards to another landing craft and directed it to the sinking craft, thus permitting his comrades to reach the beach and take up the fire fight with the enemy. Distinguished Service Cross, GO 29, HQ, First United States Army, June 29, 1944.

PFC JAMES A. CLARKE, 33181894; when Clarke's unit was forced to withdraw slightly because of concentration of enemy artillery and machine gun fire, he unit was unable to evacuate some of its wounded, Clarke secured a horse and cart from a nearby farmyard and succeeded in reaching and evacuating two badly wounded man. Distinguished Service Cross, GO 29, HQ, First United States Army, June 29, 1944.

Captain WILLIAM B. WILLIAMS, 0379493; in initial assault on coast of France, while leading his boat team through a hail of enemy fire, Captain Williams located an enemy mortar emplacement. Thrown back five times when he charged the position with hand grenades, he nevertheless persisted, though wounded, and destroyed the enemy positi0n on his next effort. Distinguished Service Cross, GO 75, HQ, Ninth United States Army, December 20, 1944.

1st Lt. WALTER P. TAYLOR, 01312356; disregarding personal safety, Lt. Taylor after having his weapon shot from his hand, went forward under heavy fire and rescued a wounded man. In the days following, Lt. Taylor demonstrated outstanding courage and coolness in leading his men in numerous attacks on enemy positions. Distinguished Service Cross, GO 75, HQ, Ninth United States Army, December 20, 1944.

Tech. Sgt. L.M. ARMSTRONG, 20365625; landing in initial assault on coast of France, fearlessly exposed himself, stepped to the head of his men and shouted encouragement to the other to follow him forward. Distinguished Service Cross, GO 29, HQ, First United States Army, June 29, 1944.

\\\

1st Sgt. WILLIAM M. PRESSLEY, 33147994; organized and led volunteer squad which rescued wounded men. Silver Star, GO 48, 1July 1.

2nd Lt. ORMAN L. KIMBROUGH, 01299754; advanced while men were pinned down by machine gun fire; knocked out machine gun nest. Silver Star, GO 47, July 10.

1st Lt. NORVAN NATHAN, 01315349; saved lives of many men on the beach by prompt and skilful action and superior leadership under fire. Silver Star, GO47, July 10

2nd Lt. DONALD C. ANDERSON, 0438426; pioneered route through minefield on the beach so following units might advance safely. Silver Star, GO 57, July 20.

Sgt. CARL W. RAYMOND, 33195210; engaged enemy in fire fight while boat team withdrew to more favourable positions. Silver Star, GO 57, July 20.

Sgt. JOHN YODER, 33152827; when entire company was pinned down, set up mortar and effectively fired the weapon himself, dispersing the enemy and making an advance possible. Silver Star, GO 45, July 8.

Sgt. PETER J. AMBROSE, 33061660; while under heavy enemy fire, advanced across minefield and set up machine gun, permitting the unit to advance and secure its objective. Silver Star, GO 44, July 7

Sgt. CARROLL E. HARRIS, 20365481; while under heavy enemy fire, advanced across minefield and set up machine gun, permitting unit to advance and secure its objective. Silver Star, GO 44, July 7.

PFC GEORGE T. MULLIGAN, 11117915; while under heavy enemy fire, advanced across minefield to administer first aid to wounded men. Silver Star, GO 38, July 1.

S.Sgt. RAYMOND A. MOKENNA, 31067702; under deadly enemy fire and with utter disregard for his own safety, established an aid station in the first phase of the beach operations and carried many wounded men to safety. Silver Star, GO 92, August 30.

1st Lt. EUGENE M. REGGETT, 01302519; though seriously wounded in both legs, led his unit to a vantage point from which effectual fire could be place on the enemy. Silver Star, GO 92, August 30.

1st Lt. RAY G. HELLEKSON, 01291818; organized all available men on his portion of the beach and personally led them on their advance inland. Silver Star, GO 90, August 27.

Lt Colonel LAWRENCE E. MEEKS, 029917; personally organized and led his troops while under heavy enemy fire during earliest phase of beach operations. Silver Star, GO 74, August 2.

1st Lt JAMES S. KNIGHT, JR., 0463443; knocked out enemy pill box with hand grenades, Silver Star, GO 119, October 5.

S.Sgt. JOHN H. WOODS, 20363311; while transporting ammunition in his capacity as supply sergeant, manned machine gun and accounted for twelve enemy snipers. Silver Star, GO 119, October 5.

Pvt. JERRY A. GREENE, 12085888; though wounded himself, saved wounded men from drowning. Silver Star, GO 132, October 19.

1st Lt RICHARD P. HANSEN, 01296026; coolly directed disembarkation of his craft; aided wounded solider and carried him from perilous surf, under fire, and salvaged vital equipment from main-infested waters. Silver Star, GO 120, October 6.

S.Sgt. HENRY E. BRENT, 33042688; under fire, place mortar in position, engaging enemy antitank gun which was firing on incoming assault boats. This action enabled boats to land safely in that sector. Silver Star, GO 169, November 29.

\\\\

Captain JOHN L. FLORA, 0409389; organized and led assault across the beach. Bronze Star, GO 48, July 11.

PFC HENRY B. KRZCIOK, 36516110; displayed superior courage against enemy in occupying he town of Vierville sur Mer. Bronze Star, GO 47, July 10.

Captain THOMAS J. CALLAHAN, 0390706; aided troops in scaling of cliffs and establishing the beachhead. Bronze Star, GO 47, July 10.

1st Sgt. WILLIAM M. PRESSLEY, 33147994; although wounded, reported enemy situation of CP and asked for supporting fire. Bronze Star, GO 47, July 10.

T.Sgt. WELDON L. KRATZER, 20364175; inspired men by his cool leadership and courage. Bronze Star, GO 47, July 10.

S.Sgt. CLABORNE W. DUDLEY, 20365474; displayed superior courage against the enemy in the occupation of the town of Vierville sur Mer. Bronze Star, GO 47, July 10.

S.Sgt. CURTIS G. GENTRY, 20365432; displayed superior courage against the enemy in the occupation of the town of Vierville sur Mer. Bronze Star, GO 47, July 10.

S.Sgt. CHARLES E. HANISKO, 33152992; inspired men by superb leadership in the face of the enemy. Bronze Star, GO 47, July 10.

S.Sgt. HENRY C. JOHNSON, 33047954; kept his platoon well-organized and, as a result, minimized casualties. Bronze Star, GO 47, July 10.

S.Sgt. JOHN F PORTER, 32300271; displayed superior courage against enemy in the occupation of the town of Vierville sur Mer. Bronze Star, GO 47, July 10.

S.Sgt. DARRELL R. SPICER, 20363121; repaired wire to rear echelon through the enemy lines. Bronze Star, GO 47, July 10.

Sgt. MORTIMER H. CHRISTIAN, 20365469; displayed superior courage against the enemy in the occupation of the town of Vierville sur Mer. Bronze Star, GO 47, July 10.

Sgt. MELVIN H. FIREDMAN, 32335527; secured valuable information from the enemy and wiped out a sniper who was holding up the advance. Bronze Star, GO 47, July 10.

Sgt. HARRY MAYES, 33009783; maintained communications with higher headquarters. Bronze Star, GO 47, July 10.

T/4 WILLIAM J. COFFEY, 32308859; saved lives of many men under heavy enemy fire on the beach. Bronze Star, GO 47, July 10.

T/5 WILLIAM F. SOLES, 33043159; while on the beach under exceptionally heavy fire, saved truck and ammunition. Bronze Star, GO 47, July 10.

PFC WILLIAM H. CAMPBELL, 20803746; under fire, evacuated seriously wounded man. Bronze Star, GO 47, July 10.

PFC DALLAS M. HARLOW, 33046748; displayed superior courage in the occupation of the town of Vierville sur Mer. Bronze Star, GO 47, July 10.

PFC ALBERT W. HORTON, 33046799; displayed superior courage in the occupation of the town of Vierville sur Mer. Bronze Star, GO 47, July 10.

PFC ANDREW LABONICH, 33151405; displayed superior courage in the occupation of the town of Vierville sur Mer. Bronze Star, GO 47, July 10.

Sgt. WATSON R. DAVISON, 33110212; provided assault for Infantry. Bronze Star, GO 47, July 10.

PFC ELWOOD J. WATTS, 33042522; placed BAR fire on enemy troops, enabling his unit to advance successfully. Bronze Star, GO 55, July 18.

Pvt. JACOB L. LUDWIG, 33505118; aided in making two successful assaults. Bronze Star, GO 55, July 18.

S.Sgt. EARL P. TALLEY, 20365645; voluntarily attempted to attend wounded man while under heavy enemy fire. Bronze Star (posthumous), GO 55, July 18.

PFC HARRY L. ZERBE, JR., 33076927; displayed superior courage against enemy in attack on town of Vierville sur Mer. Bronze Star (posthumous), GO 55, July 18.

Pvt. THOMAS S. OFFUTT, 6285527; maintained contact with headquarters and alternate headquarter groups. Bronze Star (posthumous), GO 55, July 18.

T.Sgt. JAMES R. VAN FOSSEN, 20365666; gained valuable information by capturing enemy officer. Bronze Star, GO 54, July 17.

S.Sgt. SAMUEL FARRER, 20365707; aided in successful advance by locating enemy machine gun position. Bronze Star, GO 54, July 17.

S.Sgt. DAVID W. SMITH, 20363896; scaled cliff under deadly machinegun fire. Bronze Star, GO 54, July 17.

PFC IRVING W. BENDER, 33133700; aided moral and inspired men. Bronze Star, GO 54, July 17.

PFC ALVIN J. BURKHOLDER, 33153091; provided covering fire so that enemy barbed wire could be cut. Bronze Star, GO 54, July 17.

PFC CHARLES H. CAMPBELL, 33047865; aided in assault of beach and fortified positions. Bronze Star, GO 54, July 17.

Pfs WELFORD D. HUDGINS, 33054233; aided in successful initial assault. Bronze Star, GO 54, July 17.

PFC LESTER RICHARDSON, 33046936; aided advance by spotting emplacement and snipers. Bronze Star, GO 54, July 17.

PFC ROBERT L. SALES, 20363891; demonstrated superior courage in beach operations. Bronze Star, GO 54, July 17.

PFC STEVE C. SIMCO, 33153177; showed courage and ability in landing on beach and scaling cliff. Bronze Star, GO 54, July 17.

PFC WILLIAM O. SORROW, 34676839; cleared snipers from beach area at great personal risk. Bronze Star, GO 54, July 17.

PFC ERNEST L, KISER, 33046917; displayed superior courage against the enemy in attack on Vierville sur Mer. Bronze Star, GO 53, July 16.

T.Sgt. JOHN E. MADDOX, Jr., **20363893**; displayed superior courage in beach operations. Bronze Star, GO 53, July 16.

Sgt. JAMES A. SLIGH, **20363893**; displayed initiative and courage in organizing and concentrating fire of machine gun section. Bronze Star, GO 53, July 16.

PFC RUFFNER WHITE, 35264970; without regard or personal safety, rendered first aid to wounded. Bronze Star, GO 52, July 15.

1st Lt HALLIE F. WILLIAMS, 01296132; saved men, vehicles and equipment from sinking LCT. Bronze Star, GO 38, July 1.

1st Lt NORVIN NATHAN, 01315349; inspired and led men in beach operations. Bronze Star, GO 38, July 1.

1st Sgt. JAMES W. GRAVETT, 20363571; though seriously wounded kept up morale of men. Bronze Star, GO 38, July 1.

PFC JOHN E. SULLIVAN, 36713017; while under fire, left point of comparative safety and attempted to rescue wounded man. Bronze Star, GO 38, July 1.

Pvt. BERNARD KASKU, 32158670; advanced through withering fire to administer first aid to wounded man. Bronze Star, GO 38, July 1.

Pvt. HOWARD C. SUTHERS, 20366078; advanced through withering fire to administer first aid to wounded man. Bronze Star, GO 38, July 1.

Captain MIFFLIN B. CLOWE, Jr., 0408173; helped clear beach and knocked out machine gun nest while under intense artillery fire. Bronze Star, GO 38, July 1.

Major MALCOLM R. WELLER, 0330579; demonstrated superb leadership under deadly enemy fire. Bronze Star, GO 38, July 1.

Captain CHARLES W. EAST, 0323710; inspired men to cross beach and knock out enemy machine gun nest. Bronze Star, GO 38, July 1.

Captain CHARLES H. KIDD, 0396656; assisted and inspired men to cross beach. Bronze Star, GO 38, July 1.

Captain CARROLL B. SMITH, 0425826; inspired and assisted men to cross beach under deadly enemy fire. Bronze Star, GO 38, July 1.

S.Sgt. JOHN H. DILLON, 20363385; carried supplies to isolated groups. Bronze Star, GO 38, July 1.

S.Sgt. GUILLERMO A. GARCIA, 38068433; secured cover for disorganized men and helped to organize them into a fighting unit while under heavy enemy fire. Bronze Star, GO 34, June 27.

S.Sgt. ELI JAH W. MARTIN, 20364763; secured cover for disorganized men and helped to organize them into a fighting unit while under heavy enemy fire. Bronze Star, GO 34, June 27.

T/5 CLAIR J. BLACK, 33364086; while under heavy enemy fire, saved lives of many men. Bronze Star, GO 34, June 27.

PFC CLIFFORD S. CULBREATH, 34812286; successfully led men over mine fields without casualties. Bronze Star, GO 56, July 19.

Major THOMAS D. HOWIE, 0261582; succeeded in establishing perimeter defenses. Bronze Star, GO 55, July 18.

Sgt. LARRY W. CURRY, 38531232; successfully led men and knocked out machine gun nest. Bronze Star, GO 55, July 18.

T/5 IGNAZIO A. TRAPANI, 32215835; despite heavy enemy fire, mines and booby traps, rendered first aid to wounded men. Bronze Star, GO 55, July 18.

PFC WILLIAM A. LANDRAM, 20365421; though wounded, located enemy gun position and directed fire to knock out same. Bronze Star, GO 55, July 18.

PFC JAMES T. LAMBERT, 33046995; displayed superior courage in the attach on Vierville sur Mer. Bronze Star, GO 47, July 10.

PFC ARTHUR H. MOSLEY, 33046452; displayed superior courage in the attack on Vierville sur Mer. Bronze Star, GO 47, July 10.

PFC LOUIS G. P SICARD, 38329426; under heavy enemy fire, inspired and led attack on wooded area, enabling unit to take objective. Bronze Star, GO 47, July 10.

Pvt. JAMES M. MACEY, 33689917; displayed superior courage in the attache on Vierville sur Mer. Bronze Star, GO 47, July 10.

Pvt. FELIX P. BRANHAM, 20365464; at great personal risk, saved lives of many men. Bronze Star, GO 46, July 9.

Pvt. ANTHONY GIGLIOTTI, 33459537; displayed superior courage in the attack on Vierville sur Mer. Bronze Star, GO 46, July 9.

Pvt. STEPHEN P. KAVALIS, 33694929; displayed superior courage in the attach on Vierville sur Mer. Bronze Star, GO 46, July 9.

Pvt. PAUL KOREN, 33674896; displayed superior courage in the attack on Vierville sur Mer. Bronze Star, GO 46, July 9.

2nd Lt LEON D. VAN DE VOORT, 0885530; led company in heavy crossfire; continued leadership though severely wounded and refused medical aid until ordered to leave. Bronze Star, GO 44, July 7.

T/5 IVA KATZ, 32344772; despite heavy enemy fire, maintained communications from Division to Regiment. Bronze Star, GO 44, July 7.

T/5 THOMAS J. KELLY, 31064225; under fire, evacuated seriously wounded men. Bronze Star, GO 44, July 7.

PFC MERTON J. FITZGERALD, 32850069; secured road junction and made contacts with elements on right, permitting units to advance. Bronze Star, GO 44, July 7.

Pvt. KENNETH F. STANTON, 37120976; rendered first aid under heavy enemy fire. Bronze Star, GO 44, July 7.

1st Lt WAYLAND C. HOOKS, 01291825; knocked out fortified positions, making it possible for the unit to advance. Bronze Star, GO 41, July 4.

2nd Lt DAVID R. HALL, 01322546; knocked out machine gun nest, making it possible for the unit to advance. Bronze Star, GO 41, July 4.

S.Sgt. ROY J. SEGAL, 34027669; while under heavy enemy fire, gained valuable information by interrogating prisoners. Bronze Star, GO 41, July 4.

PFC DELBERT S. NURNEY, 33042415; while under heavy enemy fire, directed mortar fire and knocked out two enemy machine gun nests. Bronze Star, GO 41, July 4.

Pvt. LESTER C. BRUNDAGE, 35918079; killed group of enemy guards, thus insuring the passage of a patrol which gained valuable information. Bronze Star, GO 41, July 4

M/Sgt. GORDON MCDONALD, 20363109; saved valuable communications equipment and the lives of several men. Bronze Star, GO 39, July 2.

S.Sgt. JOHN R. COX, 20365451; helped clear beach and raised the morale of the men. Bronze Star, GO 38, July 1.

Captain BERTHIER B. HAWKS, 0415402; though painfully wounded, led his troops and inspired them to cross the beach. Bronze Star, GO 38, July 1.

2nd Lt JOHN A. MARTINEAU, 01306298; saved materiel and gave drivers confidence to get their vehicles off the beach. Bronze Star, GO 51, July 14.

2nd Lt VARAD S. VARADIAN, 01324304; though wounded, continued to lead his platoon and showed exceptionally skilful leadership. Bronze Star, GO 51, July 14.

T.Sgt. ROBERT M. CAMPBELL, 3544165; assisted in establishing initial beachhead. Bronze Star, GO 51, July 14.

T.Sgt. ROBERT R. DRISKILL, 20363826; assisted in establishing initial beachhead. Bronze Star, GO 51, July 14.

T.Sgt. ODELL L. PADGETT, 20363837; provided cover fro initial Infantry assault. Bronze Star, GO 51, July 14.

Sgt. CHARLES W. HARTIGAN, 33043695; kept communications of unit up to exceptionally high standard. Bronze Star, GO 51, July 14.

Sgt. EARL J. MARTIN, 38486347; aided in forward movement of assault. Bronze Star, GO 51, July 14.

S.Sgt. JAMES A. BRENNAN, 32301899; showed exceptional courage under fire in making initial assault effective. Bronze Star, GO 50, July 13.

Captain CHARLES R. CAWTHON, 0407674; braved intense enemy fire and saved numerous lives. Bronze Star, GO 60, July 23.

S.Sgt. WOODROW F. WILSON, 20364384; exposed himself to direct enemy fire in leaving cover to rescue wounded soldier. Bronze Star, GO 60, July 23.

Sgt. ALLEN E. BEVERLEY, 33048009; at great personal risk, maintained fire on enemy, enabling troops to advance across beach. Bronze Star, GO 60, July 23.

T/5 ROBERT L. NEWMAN, 36713542; under fire, aided wounded men. Bronze Star, GO 60, July 23.

PFC JOSEPH F. DEGREGORIO, 32329545; saved wounded men from death or further injury. Bronze Star, GO 60, July 23.

PFC DANIEL O. DILLON, 20365063; displayed unusual courage during beach operations. Bronze Star, GO 60, July 23.

T/4 JAMES W. HOLLAND, 34496011; maintained excellent communications between Bn and companies under heavy enemy barrages. Bronze Star, GO 73, August 6.

Cpl ARTHUR G. SHELDON, 31274684; saved life of wounded man. Bronze Star, GO 73, August 6.

1st Lt ARTHUR J. EICHELBAUM, 0439251; inspired troops to cross beach under extremely heavy enemy fire. Bronze Star, GO 72, August 5.

T/5 CHARLES W. DAWSON, Jr., 31242404; under heavy enemy ire, maintained communications between Bn and companies. Bronze Star, GO 72, August 5.

T.Sgt. ROBERT J. AUSTIN, 35595852; saved wounded officer from possible death or further injury. Bronze Star, GO 72, August 5.

Pvt. JAMES R. YARBROUGH, 34737452; although wounded, assisted in operations against Vierville sur Mer. Bronze Star, GO 72, August 5.

PFC JOSEPH P. ROCHE, 32300620; cleared enemy strongpoint. . Bronze Star, GO 72, August 5.

PFC FRANK STRIZAK, 35172990; although wounded, demonstrated great courage during assault on beach. Bronze Star, GO 72, August 5.

T/5 JOHN F. BROOKER, 33047819; rid beaches of sniper fire and aided in holding cliff. Bronze Star, GO 85, August 19.

T/5 GEORGE J. ELLIOTT, 32205967; while under heavy enemy fire from mortars and machine guns, administered first aid to many wounded soldiers. Bronze Star, GO 85, August 19.

T.Sgt. HARLYN WOOD, 37300346; knocked out pillbox which was holding up advance of unit. Bronze Star, GO 84, August 18.

S.Sgt. WOODROW W. JONES, 33043077; succeeded in knocking out enemy pillbox. Bronze Star, GO 84, August 18.

Sgt. FRANK A. RUDA, 33055543; established contact with unit on right flank. Bronze Star, GO 84, August 18.

Sgt. WILLIAM P. VECHO, 33153318; at risk of life , crawled forward with flamethrower and knocked out pillbox. Bronze Star, GO 84, August 18.

PFC SERGIO MADDALENA, 32706272; demonstrated unusual courage in repulsing enemy. Bronze Star, GO 84, August 18.

T.Sgt. ROBERT G. CHIEF, 6713258; knocked out enemy mortar that was holding up advance and permitted units to go forward to their objective. Bronze Star, GO 84, August 18.

S.Sgt. MELVIN L. LANDRAM, 20365641; released troops that had been pinned down by constantly exposing himself and drawing fire from the enemy. Bronze Star, GO 116, October 2.

PFC RUSSELL G. DAHLBERG, 36675644; released troops that had been pinned down by constantly exposing himself and drawing fire from the enemy. Bronze Star, GO 116, October 2.

Captain WILLIAM E. BRYAN, 03755180; when Regimental S-4 became a casualty, he assumed the position and duties with minimum of personnel and supplied entire combat team with vital supplies. Many times he exposed himself to severe enemy fire to make sure that supplies reached the companies. Silver Star, GO 138, October 25

Sgt. ORVILLE D. OWEN, 35547260; relieved troops pinned down by heavy enemy fire. Bronze Star, GO 117, October 3.

PFC PEARL M. ROBERTSON, 20365693; gave life attempting to knock out enemy machine gun. Bronze Star (posthumous), GO 171, December 1.

Major MILLARD R. BUCKLEY, 0319502; saved lives and aided in evacuation of wounded. Bronze Star.

PFC KENNETH F. O'HARA, 32934509; inspired troops to advance across beach. Bronze Star, GO 52, July 15.

Captain RUSSELL J. MOWADE, 01290104; made possible reclamation of many combat team vehicles and ammunition. Bronze Star, GO 51, July 14.

T/4 ALBERT SLAUGHTER, 33009676; retrieved vehicles and supplies from beach under fire. Bronze Star, GO 51, July 14.

PFC CARMINE DELLOIACONO, 32769398; inspired troops to advance across beach. Bronze Star, GO 51, July 14.

PFC CHARLIE W. WHITLOW, 33047017; rescued and treated wounded at great person risk. Bronze Star, GO 51, July 14.

Pvt. FRANK L. MEANS, 34823562; under heavy fire, inspired troops to cross beach. Bronze Star, GO 51, July 14.

PFC ERNEST W. BOLLING, 33048012; maintained communications with higher headquarters. Bronze Star, GO 48, July 11.

PFC LOUIS E. BOTTS, 37530705; treated wounded men under fire. Bronze Star, GO 55, July 18.

S.Sgt. GEORGE W. BOWMAN, 20365656; displayed unusual courage during beach operations. Bronze Star, GO 54, July 17.

Ch (Captain) CHARLES D. REED, 0463522; though wounded, saved enlisted man from drowning. Silver Star, GO 143, October 30.

APPENDIX 4

Casualties Recorded on the Graignes Memorial

Ernest Mosqueron
Desire Palla
Joseph Perrette
Madeleine Pezeril
Paulette Pezeril
Louis Rigault
Louis Thereze
Georges Turpin
Louis Vardon

American Armed Forces

Major Charles Johnson
Captain Loyal Bogart
Captain Abraham Sophain Jr.
Lieutenant Elmer Farnham
Lieutenant Elmer Hoffman
Lieutenant Lowell Maxwell
1st Sergeant Cyril McIntyre
Staff Sergeant Jean Tessier
Staff Sergeant Nelson Hornbaker
Staff Sergeant Harry Murray
Sergeant Marvin Allen
Sergeant George Baragona
Sergeant Benton Broussard
Sergeant Walter Choquette
Sergeant Raymond Collabam
Sergeant Kenneth Gunning
Corporal Jesus Casas
Corporal Reuben Lempke
Corporal William Lucas
Corporal James Noff
Corporal Leopold Parklom
Corporal Edward Pittis
Corporal Thomas Travers
PFC William Love
PFC Arnold Martinez
PFC Robert Miller
PFC David Purcell
PFC Lacy Reaves
PFC Robert Rochwell
PFC Joseph Stachowiak
PFC H. Weiss

Notes

INTRODUCTION

1. Sydney Race Diary, May 10, 1944, Nottinghamshire Archives M24480/A/1-6.

2. See for example M. K. A. Morgan, *Down to Earth: The 507th Parachute Infantry Regiment in Normandy* (Pennsylvania: Schiffer, 2004).

3. S. Ball, *World War II Infantry Tactics: Squad and Platoon* (Oxford: Osprey, 2004), 23.

4. Paul Fussell, "My War," in *The Boy Scout Handbook and Other Observations* (Oxford: Oxford University Press, 1985), 253–80.

5. Stephen Ambrose, *D-Day* (New York: Touchstone, 1994), 395.

6. An army camera unit under the command of Major W. Ullman also went ashore on D-Day. Ullman eventually went ashore to find out what had happened to his men but he was "unable to locate any film or cameramen." To: HQ FUSA, From: Eisenhower, Supreme Headquarters Allied Expeditionary Force Papers, R.G. 331, Entry 23, U.S. National Archives and Records Administration II, College Park, MD.

7. Ambrose, *D-Day,* 397.

8. http://www.flickphilosopher.com (accessed March 26, 2006).

CHAPTER 1

1. "U.S. Estimate of Casualties" (n.d.), WO219/3408, British National Archives, London.

2. "Notes on the Planning of Operation Overlord, 1944," WO232/15, British National Archives. London.

3. "Key plan for the Reception, Accommodation and Maintenance of the U.S. Forces," 4th ed., July 12, 1943, WO199/2301, British National Archives, London.

4. "Estimated Costs of Works Services in Connection with the Bolero and Overlord Schemes," December 6, 1942, T161/1194, British National Archives, London.

5. "Key plan for the Reception, Accommodation and Maintenance of the U.S. Forces," 4th ed., July 12, 1943.

6. "Overlord: Administrative Appreciation," December 14, 1943, R.G. 331, Entry 23, U.S. National Archives and Records Administration II, College Park, MD.

7. "Key plan for the Reception, Accommodation and Maintenance of the U.S. Forces," 4th ed., July 25, 1942, WO199/2300, British National Archives, London.

8. *A Short Guide to Great Britain* (Washington DC: War and Navy departments, 1942), 4.

9. Ibid., 8

10. *Yank,* July 15, 1942, 5.

11. *A Short Guide to Northern Ireland* Washington DC: War and Navy departments, 1942), 4.

12. J.P. McCann, *Passing Through: The 82nd Airborne Division in Northern Ireland 1943–44* (Newtonards: Colourpoint Books, 2005), 58.

13. Paul Fussell, *The Boy's Crusade: American G.I.'s in Europe: Chaos and Fear in World War II* (London: Weidenfeld and Nicolson, 2004), 15–16.

14. *Exeter Express and Echo,* January 20, 1944, 3.

15. Report by R.A. Humphreys, June 1941, FO371/26228, British National Archives, London.

16. L. MacNeice, *Meet the US Army* (London: HMSO, 1943), 6.

CHAPTER 2

1. Ever Forward by Sergeant Edley Craighill Jr., Co. B, 116th Infantry Regiment, R.G. 407, Entry 427, U.S. National Archives and Records Administration II, College Park, MD.

2. Speech by Madeleine Carroll, March 14, 1942, R.G. 407, Entry 427, U.S. National Archives and Records Administration II, College Park, MD.

3. C.B. McCoid, to Clay Blair, January 16, 1984, Blair Papers, Box 54, U.S. Army Military History Institute, Carlisle, PA.

4. J. McKenzie, *On Time on Target: The World War II Memoir of a Paratrooper in the 82nd Airborne* (California: Presidio, 2000), 27–28.

CHAPTER 3

1. J. Gardner, *D-Day: Those Who Were There* (London: Collins and Brown, 1994), 93.

2. Interview with Felix Branham in Eisenhower Center, Louisiana, reproduced in R. Miller, *Nothing Less Than Victory* (New York: William Morrow and Co., 1993), 54.

3. Unknown, May 1944. Reproduced in E.P. Hoyt, *The GI's War: The Story of American Soldiers in Europe in World War II* (New York: McGraw Hill, 1988), 289–90.

4. Interview in Eisenhower Center, reproduced in Miller, 57.

5. *History of the 22nd Infantry Regiment,* January 1, 1944 to January 1, 1946, 16. R.G. 407, Entry 427, U.S. National Archives and Records Administration II, College Park, MD.

6. Major General R.O. Barton to SHAEF, April 8, 1944, WO219/550, British National Archives, London.

7. Morgan, 77. See alsoMcCann, 42–44.

8. D. Reynolds, *Rich Relations: The American Occupation of Britain 1942–1945* (London: Harper Collins, 1995), 257.

9. McCann, 77.

10. Verret would be killed during the Battle of the Bulge while rescuing a wounded NCO. For his actions he would be awarded the Purple Heart and Silver Star.

11. See "Particulars, Plan and Condition of Sale, Roclaveston Manor Estate, Tollerton, Nottinghamshire, 1894," Nottinghamshire Archives DDH 137/1.

12. General Gavin diary, March 7, 1944, U.S. Army Military History Institute, Carlisle, PA.

13. General Gavin diary, March 19, 1944.

14. General Gavin diary, March 24, 1944.

15. C.B. McCoid to Clay Blair, January 16, 1984.

16. General Gavin diary, March 23, 1944.

CHAPTER 4

1. Sergeant Gorman T. Filoia (Quartermaster Corps) to his wife, July 28, 1944, Filoia Papers, privately held by author.

2. "Security Report on Mail from Far Shore by ETO Theater Censor," July 1, 1944, WO219/1783, British National Archives, London.

3. Sergeant J. Robert Slaughter, unpublished MS, MSS2SL155a1, Richmond Historical Society, Richmond, VA.

4. *Western Evening Herald,* December 23, 1943, 4. American forces held children's Christmas parties across Britain. For example, at Yeovil in Somerset, some 700 children from the town and 28 surrounding villages were entertained. See *Pulman's Weekly News,* January 4, 1944.

5. *Western Evening Herald,* December 20, 1943, 5.

6. Sergeant Gorman T. Filoia (Quartermaster Corps) to his wife, June 21, 1944, Filoia Papers.

7. Sergeant Gorman T. Filoia (Quartermaster Corps) to his wife, April 17, 1944, Filoia Papers.

8. Harold Nicolson diary entry, January 7, 1943, in N. Nicolson, *Harold Nicolson Diaries and Letters 1939–1945* (London: Collins, 1967), 275.

9. *Western Gazette,* November 5, 1943, 5.

10. See, for example, "Baseball game played in Leicester, December 26, 1943," *Illustrated Leicester Chronicle,* January 1, 1944, 1.

11. Reynolds, 370.

12. Technical Sergeant William D. Rowell, 29th Infantry, 116th Infantry, Company M, reproduced in L. Lefebvre, *They Were on Omaha Beach* (France: Chatenay-Malabry, 2003), 46–47.

13. J.H. Ewing, *29 Lets Go: A History of the 29th Infantry Regiment in World War II* (Washington DC: Infantry Journal Press, 1948), 24.

14. *Western Evening Herald,* December 23, 1943, 8.

15. J. Keegan, *Six Armies in Normandy* (New York: The Viking Press, 1982), 12.

16. *Western Evening Herald,* December 6, 1943.

17. Report by Regional Information Officer (North West Region), July 23, 1942, TNA: PRO CAB123/176, British National Archives, London.

18. Arthur L. Clamp, *Ivybridge During the Second World War* (Plympton: PDS Printers, n.d.), 30

19. D. Rothbart, *A Soldier's Journey: With the 22nd Infantry Regiment in World War II* (New York: i books, 2003), 172.

20. *Western Evening Herald,* December 1, 1943, 10.

21. J. Jenkins, *Langham's Wartime Experience American Style* (Privately Printed, 2002), 2.

22. L. Lefebvre, *They Were on Utah Beach* (France: Malabry, 2005), 27–28

23. *Devon and Somerset News* October 27, 1943, 7.

24. *Exeter Express and Echo* January 25, 1944, 5.

25. *Exeter Express and Echo* March 13, 1944, 3.

26. *Mid-Devon Advertiser* May 27, 1944, 5.

27. *Western Evening Herald* December 23, 1943, 6.

28. *Somerset Country Gazette* June 17, 1944, 4.

29. N. Longmate, *The G.I.'s: The Americans in Britain 1942–1945* (London, Hutchinson, 1975), 280.

30. Metropolitan Police Report for West End Central Station, August 27, 1942, MEPO3/2138, British National Archives, London.

31. Private correspondence, December 14, 2001.

32. Metropolitan Police Report for West End Central Station, August 27, 1942, MEPO 3/2138, British National Archives, London..

33. Captain R. W. Townsend, *Exeter City Constabulary 1939–1945* (Exeter: privately printed, 1946), 5.

34. R. Ingleton, *The Gentlemen at War: Policing Britain 1939–45* (Kent: Cranborne Publications, 1994), 251.

35. Ernest Links or Ernest Fitzgerald of Dennis, MA, to home, November 30, 1944, author's miscellaneous collection.

36. Ingleton, 296.

37. T. Gray, *Exeter Remembers the War: Life on the Home Front* (Exeter: Mint Press, 2005), 164.

38. Longmate, 286.

39. Captain Francis L. Ware, unpublished ms., Veterans Memories project, 4th Infantry Files, U.S. Army Military History Institute, Carlisle, PA.

40. K. Wakefield, *Operation Bolero: The Americans in Bristol and the West Country, 1942–45* (Bodmin: Crecy Books, 1994), 32.

41. Vincent Edward Baker to author, June 20, 2002.

42. "Exmouth Bride and US Bridegroom," *The Exmouth Journal,* April 15, 1944, 6.

43. *Yank,* July 1, 1942, 2.

44. J. Gardiner, *D-Day: Those Who Were There* (London: Collins & Brown, 1994), 45.

45. *Western Gazette,* April 14, 1944, 5.

46. *Somerset County Gazette,* May 20, 1944, 3.

47. *Western Evening Herald,* December 6, 1943, 7.

48. H. Bergmeierand R. Lotz, *Hitler's Airwaves: The Inside Story of Nazi Radio* (New Haven and London: Yale University Press, 1997), 127.

49. *Daily Mail,* May 27, 1944, 1

50. *New York Times,* May 26, 1944, 7.

51. *News Chronicle,* June 5, 1944, 3.

52. *Devon and Somerset News,* April 5, 1944, 5.

53. *Devon and Somerset News,* May 31, 1944, 5.

54. *Devon and Somerset News,* August 2, 1944, 2.

55. See MH102/895, British National Archives, London..

56. Roger A. Freeman, *The American Airman in Europe* (London: Arms and Armor, 1991), 50.

CHAPTER 5

1. N. A. Wynn, *The Afro-American Soldier and the Second World War* (London: Eleck Books Ltd., 1976), 33.

2. U. Lee, *United States Army in World War II: The Employment of Negro Troops* (Washington DC: Office of the Chief of Military History, U.S. Army, 1966), 305.

3. "United States Coloured Troops in the United Kingdom, Memorandum by the Home Secretary," October 10, 1942, CO 876/14, British National Archives, London.

4. Sergeant Walrond to Secretary of State for the Colonies, June 29, 1943, CO876/15, British National Archives, London.

5. *Sunday Pictorial,* August 19, 1943, 7.

6. Lea M. Crawley (World War II Quartermaster Department), interview, November 1994, Rutgers Oral History Archives of World War II, http://fas-history.rutgers.edu/oralhistory/crawley.html

7. MacNeice, 14.

8. Ibid.

9. Lee, 440–41.

10. Ibid., 623–24.

11. *Mid-Devon Advertiser,* April 29, 1944, 8.

12. *Western Evening Herald,* October 5, 1943, 5.

13. Randolph A. Ginman, unpublished memoir, in U.S. Army Military History Institute, Carlisle, PA.

14. Slaughter, unpublished MS.

15. See for example, *Leicester Mercury,* April 29, 1944, 1.

16. General Gavin diary, February 22, 1944.

17. Gray, 157.

18. Rothbart, 172.

19. *Daily Mirror,* June 9, 1944, 2.

CHAPTER 6

1. Ambrose, 325.

2. A. Greenstreet, "An American Family at War-time Instow," *Devon Historian* 63 (October 2001): 23

3. "Woolacombe at War: 1939 to 1945," in B. Gunn, *The Last of the Wreckers and Woolacombe at War and Other Tales of Old Woolacombe*(Devon: Fisher, 1999), 51.

4. See, for example, V. Acton and D. Carter, *Cornish War and Peace* (Truro: Landfall Publications, 1995), 14, for some details on a training accident at Tolverne in Cornwall.

5. *Western Gazette* March 24, 1944, 8.

6. "Woolacombe at War: 1939 to 1945," 44.

7. Hoyt, 288.

8. D. Howarth, *Dawn of D-Day* (London: Collins, 1959), 152.

9. G. Bradbeer, *The Land Changed its Face: The Evacuation of the South Hams 1943–44* (Devon: Halsgrove, 1997).

10. Arthur L. Clamp, *Exercises Tiger and Fabius* (Plymouth: P.D.S. Printers, n.d.), 5.

11. Medical Report Exercise Fox, March 13, 1944, Office of the Surgeon Headquarters of the 29th Infantry Division, R.G. 94, Entry 6, U.S. National Archives and Records Administration II, College Park, MD.

12. General Thrasher to ETOUSA, April 29, 1944, Exercise Fabius, R.G. 331, Entry 7, U.S. National Archives and Records Administration II, College Park, MD.

13. E. Eckstam, Oral History (Exercise Tiger), http://www.history.navy.mil/faq/faq87-3g. htm (Accessed December 14, 2001).

14. BBC People's War Web site, Article 3565587, January 24, 2005, article 3565587, http://www.bbc.co.uk/dna/ww2/ (accessed June 17, 2005).

15. CTF 125 to COMINCH, April 29, 1944, Exercise Fabius, R.G. 331, Entry 7, U.S. National Archives and Records Administration II, College Park, MD.

16. 135. R. Legg, *Wartime Dorset: The Complete History* (Somerset: Dorset Publishing, 2000), 218

17. Memorandum by SHAEF Public Relations Department, April 27, 1944, WO219/ 184, British National Archives, London.

18. Chief Umpire and Major Mullholland, 115th Infantry Regiment, Reports on exercise Duck (n.d.), Adjutant General's papers, R.G. 94, Entry 427, U.S. National Archives and Records Administration II, College Park, MD.

19. Robert H. Poole, Reports on exercise Duck (n.d.), Adjutant General's papers, R.G. 94, Entry 427, U.S. National Archives and Records Administration II, College Park, MD.

20. Report by Lieutenant Colonel Partin on the performance of 2nd Battalion, 175th Infantry, January 8, 1944, Adjutant General's papers, R.G. 94 Entry 427, U.S. National Archives and Records Administration II, College Park, MD.

21. Report by Colonel Henion on Exercise Duck, January 10, 1944, Adjutant General's papers, R.G. 94 Entry 427, U.S. National Archives and Records Administration II, College Park, MD.

22. Critique Exercise Fox, March 15, 1944, Adjutant General's papers, R.G. 94, Entry 427, U.S. National Archives and Records Administration II, College Park, MD.

CHAPTER 7

1. See J. Perrigualt and R. Meister, *Gotz von Berlichingen* (Caen: Editions Heimdal, 2004), 86.

2. *The Rise and Fall of the German Air Force 1933–1945,* Air Ministry Pamphlet No. 248 (1948; reprint, London: Public Record Office, 2001), 329.

3. Tactical Problems of an Invasion of North West Europe, May 1943, WO 232/15, British National Archives, London.

4. F. Ruge (former Admiral Kriegsmarine), "The Invasion of Normandy," in *Decisive Battles of World War II: The German View,* ed. Hans-Adolf Jacobsen and J. Rohwer (London: Andre Deutsch, 1965), 326

5. J. Keegan, *The Battle For History: Re-fighting World War II* (London: Pimlico, 1995), 75.

CHAPTER 8

1. Gardner, 1994, 109–10.

2. Slaughter, Sergeant J. Robert, unpublished MS, Richmond Historical Society, MSS2SL155a1.

3. BBC People's War Web site, May 20, 2005, article 4095281

4. BBC People's War Web site, February 17, 2004, article 2304398.

5. Hoyt, 388.

6. Lt. Jack Shea, Notes on D-Day, Norman Cota Papers, Box 2, Eisenhower Presidential Library, Abilene, KS.

7. Major General H.R. Bull to Deputy Chief of Staff, March 18, 1944, R.G. 331, Entry 7, U.S. National Archives and Records Administration II, College Park, MD.

8. Norbonne P. Gatling, unpublished MS, U.S. Army Military History Institute, Carlisle, PA, 20.

9. R. Freeman, *A Wren's-Eye of Wartime Darmouth* (Dartmouth: Dartmouth History Research Group, 1994), 23.

10. *Mission Accomplished: The Story of the Campaigns of the VII Corps United States Army in the War Against Germany* (Leipzig: J.J. Weber, 1945), 12.

11. Longmate, 301.

12. D. Francois, *The 507th Parachute Infantry Regiment* (Caen: Heimdal, 2002), 21.

13. General Gavin diary, May 27, 1944.

14. Counter intelligence plan, Intelligence Officer 507th Infantry, May 22, 1944, R.G. 407, Box 7661, U.S. National Archives and Records Administration II, College Park, MD.

15. Summary of the Intelligence Situation, Intelligence Officer 507th Infantry, May 22, 1944, R.G. 407, Entry 427, U.S. National Archives and Records Administration II, College Park, MD.

16. Lefebvre, *They Were on Utah Beach*, 92.

17. For the 82nd Airborne the challenge would be "Flash" and correct response would be "Thunder." Men would also carry a cheap metal device known as a cricket, which made a clicking sound. A challenge of one click should be met with a response of two clicks.

18. Phil Nordyke, *All American All the Way: The Combat History of the 82nd Airborne Division in World War II* (St Paul, MN: Zenith Press, 2005), 274.

19. Private information supplied to author, July 2004.

20. Carlo D'Este, *Decision In Normandy* (London: Penguin, 2001), 507.

21. M. Hastings, *Overlord: D-Day and the Battle for Normandy* (New York: Simon and Schuster, 1984), 211.

22. Nordyke, 62–63. Unfortunately, Scambelluri's injuries were such that he died in 1944.

23. Rothbart, 187.

24. See H. Cole, *The Ardennes: Battle of the Bulge* (Old Saybrook, CT: Konecky & Konecky, n.d.), 264.

25. Sydney Race Diary, June 6, 1944, Nottinghamshire Archives, M24480/A/1-6.

CHAPTER 9

1. Giles Bre, *A Bridge in Normandy* (France: Bre, 2004), 60.

2. Lefebvre, *They Were on Utah Beach*, 93.

3. Regimental Unit Study Number 5: Preliminary Operations Around the La Fiere Bridgehead, Merderet River, Normandy, June 6–9, 1944, p.2. R.G. 427, Entry 427, U.S. National

Archives and Records Administration II, College Park, MD.

4. Don Glen Reiland, "An Ancient Paratrooper Recalls D-Day" unpublished MS, U.S. Army Military History Institute, Carlisle, PA.

5. Regimental Unit Study Number 5: Preliminary Operations Around the La Fiere Bridgehead, Merderet River, Normandy, June 6-9 1944, 10.

6. Ewing, 36–37.

7. Appendix 16 (Meteorological Report) to Report by the Allied Naval Commander-in-Chief, Expeditionary Force, Operation Neptune, Eisenhower Presidential Library, Abilene, KS.

8. Samuel E. Morison, *History of United States Naval Operations in World War II*, vol.XI (Boston: Little Brown and Co., 1959), 120

9. Cecil Breedin, Co. A 116th Infantry Regiment, interview by Robert A. Rowe, Robert A. Rowe Papers, U.S. Army Center for Military History, Carlisle PA.

10. Morison, 120.

11. Interview with John Barnes at Eisenhower Center, New Orleans, LA, reproduced in Miller, 294.

12. Hoyt, 339.

13. Ambrose, 328.

14. Ewing, 43.

15. Theatre Historian's interview [late 1944] with survivors of the 116th Infantry Regiment, Robert A. Rowe Papers, U.S. Army Military History Institute, Carlisle, PA, 11.

16. Ambrose, 339.

17. S.L.A. Marshall, "First Wave at Omaha Beach," *Atlantic Monthly*, vol. 206, no.5, 1960, 69.

18. Randolph A. Ginman, unpublished memoir.

19. Interview with George Kobe at Eisenhower Center, New Orleans, LA, reproduced in R.J. Drez, *Voices of D-Day* (Baton Rouge: Louisiana State University Press, 1996), 220.

20. Interview with William Otlowski at Eisenhower Center, New Orleans, LA, reproduced in Miller, 296.

21. Interview with Harry Parley at Eisenhower Center, New Orleans, LA, reproduced in Drez, 211.

22. Interview with Harold Baumgarten at Eisenhower Center, New Orleans, LA, reproduced in Drez, 217.

23. Randolph A. Ginman, unpublished memoir.

24. Interview with Harold Baumgarten, reproduced in Drez, 217.

25. *Saving Private Ryan* press pack, http://www.spielbergfilms.com.

26. P. Grainge, *Memory and Popular Film* (Manchester: Manchester University Press, 2003), 223.

27. J. Baudrillard, *Simulacra and Simulation* (Ann Arbor: University of Michigan Press, 1994), 1.

28. Morison, 115.

29. Ibid., 115.

30. A.R. Lewis, *Omaha Beach: A Flawed Victory* (Chapel Hill: University of North Carolina Press, 2001), 291.

31. Ambrose, 342.

32. C. Whiting, *'44: In Combat from Normandy to the Ardennes* (Staplehurst: Spellmount, 2000), 155.

33. *Combat Lessons, No. 5* (Washington, DC: U.S. Army, 1945), 59.

34. Report by Commander, Assault Force U on Operation Neptune, June 26, 1944 (Eisenhower Presidential Library, Abilene, KS), 7.

35. Miller, 369.

36. William S. Boice, "History of the 22nd United States Infantry in World War II," unpublished MS, U.S. Army Military History Institute, Carlisle, PA (circa 1959), 11.

37. "History of the 22nd Infantry Regiment, January 1, 1944 to January 1, 1946," R.G. 407, Entry 427, U.S. National Archives and Records Administration II, College Park, MD, 16.

38. Boice, 19.

39. Signal Log 22nd Infantry Regiment, June 6 1944, R.G. 407, Entry 427, U.S. National Archives and Records Administration II, College Park, MD.

CHAPTER 10

1. S.L.A. Marshall, *Night Drop: The American Airborne Invasion of Normandy* (New York: Jove Books, 1984), 63.

2. Nordyke, 269.

3. Flight Officer Irwin Morales and Lieutenant Thomas Ahmad of the 74th Troop Carrier Squadron had landed some 12 miles from their intended landing zone at Hiesville.

4. "Third Battaltion S-3 Journal," June 1944, R.G. 94, Entry 427, U.S. National Archives and Records Administration II, College Park, MD.

5. *Au Nom de La Liberte* (St Lo: La Presse De La Manche, 2004), 37.

CHAPTER 11

1. Signal log 22nd Infantry Regiment, June 8 1944, R.G. 407, Entry 427, U.S. National Archives and Records Administration II, College Park, MD.

2. Ibid.

3. Ibid.

4. History of the 22nd Infantry Regiment January 1 1944 to January 1 1946, 16.

5. Boice, 20.

6. Rothbart, 185–86.

7. Nordyke, 347–48.

CHAPTER 12

1. 223. After Action Report, Major D.E. Thomas, June 15, 1944, R.G. 407, Entry 427. U.S. National Archives and Records Administration II, College Park, MD.

2. Francois, 32.

3. After Action Report, Major D.E. Thomas, June 15, 1944.

4. Statement of Captain Brummitt, S-3, 3rd Battalion, 507th Parachute Infantry Regiment R.G. 94, Entry 427, U.S. National Archives and Records Administration II, College Park, MD.

5. Third Battalion S-3 Journal June 1944, R.G. 94, Entry 427, U.S. National Archives and Records Administration II, College Park, MD.

6. T.M. Rice, *Trial By Combat: A Paratrooper of the 101st Airborne Division Remembers the 1944 Battle of Normandy* (Bloomington, IN: Authorhouse, 2004), 159.

7. Speech given by Alphonse Voydie, Mayor of Graignes, at the inauguration of the new town of Graignes on June 11, 1964, courtesy of Monsieur Mairie D. Small, Graignes, August 2005.

8. *Au Nom de La Liberte,* 38.

9. Third Battaltion S-3 Journal, June 1944.

10. *La Manche Libre,* June 3, 1984, 11.

11. Letter by R.P. Paseal, May 17, 1994, courtesy Diocesan Archives Coutances.

12. Speech given by Alphonse Voydie, June 11, 1964, courtesy of Monsieur Mairie D. Small, Graignes, Argent 2005.

13. Morgan, 241.

14. Rice, 164.

15. Ibid., 164.

16. Ibid., 178.

17. Gary N. Fox, *Graignes: The Franco-American Memorial* (Estoria, OH: Gray Printing Co., 1990), 42–43.

18. *Demain La Liberte* (St. Lo: La Manche Libre, 2004), 52.

19. F. Juliano to E. Mohan, April 19, 1980, 82nd Airborne Museum, Fort Bragg, NC.

20. Morgan, 251–56.

21. *Au Nom de La Liberte,* 38.

22. *Demain La Liberte,* 52.

23. Nordyke, 366.

24. Perrigualt, 242.

25. J. Binkoski and A. Plaut, *The 115th Infantry Regiment in World War II* (Washington, DC: Infantry Journal Press, 1948), 19.

26. R. Bowen, *Fighting with the Screaming Eagles: With the 101st Airborne from Normandy to Bastogne* (London: Greenhill, 2001), 57.

27. C. Ryan, *The Longest Day* (London: Corgi, 1971), 187.

28. G. Duboscq, *My Longest Night: An Eleven Year Old French Girl's Memories of D-Day* (London: Leo Cooper, 1984), 123.

29. SHAEF intelligence summary for week ending July 1, 1944, Eisenhower papers, Eisenhower Presidential Library, Abilene, KS.

CHAPTER 13

1. Randolph A. Ginman, unpublished memoir.

2. After action report for 111 Field Artillery Battalion, June 1944 in the papers of Lt. Col. David G. MacIntosh III, Richmond Historical Society, MSS UN329a.

3. Lt. Col. David G. MacIntosh III, "History of 111 Field Artillery Battalion," June 1944, MSS UN329a, Richmond Historical Society, Richmond, VA.

4. Ryan, 219.

5. Interview with Harold Baumgarten, reproduced in Drez, 215–16.

6. *Trinity Parish Newsletter,* August 1944, courtesy of Fairfield Historical Society, Fairfield, CT.

7. See MS B25, Box V, Folder D, Fairfield Historical Society, Fairfield, CT.

8. A. Kershaw, *The Bedford Boys: One Town's Ultimate D-Day Sacrifice*(Cambridge, MA: Da Capo Press, 2003), 199.

9. D. Cooke and W. Evans, *Kampfgruppe Peiper* (Barnsley: Pen and Sword, 2005), 169.

10. Davis, B., quoted msnbc.msn.com/id/5138079 (accessed June 24, 2005).

11. Nordyke, 406.

12. 82nd Airborne Division Casualties, RG407, Entry 427, National Archives II, College Park , Maryland.

13. *Ouest-France Nord,* June 12, 1959, 7.

14. *Ouest-France,* June 10, 1989, 4.

15. See B.N. Siddall, *507th In Normandy: The Complete Jump Rosters & Aircrews for Operation Neptune* (Ithaca: EQS Press, 2005), 49–57. PFC Allison T. Bliss, PFC Stanley Pytel, PFC Shuford N. Humphries, PFC Loyal I. Anderson, Pvt. Lloyd Grady, PFC George E. Tillett, Pvt. Harold J. Premo, and Pvt. Walter Zielinski of the 507th were dropped around Graignes on June 6. According to Army records they became casualties or went missing in action between June 6 and June 11.

16. T. McCrisken and A. Pepper, *American History and Contemporary Hollywood Film* (Edinburgh: Edinburgh University Press, 2005), 125.

17. G. Wilson, *If You Survive* (New York: Random House, 1987), 7.

18. Private Paul Berkins (35th Signal Company), *Connecticut Men in the 35th Santa Fe Division* (Connecticut: State of Connecticut, 1945), 6.

19. Reproduced in *D Day to VE Day, 1944–45: General Eisenhower's Report on the Interior of Europe* (London: HMSO, 2000), 50–51.

Sources

PRIMARY SOURCES

Newspapers

Illustrated Leicester Chronicle

Leicester Mercury

Mid-Devon Advertiser

Exmouth Journal

Daily Telegraph

Daily Mail

Daily Herald

Picture Post

Manchester Guardian

News Chronicle

Daily Mirror

Exeter Express and Echo

Pulman's Weekly News

Western Evening Herald

The Somerset Country Gazette

New York Times

London Times

Yank

American Military Records

Adjutant Generals Papers, National Archives, College Park, Maryland

V Corps Papers, National Archives, College Park, Maryland

VII Corps Papers, National Archives, College Park, Maryland

4th Infantry Division Papers, National Archives, College Park, Maryland

22nd Infantry Regiment papers, National Archives, College Park, Maryland

29th Infantry Division Papers, National Archives, College Park, Maryland

82nd Airborne Division Papers, National Archives, College Park, Maryland

115th Infantry Regiment papers, National Archives, College Park, Maryland

116th Infantry Regiment papers, National Archives, College Park, Maryland

175th Infantry Regiment papers, National Archives, College Park, Maryland

501st Parachute Infantry Regiment papers, National Archives, College Park, Maryland

507th Parachute Infantry Regiment papers, National Archives, College Park, Maryland

Yearbook 507th Parachute Infantry Regiment, 1943.

508th Parachute Infantry Regiment papers, National Archives, College Park, Maryland

British Military and Civilian Records

Cabinet Papers, National Archives, London

Foreign Office Papers, National Archives, London

Treasury Papers, National Archives, London

Metropolitan Police Files, National Archives, London

The BBC Peoples War Archive. http://www.bbc.co.uk/dna/ww2/

Private Papers

Olin Dows Papers, Franklin D. Roosevelt Library, Hyde Park, New York

Gorman Filoia, author's collection

Miscellaneous correspondence, author's collection

Norman Cota Papers, Eisenhower Presidential Library, Abilene, Kansas.

Robert A. Rowe Papers, U.S. Army Military History Institute, Carlisle Pennsylvania.

Robert Slaughter, Richmond Historical Society

Rotary Club, Fairfield Historical Society

Frank Juliano, 82nd Airborne Division Museum

Correspondence

James H. Drumwright Jr. (58th Field Artillery Battalion). Privately held by author.

Vincent Edward Baker (58th Field Artillery Battalion). Privately held by author.

Ray Summers (29th Infantry Division). Privately held by author.

SECONDARY SOURCES

Acton, V., and D. Carter. *Operation Cornwall 1940–1944*. Truro: Landfall Publications, 1994.

———. *Cornish War and Peace*. Truro: Landfall Publications, 1995.

Ambrose, S. *D-Day*. New York: Touchstone, 1994.

———. *Band of Brothers*. London: Simon and Schuster, 1992.

Au Nom de La Liberte. St. Lo: La Presse De La Manche, 2004.

Babcock, R. *War Stories: The 4th Infantry Division from Utah Beach to Pleiku*. Baton Rouge, LA: St. John's Press, 2001.

Balkoski, J. *Omaha Beach*. Mechanicsburg, PA: Stackpole Books, 2005.

———. *Utah Beach* Mechanicsburg, PA: Stackpole Books, 2005.

Bass, R. T. *Spirits of the Sand, Exeter*. Short Run Press, 1992.

———. *The Brigades of Neptune: The US Army Engineer Special Brigades in Normandy*. Exeter: Lee Publishing, 1994.

———. *Clear the Way! The History of the U.S. Army's 146th Engineer Combat Battalion*. Exeter: Short Run Press, 1996.

Baudrillard, J. *Simulacra and Simulation*. Ann Arbor: University of Michigan Press, 1994.

Beck, P. *Oradour: The Death of a Village*. Barnsley: Pen & Sword, 2004.

Bennett, G.H., and R. Bennett. *Hitler's Admirals*. Annapolis, MD: United States Naval Institute Press, 2004.

Bergmeier, H. and R. Lotz. *Hitler's Airwaves: The Inside Story of Nazi Radio*. New Haven and London: Yale University Press, 1997.

Blair, C. *Ridgeway's Paratroopers: The American Airborne in WWII*. New York: Morrow, 1985.

Boussel, P. *D-Day Beaches Pocket Guide*. London: Macdonald, 1964.

Bowen, R. *Fighting with the Screaming Eagles: With the 101st Airborne from Normandy to Bastogne*. London: Greenhill, 2001.

Bradbeer, G. *The Land Changed its Face: The Evacuation of the South Hams 1943–44*. Devon: Halsgrove, 1997.

Bradley, O. *A Soldier's Story*. New York: Henry Holt, 1951.

Bre, G. *A Bridge in Normandy*. France: Bre, 2004.

Brewer, J.H.F. *History of the 175th Infantry (Fifth Regiment)*. Baltimore: War Records Division, Maryland Historical Society, 1955.

Brode, P. *Casual Slaughters and Accidental Judgements: Canadian War Crimes Prosecutions, 1944–1948*. Toronto: Osgoode Society for Canadian Legal History, 1997.

Brokaw, T. *The Greatest Generation*. London: Pimlico, 2002.

Bourke, J. *An Intimate History of Killing*. London: Granta, 1999.

Calder, A. *The People's War: Britain 1939–45*. New York: Ace Books, 1969.

Cawthon, Charles R. "Fortuitous Fire — A D-Day Memory." *Winchester-Frederick County Historical Society Journal* 8 (1994–95).

Clamp, Arthur L. *Ivybridge During the Second World War*. Plympton: PDS Printers, n.d.

———. *Darmouth and Kingswear During the Second World War.* Plympton: PDS Printers, n.d.

———. *United States Naval Advanced Amphibious Base Plymouth 1943–45.* Plympton: PDS Printers, n.d.

Clark, B. "Olin Dows World War II Photograph Collection." *The View From Hyde Park: The Newsletter of the Roosevelt Institute and Library* 17, no. 1 (Spring 2003), 5–6.

Colby, J. *War from the Ground Up: The 90th Division in World War II.* Austin, TX: Nortex Press, 1991.

Cole, H. *The Ardennes: Battle of the Bulge.* Old Saybrook, CT: Konecky & Konecky, n.d.

Combat Lessons, No. 5. Washington, DC: U.S. Army, 1945.

Cooke, D., and W. Evans. *Kampfgruppe Peiper.* Barnsley: Pen and Sword, 2005.

Copp, T. *No Price Too High: Canadians and the Second World War.* Toronto: McGraw Hill, 1995.

Cosmas, G.A., and A.E. Cowdrey. *The Medical Department: Medical Service in the European Theater of Operations.* Washington DC: Center of Military History, 1992.

Courtney, G.B. *SBS in World War Two: The Story of the Orignal Special Boat Section of the Army Commandos.* London: Grafton Books, 1983.

Demain La Liberte. St. Lo: La Manche Libre, 2004.

D Day to VE Day, 1944–45: General Eisenhower's Report on the Interior of Europe. London: HMSO, 2000.

D-Day: Operation Overlord From its Planning to the Liberation of Paris. London: Salamander, 1999.

D'Este, C. *Decision In Normandy.* London: Penguin, 2001.

Dows, O. "New Deal's Treasury Art Programs — A Memoir." *Arts in Society: Government in Art* 2, no. 4 (1963).

Drez, R.J. *Voices of D-Day.* Baton Rouge: Louisiana State University Press, 1996.

Duboscq, G. *My Longest Night: An Eleven Year Old Girls Memories of D-Day.* London: Leo Cooper, 1984.

Ewing, J.H. *29 Lets Go: A History of the 29th Infantry Regiment in World War II.* Washington, DC: Infantry Journal Press, 1948.

Foster, T. *Meeting of Generals.* Toronto: Methuen, 1986.

Fowler, W. *D-Day: The First 24 Hours.* Leicester: Silverdale, 2004.

Fox, G.N. *Graignes: The Franco-American Memorial.* Estoria, OH: Gray Printing Co., 1990.

Fussell, P. *The Boys' Crusade: American G.I.'s in Europe: Chaos and Fear in World War Two.* London: Weidenfeld & Nicholson, 2003.

Gardner, J. *D-Day: Those Who Were There.* London: Collins and Brown, 1994.

Grainge, P. *Memory and Popular Film.* Manchester: Manchester University Press, 2003.

Gray, T. *Exeter Remembers the War: Life on the Home Front.* Exeter: Mint Press, 2005.

Greenstreet, A. "An American Family at War-time Instow." *The Devon Historian* 63 (October 2001).

Gunn, Ben. "Woolacombe at War: 1939 to 1945." In *The Last of the Wreckers and Woolacombe at War and other Tales of Old Woolacombe.* Devon: Fisher, 1999.

Hastings, M. *Overlord: D-Day and the Battle for Normandy.* New York: Simon and Schuster, 1984.

Howarth, D. *Dawn of D-Day.* London: Collins, 1959.

Hoyt, E.P. *The GI's War: The Story of American Soldiers in Europe in World War II.* New York: McGraw Hill, 1988.

Ingleton, R. *The Gentlemen at War: Policing Britain 1939–45.* Kent: Cranborne Publications, 1994.

Isby, D., ed. *Fighting the Breakout: The German Army in Normandy from 'Cobra' to the Falaise Gap.* Pennsylvania: Stackpole Books, 2004.

Jacobsen, Hans-Adolf, and J. Rohwer, eds. *Decisive Battles of World War II: The German View.* London: Andre Deutsch, 1965.

Jenkins, J. *Langham's Wartime Experience American Style.* Privately printed, 2002.

Keegan, J. *Six Armies in Normandy: From D-Day to the Liberation of Paris.* New York: Viking, 1992.

———. *The Battle For History: Re-fighting World War II.* London: Pimlico, 1995.

Kemp, A. *D-Day: The Normandy Landings and the Liberation of Europe.* London: Thames and Hudson, 1994.

Kershaw, A. *The Bedford Boys: One Town's Ultimate D-Day Sacrifice.* Cambridge, MA: Da Capo, 2003.

Kliger, S., ed. *Yank: The Army Weekly.* New York: St. Martins, 1991.

Lebarbenchon, R.J. *Amerians et Normands Dans La Battaile.* Azeville: Azer, 1993.

Lee, U. *United States Army in World War II: The Employment of Negro Troops.* Washington, DC: Office of the Chief of Military History, U.S. Army, 1966.

Lefebvre, L. *They Were on Omaha Beach,* American D-Day Edition. France: Malabry, 2003.

———. *They Were on Utah Beach,* American D-Day Edition. France: Malabry, 2005.

Legg, R. *Wartime Dorset: The Complete History.* Somerset: Dorset Publishing, 2000.

Lewis, A.R. *Omaha Beach: A Flawed Victory.* Chapel Hill: University of North Carolina Press, 2001.

Lewis, N. *Exercise Tiger.* New York: Prentice Hall, 1990.

Longmate, N. *The G.I.'s: The Americans in Britain 1942–1945.* London: Hutchinson, 1975.

McCann, J.P. *Passing Through: The 82nd Airborne Division in Northern Ireland 1943–44.* Newtonards: Colourpoint Books, 2005.

McCrisken, T., and A. Pepper. *American History and Contemporary Hollywood Film.* Edinburgh: Edinburgh University Press, 2005.

McKenzie, J. *On Time on Target: The World War II Memoir of a Paratrooper in the 82nd Airborne.* California: Presidio, 2000.

MacNeice, L. *Meet the US Army.* London: HMSO, 1943.

Margolian, H. *Conduct Unbecoming: The Story of the Murder of Canadian Prisoners of War in Normandy.* Toronto: University of Toronto Press, 1998.

Marshall, S.L.A. "First Wave at Omaha Beach." *Atlantic Monthly* 206, no. 5 (1960) 67–72.

———. *Night Drop: The American Airborne Invasion of Normandy.* New York: Jove Books, 1984.

Miller, R. *Nothing Less Than Victor: An Oral History of D-Day.* New York: William Morrow and Co., 1993.

Mission Accomplished: The Story of the Campaigns of the VII Corps United States Army in the War Against Germany. Leipzig: J.J. Weber, 1945.

Morgan, M.K.A. *Down to Earth: The 507th Parachute Infantry Regiment in Normandy.* Pennsylvania: Schiffer, 2004.

Morison, S.E. *History of United States Naval Operations in World War II.* Vol. XI. Boston: Little Brown and Co., 1959.

Munoz, A.J. *Iron Fist: A Combat History of the 17th SS Panzergrenadier Division "Gotz von Berlichingen."* N.p.: Axis Europa Books, 1999.

Murch, D., and M. Murch. *The American Forces at Salcombe and Slapton during WWII.* Plymouth: PDS Printers, 1984.

Neilands, R., and R. De Norman. *D-Day 1944: Voices from Normandy.* London: Weidenfeld and Nicolson, 1993.

Nicolson, N. *Harold Nicolson Diaries and Letters 1939–1945.* London: Collins, 1967.

Nordyke, P. *All American All the Way: The Combat History of the 82nd Airborne Division in World War II.* St. Paul, MN: Zenith Press, 2005.

Pearce, R. *Seven Months to D-Day: An American Regiment in Dorset.* Dorset: Dovecote, 2000.

———. *Dorset Attacked, Dorset Defended: A Historical Guide to Some of the Places of Interest connected with World War II.* Dorset: Hamblin Books, 1999.

Perrigualt, J., and R. Meister *Gotz von Berlichingen.* Caen: Editions Heimdal, 2004.

Potter, S.P. *A History of Tollerton.* Nottingham: Saxton, 1929.

Rennison, J. *Wings over Rutland.* Rutland: Spiegl Press, 1980.

Reynolds, D. *Rich Relations: The American Occupation of Britain 1942–1945* London: Harper Collins, 1995.

Reynolds, M. *Steel Inferno: I SS Panzer Corps in Normandy.* Staplehurst: Spellmount, 1997.

Rice, T.M. *Trial By Combat: A Paratrooper of the 101st Airborne Division Remembers the 1944 Battle of Normandy.* Bloomington, IN: Authorhouse, 2004.

The Rise and Fall of the German Air Force 1933–1945. London: Air Ministry Pamphlet No. 248, 1948. Reprint, Public Record Office, 2001.

Rothbart, D. *A Soldier's Journal: With the 22nd Infantry Regiment in World War II.* New York: i books, 2003.

Rush, R.S. *US Infantryman in World War II (3).* Oxford: Osprey, 2002.

Ryan, C. *The Longest Day.* London: Corgi, 1971.

Siddall, B. N. *507th In Normandy: The Complete Jump Rosters & Aircrews for Operation Neptune.* Ithaca, NY: EQS Press, 2005.

Small, K. *The Forgotten Dead.* London: Bloomsbury, 1988.

Thompson, R. W. *D-Day: Spearhead of Invasion.* London: Pan, 1968.

Townsend, Captain R. W. *Exeter City Constabulary 1939–1945.* Exeter: Privately printed, 1946.

Wakefield, K. *Operation Bolero: The Americans in Bristol and the West Country, 1942–45.* Bodmin: Crecy Books, 1994.

Whitaker, D., and S. Whitaker. *Normandy: The Real Story.* New York: Ballantine Books, 2004.

Whiting, C. *'44: In Combat from Normandy to the Ardennes.* Staplehurst: Spellmount, 2000.

Whitlock, F. *Given up For Dead: American GI's in the Nazi Concentration Camp at Berga.* Boulder, CO: Westview Press, 2005.

Wilson, G. *If You Survive.* New York: Random House, 1987.

Wynn, N. A. *The Afro-American Soldier and the Second World War.* London: Eleck Books Ltd., 1976.

Index

217

Vierville-sur-mer. *See* Normandy
Virginia, xvii, 8–9, 20, 44, 88, 131;
   Bedford, 31, 88, 131, 137; Danville, 7;
   Pollard, John, governor of, 7
Von Rundstedt, 65
Voydie, Alphonse, 106, 120

Washington, DC, xvii, 8
Weapons and equipment: 57-mm antitank
   gun, 103, 113; 75-mm antitank gun,
   119; 105-mm howitzer, 8, 49, 89;
   bazooka, 49, 88, 103; Browning
   automatic rifle (BAR), xvi, 49; Browning
   machine gun, 49, 88, 123, 125; C-47,

27, 79, 81, 104; DUKW, 89–90, 129;
flame thrower, 49, 87, 111; M-1
Carbine, 49, 123; M-1 Garand, xvi, 49,
97; M-4 Sherman, xx, 49, 85, 93;
mortar, 49, 88, 103; Thompson SMG,
xvi
West Bromwich, 9
Wiltshire: Bath, 48; Malmesbury, 3;
   Stonehenge, 30; Tidworth Barracks,
   9–10
Wright Brothers, 15

Yank, 36

Stackpole Military History Series

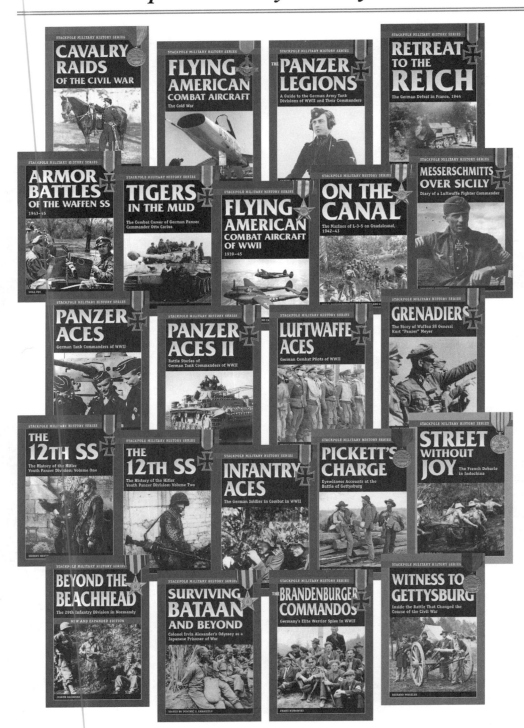

Real battles. Real soldiers. Real stories.

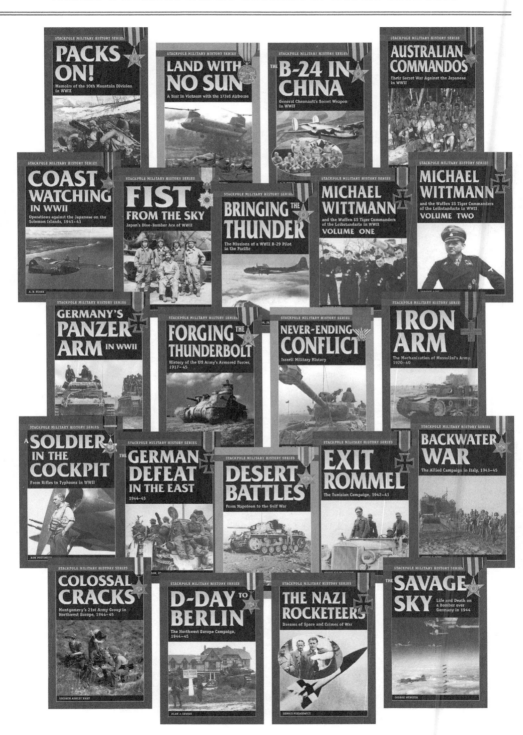

Stackpole Military History Series

Real battles. Real soldiers. Real stories.

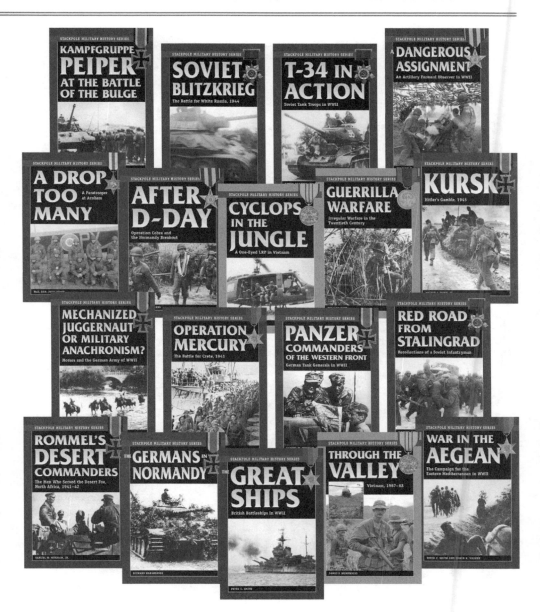

Stackpole Military History Series

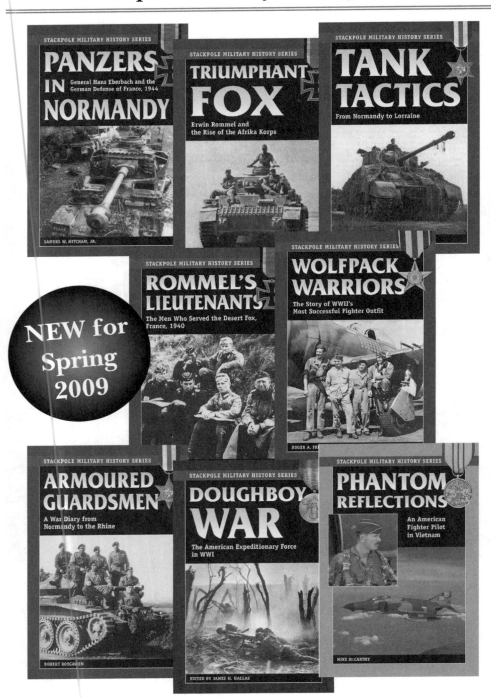

Real battles. Real soldiers. Real stories.

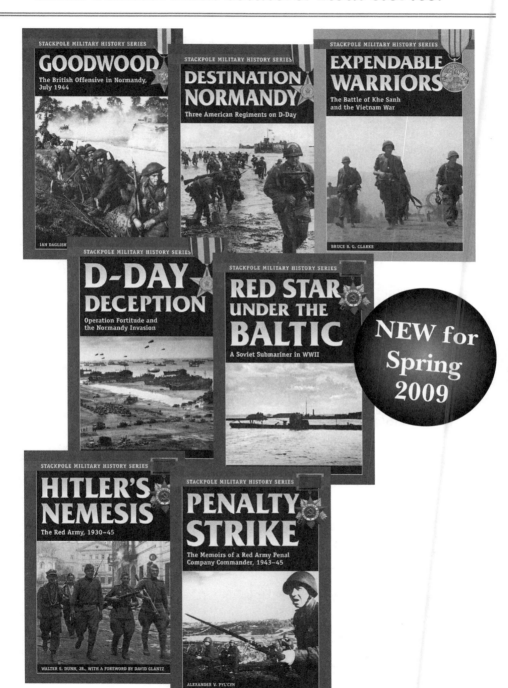

STACKPOLE MILITARY HISTORY SERIES

GOODWOOD
The British Offensive in Normandy, July 1944

IAN DAGLISH

STACKPOLE MILITARY HISTORY SERIES

DESTINATION NORMANDY
Three American Regiments on D-Day

STACKPOLE MILITARY HISTORY SERIES

EXPENDABLE WARRIORS
The Battle of Khe Sanh and the Vietnam War

BRUCE B. G. CLARKE

STACKPOLE MILITARY HISTORY SERIES

D-DAY DECEPTION
Operation Fortitude and the Normandy Invasion

STACKPOLE MILITARY HISTORY SERIES

RED STAR UNDER THE BALTIC
A Soviet Submariner in WWII

NEW for Spring 2009

STACKPOLE MILITARY HISTORY SERIES

HITLER'S NEMESIS
The Red Army, 1930–45

WALTER S. DUNN, JR., WITH A FOREWORD BY DAVID GLANTZ

STACKPOLE MILITARY HISTORY SERIES

PENALTY STRIKE
The Memoirs of a Red Army Penal Company Commander, 1943–45

ALEXANDER V. PYL'CYN

Stackpole Military History Series

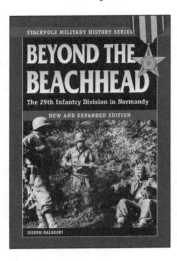

BEYOND THE BEACHHEAD
THE 29TH INFANTRY DIVISION IN NORMANDY
Joseph Balkoski

Previously untested in battle, the American 29th
Infantry Division stormed Omaha Beach on D-Day and
began a summer of bloody combat in the hedgerows
of Normandy. Against a tenacious German foe, the
division fought fiercely for every inch of ground and,
at great cost, liberated the town of St. Lô. This new
and expanded edition of Joseph Balkoski's classic
follows the 29th through the final stages of the
campaign and the brutal struggle for the town of Vire.

$19.95 • Paperback • 6 x 9 • 352 pages
36 b/w photos, 30 maps

WWW.STACKPOLEBOOKS.COM
1-800-732-3669

Stackpole Military History Series

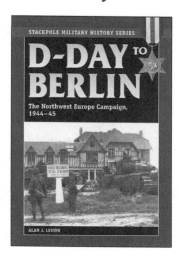

D-DAY TO BERLIN
THE NORTHWEST EUROPE CAMPAIGN, 1944–45
Alan J. Levine

The liberation of Western Europe in World War II
required eleven months of hard fighting, from the beaches
of Normandy to Berlin and the Baltic Sea. In this crisp,
comprehensive account, Alan J. Levine describes the Allied
campaign to defeat Nazi Germany in the West: D-Day, the
hedgerow battles in France during the summer of 1944, the
combined airborne-ground assault of Operation Market-
Garden in September, Hitler's winter offensive at the Battle
of the Bulge, and the final drive across the Rhine that
culminated in Germany's surrender in May 1945.

$16.95 • Paperback • 6 x 9 • 240 pages

WWW.STACKPOLEBOOKS.COM
1-800-732-3669

Stackpole Military History Series

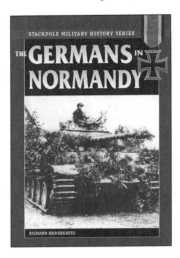

THE GERMANS IN NORMANDY

Richard Hargreaves

Richard Hargreaves recounts the Normandy campaign
from the perspective of the German soldiers who
manned the Atlantic Wall when the Allies invaded
France in June 1944 and then put up a bitter but
ultimately hopeless defense throughout that horrific
summer. These are the stories of the troops—like
Michael Wittmann, Kurt Meyer, and the boy soldiers of
the 12th SS Panzer Division—who looked out from
pillboxes on Omaha Beach, fired machine guns over
hedgerows, commanded panzers, defended the
bombed-out ruins of St. Lô and Caen, and suffered
through the nightmare of the Falaise Gap.

$19.95 • Paperback • 6 x 9 • 320 pages • 19 b/w photos, 2 maps

WWW.STACKPOLEBOOKS.COM
1-800-732-3669

Stackpole Military History Series

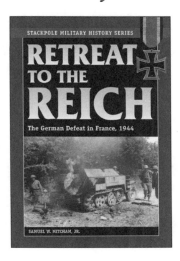

RETREAT TO THE REICH
THE GERMAN DEFEAT IN FRANCE, 1944
Samuel W. Mitcham, Jr.

The Allied landings on D-Day, June 6, 1944, marked the beginning of the German defeat in the West in World War II. From the experiences of soldiers in the field to decision-making at high command, military historian Samuel Mitcham vividly recaptures the desperation of the Wehrmacht as it collapsed amidst the brutal hedgerow fighting in Normandy, losing its four-year grip on France as it was forced to retreat back to the German border. While German forces managed to temporarily halt the Allied juggernaut there, this brief success only delayed the fate that had been sealed with the defeat in France.

$17.95 • Paperback • 6 x 9 • 304 pages • 26 photos, 12 maps

WWW.STACKPOLEBOOKS.COM
1-800-732-3669

Stackpole Military History Series

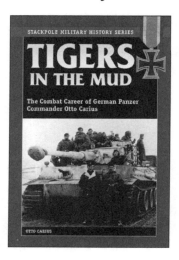

TIGERS IN THE MUD
THE COMBAT CAREER OF GERMAN PANZER
COMMANDER OTTO CARIUS

Otto Carius,
translated by Robert J. Edwards

World War II began with a metallic roar as the
German Blitzkrieg raced across Europe, spearheaded
by the most dreadful weapon of the twentieth century:
the Panzer. Tank commander Otto Carius thrusts the
reader into the thick of battle, replete with the
blood, smoke, mud, and gunpowder so common
to the elite German fighting units.

$19.95 • Paperback • 6 x 9 • 368 pages
51 photos • 48 illustrations • 3 maps

WWW.STACKPOLEBOOKS.COM
1-800-732-3669

Stackpole Military History Series

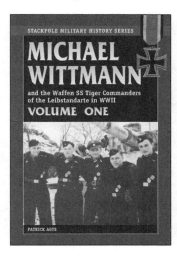 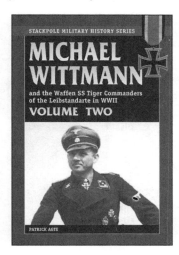

MICHAEL WITTMANN AND THE WAFFEN SS TIGER COMMANDERS OF THE LEIBSTANDARTE IN WORLD WAR II

Patrick Agte

By far the most famous tank commander on any side in World War II, German Tiger ace Michael Wittmann destroyed 138 enemy tanks and 132 anti-tank guns in a career that embodies the panzer legend: meticulous in planning, lethal in execution, and always cool under fire. Volume One covers Wittmann's armored battles against the Soviets in 1943–44 at places like Kharkov, Kursk, and the Cherkassy Pocket. Volume Two picks up with the epic campaign in Normandy, where Wittmann achieved his greatest successes before being killed in action. The Leibstandarte went on to fight at the Battle of the Bulge and in Austria and Hungary before surrendering in May 1945.

Volume One: $19.95 • Paperback • 6 x 9 • 432 pages
383 photos • 19 maps • 10 charts
Volume Two: $19.95 • Paperback • 6 x 9 • 400 pages
287 photos • 15 maps • 7 charts

WWW.STACKPOLEBOOKS.COM
1-800-732-3669

Also available from Stackpole Books

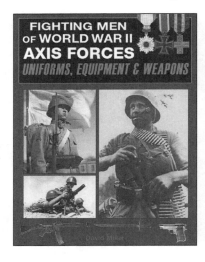
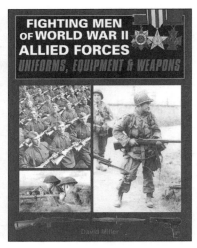

FIGHTING MEN OF WORLD WAR II
VOLUME 1: AXIS FORCES
VOLUME 2: ALLIED FORCES
David Miller

These comprehensive volumes present a full-color
look at Axis and Allied soldiers in World War II,
covering their weapons, equipment, clothing,
rations, and more. The Axis volume includes Germany,
Italy, and Japan while the Allied volume presents
troops from the United States, Great Britain, and the
Soviet Union. These books create a vivid picture of
the daily life and battle conditions of the fighting
men of the Second World War.

$49.95 • Hardcover • 9 x 12 • 384 pages • 600 color illustrations

WWW.STACKPOLEBOOKS.COM
1-800-732-3669